DEVELOPING
MOBILE WEBSITES
WITH HTML5

DAVID KARLINS

Cengage Learning PTR

CENGAGE
Learning·

Professional • Technical • Reference

Australia • Brazil • Japan • Korea • Mexico • Singapore • Spain • United Kingdom • United States

Professional • Technical • Reference

**Developing Mobile Websites
with HTML5**
David Karlins

**Publisher and General Manager,
Cengage Learning PTR:** Stacy L. Hiquet

Associate Director of Marketing:
Sarah Panella

Manager of Editorial Services:
Heather Talbot

Product Manager: Heather Hurley

Senior Marketing Manager:
Mark Hughes

Project/Copy Editor: Kezia Endsley

Technical Editor: Richard Joergensen

Interior Layout: MPS Limited

Cover Designer: Luke Fletcher

Proofreader: Sam Garvey

Indexer: Sharon Shock

Library of Congress Control Number: 2014937091

ISBN-13: 978-1-305-09053-8

ISBN-10: 1-305-09053-5

Cengage Learning PTR

20 Channel Center Street

Boston, MA 02210

USA

Cengage Learning is a leading provider of customized learning solutions
with office locations around the globe, including Singapore, the United
Kingdom, Australia, Mexico, Brazil, and Japan. Locate your local office at:
international.cengage.com/region.

Cengage Learning products are represented in Canada by Nelson
Education, Ltd.

For your lifelong learning solutions, visit **cengageptr.com.**

Visit our corporate website at **cengage.com.**

Printed in the United States of America
1 2 3 4 5 6 7 16 15 14

This book is dedicated to everyone, everywhere with limited financial resources and technical skills but with the energy and determination to get their message into the mobile world.

Acknowledgments

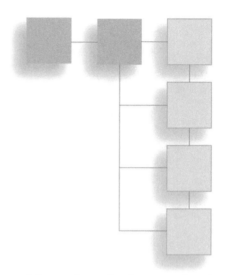

The community that made this book possible was anchored by technical editor Richard Joergensen, project editor Kezia Endsley, and product manager Heather Hurley, as well as my agent, Margot Hutchinson. Each of them made indispensible contributions in different realms to ensure that the content was relevant and accurate, and that this book would reach you.

Beyond that, I was able to draw on the work of experts in many realms of mobile web design. Some are cited directly in the book, others contributed more informally—answering late night phone calls and selflessly sharing tips from their specializations and experiences. Collectively, their contributions funneled unique insights into the final book. The whole process was an exciting and rewarding journey.

ABOUT THE AUTHOR

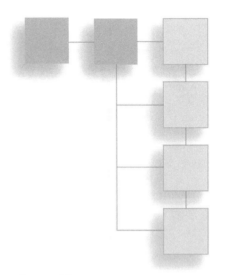

David Karlins is a consultant, writer, designer, and teacher addressing contemporary challenges in digital graphic and interactive design. He is the author of more than 40 books on web design, digital graphics, project management, online video, and animation. His consulting clients include prominent figures and institutions in theater, performance venues, music production, art, music, handicrafts, and education. Learn more about David Karlins at davidkarlins.com.

CONTENTS

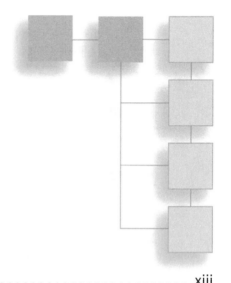

Introduction

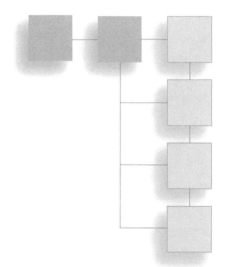

Analyst after analyst is pointing to the same phenomenon, "[T]he trend seems clear: For the vast majority of consumers worldwide, the primary computing and online experience will be on mobile devices." (This is from "What Happens to the Web Now That Smartphones and Tablets Run the Show?" by Geoff Duncan, *DIGITAL TRENDS*, December 7, 2012.)

Enterprises with massive design and development resources have gone mobile. Yes, they maintain their laptop/desktop sites. But they are pouring their energies into the dynamic realm of mobile. Sites ranging from YouTube.com to Hulu.com haven't just "gone mobile;" they have gone through several iterations in their mobile sites. They've changed the format of their videos to mobile-friendly files. They've changed the navigation schemes of their sites so that users without "hover state" experiences (that is, mobile users without a mouse pointer that can hover over an element) can navigate the sites. They've speeded up their sites, tweaked their color schemes, and added animation and effects optimized for mobile devices.

This Book in the World of Mobile Web Design

But what about the rest of us? Much of my own research focuses on surveying the state of the mobile presence of small and medium-sized enterprises. My conclusion: in brief, a huge gap exists between the state of the *audience* for these entities' websites on the one hand and the state of their mobile *presence*.

That does *not need to be the case!* The skillset required to build highly inviting, highly accessible, mobile-focused websites is no more daunting than that needed to build a similarly successful laptop/desktop site.

Options for Mobile Designers

As a web designer who recognizes the need for an inviting, accessible mobile presence, you have essentially three options: Responsive Web Design (RWD); building a native app; and building a mobile web app with HTML5. It is "option 3" (building a mobile web app) that is the focus of this book, but let me explain all three options and put mobile web apps in perspective, in the context of the world of mobile web design.

- **Responsive Web Design (RWD)** is a relatively low-cost, low-resource option for providing web content that works reasonably well in laptop/desktop, tablet, and mobile environments. RWD provides distinct page designs for different *viewports* (browser widths). Figure I.1 illustrates a responsive site viewed in a mobile viewport.

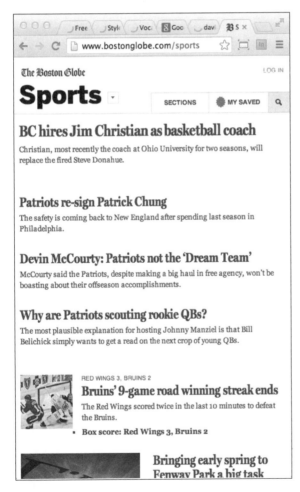

Figure I.1
The Boston Globe uses responsive design to address the needs of mobile users.
Source: *The Boston Globe™.*

- **Native apps are *native* to a specific operating system.** An app built for Apple devices (like iPads and/or iPhones) will not work in an Android device. Nor will it work in other mobile operating systems (like BlackBerry or Windows Mobile devices). And an app built for an iPhone will not work in any laptop/desktop environments. Native apps provide an optimal experience for mobile users, but they require substantial high-level coding to create and maintain. Native apps are distributed (sometimes free, sometimes for a cost) through online stores associated with specific operating systems, like iTunes and Google Play. Figure I.2 shows the native app for Bank of America.

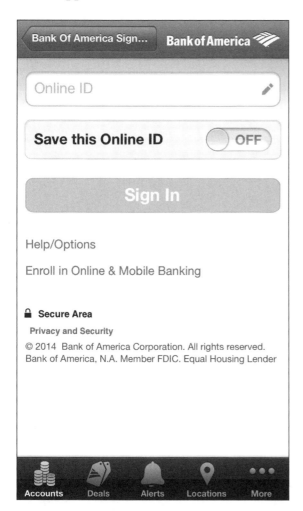

Figure I.2

The native app for Bank of America.

Source: Bank of America™.

■ **Web apps are the focus of this book.** They are built with HTML5, not high-level programming languages. They work in any mobile environment, and work in laptop/desktop environments as well. Figure I.3 shows a web app built with jQuery Mobile.

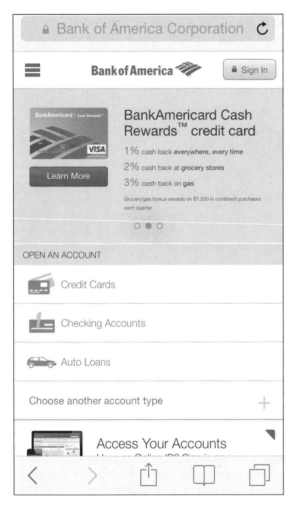

Figure I.3
The web app for Bank of America built with jQuery Mobile.
Source: Bank of America™.

The Advantages of Mobile Web Apps Built with HTML5

Mobile Web apps built with HTML5 provide a more "natural" mobile experience than RWD pages, and are much easier to build and maintain than native apps.

Mobile web apps can emulate much of the interactivity and animation mobile users get with native apps by accessing JavaScript libraries (sets of files). The most widely applied, best supported, and most stable of these mobile JavaScript libraries is jQuery Mobile. The jQuery Mobile library is built on and relies on the powerful jQuery library. It is frequently updated with new features that make mobile websites, built with HTML5, look and feel like apps.

Does this mean you need to know JavaScript to build animated, interactive mobile websites with jQuery Mobile? No, it does not. The JavaScript required for animated, interactive elements in mobile sites is built and maintained by the jQuery and jQuery Mobile development teams, and distributed free. You can download the files required for jQuery Mobile or, as I recommend throughout this book, you can simply link to versions of them saved at Content Delivery Network (CDN) sites.

Four Components of Mobile Web Design with HTML5

Let me break down the components of building mobile web apps with HTML5. There are essentially four of them:

- **JavaScript libraries supplied by jQuery and jQuery Mobile.** These files are already created; you don't create or edit them. They are stored at and linked to through a Content Delivery Network (CDN). Figure I.4 shows the resource site for jQuery Mobile, with links to the CDN files. I walk through how to connect to and use these files early and repeatedly in this book.

Figure I.4
Content Delivery Network (CDN) files for jQuery Mobile.
Source: jQuery Mobile™.

- **JavaScript widgets.** You can enhance HTML5 mobile web apps with additional JavaScript widgets (sets of features) beyond those supplied by jQuery Mobile. In this book, I introduce you to using JavaScript widgets. Figure I.5 shows some example widgets.

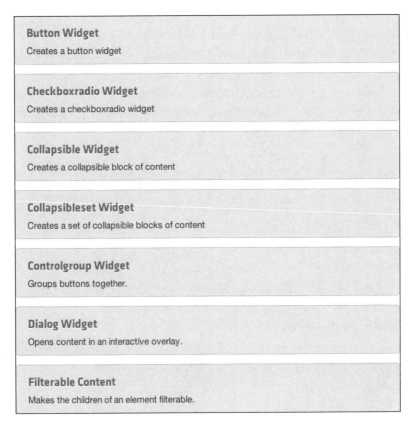

Figure I.5
jQuery Mobile widgets.
Source: jQuery Mobile™.

- **CSS, Cascading Style Sheet files.** In the main, these are supplied by jQuery Mobile. You *do* edit them. But you don't need to know CSS to do that. There is a powerful online resource (called jQuery Mobile ThemeRoller) that is used to customize the look of mobile website elements. Figure I.6 shows the jQuery Mobile ThemeRoller site. This book explains in detail how to customize the look of your mobile site with jQuery Mobile ThemeRoller.

Figure I.6
Designing styles for a mobile site with jQuery Mobile ThemeRoller.
Source: jQuery Mobile™.

- **HTML5.** As you might have guessed, HTML5 is the key and dynamic tool in building mobile web apps. The essential JavaScript is supplied by jQuery Mobile. The essential CSS is also supplied by jQuery Mobile and can be modified with ThemeRoller. But *content*—the heart and soul of your mobile site—as well as a wide range of format and style options are all invoked with HTML5.

The Dynamic Role of HTML5

If you come from a laptop/desktop design background, you are used to a routine of building content with HTML5, and styling with CSS3. That background will serve you well in building mobile web apps, but it is not a prerequisite. In this book, I'll walk through all the HTML5 you need to build mobile sites.

But if you do come from a laptop/desktop design background (or, for that matter even if you do not), it is helpful to appreciate the different role HTML5 and CSS3 play in designing mobile web apps. The JavaScript used to make jQuery Mobile pages pop open, transition with effects, and in general feel like apps, relies on a highly complex CSS file (with something like a thousand lines of code). The JavaScript in jQuery Mobile and the CSS supplied through the jQuery Mobile CDN (or customized with ThemeRoller) mesh tighltly together. For that reason, if you have advanced CSS3 design skills, you're going to leave them on the shelf, in large part, when you build mobile sites with HTML5 and jQuery Mobile.

How, then, do you customize the look and feel of mobile sites? An extensive set of jQuery Mobile-specific HTML5 parameters invoke and apply different styling. HTML5 itself, even without the styling supplied by jQuery Mobile, provides little-appreciated tools for a wide range of mobile-friendly elements.

Take input forms, for example. HTML5 allows you to present handy placeholder text that clues users in to what to enter into a form field. It includes features that display a calendar when a user is asked to enter a date, a color palette when a user is prompted to enter a color, and even a simple calculator. Figure I.7 illustrates a mobile-friendly form built with HTML5.

Figure I.7
A mobile-friendly form built with HTML5.

© 2015 Cengage Learning PTR.

In general, the work of building mobile web apps is done with HTML5. You use HTML5 to create and embed content—text, images, audio, and video. You use HTML5 to define navigation structures—navigation bars, navigation lists, navigation buttons, and other link elements.

How does all this play out for users accessing your mobile site with laptop/desktop browsers? Increasingly, laptop/desktop browsers that do not support HTML5 (here I'm talking about Internet Explorer versions 6, 7, and 8) are going extinct, and current generation browsers support HTML5. Where that is not the case with specific features, I explore options for addressing those issues in this book.

WHAT YOU'LL FIND IN THIS BOOK

This book is designed as a guide to building mobile web apps using HTML5, along with jQuery Mobile. While it is not meant as an introductory tutorial on HTML5 itself, it basically serves that function.

A basic working knowledge of HTML5 (and CSS3) will help, as it provides a useful background and context for the content of this book. But it is not a prerequisite to building inviting, accessible, attractive mobile web apps with HTML5.

After reading this book, you will know how to do the following:

- Understand how mobile web apps fit into the set of options for building mobile-friendly web content.

- Build basic, animated, interactive mobile web apps.

- Set up a preview and testing environment for mobile sites.

- Animate navigation with easy-to-tap buttons and animation.

- Understand and apply styling to mobile sites.

- Define and apply completely unique, custom styling to your mobile site.

- Pack extra content into mobile web pages without creating a cluttered look, using collapsible blocks of content.

- Design multicolumn mobile page layouts with grids.

- Stream native video into users' mobile devices.

- Produce and distribute native audio that works well and opens quickly in mobile devices.

- Size images for mobile devices.

- Build mobile-friendly forms and collect data from users.

- Employ JavaScript widgets for additional interactivity.

- Add mobile app tools like caching (so apps work when a user is offline) and geolocation.

- Expedite development with templates.

Who This Book Is For

The book will be helpful to any of the following professionals and semi-professional web designers:

- Web masters for organizations, small businesses, and communities that need a mobile presence.

- Professional and semi-professional web designers who want to add mobile site design to their skillset.

- Musicians, entertainers, performers, and others who need to project their audio and video content over mobile devices.

- Developers who want to build mobile-accessible forms.

- Web designers who want to add animation and interactivity to mobile pages.

- Anyone in the world of web design who wants to understand the most effective, accessible approach to building mobile web apps.

How This Book Is Organized

This book contains 14 chapters:

Chapter 1: "Solving Mobile Design Challenges with HTML5." This chapter surveys alternative approaches to developing a mobile presence, ranging from no mobile design, to "fluid design" (sites that adjust the size of elements based on the size of a user's browser window), to responsive web design, to native apps. It also surveys and outlines the advantages and techniques involved in building mobile websites with HTML5.

Chapter 2: "Building and Testing a Multipage Mobile Web App with HTML5." In this chapter, I show you how to begin to build and test HTML5-based pages that look and feel like mobile apps. I start walking through how to set up a testing environment, so you can preview how your pages will look in a variety of mobile devices without actually having to buy every mobile device on the market! And then, I show you how to create a basic mobile-friendly site with HTML5.

Chapter 3: "Animating Navigation." Without a useful navigation system, any mobile site is unusable. In this chapter, I cover how to enhance navigation lists (listviews), and how to make the experience of navigating your mobile site a pleasant and inviting one for users. In the course of doing that, I walk you through when and how to define listviews with filters to make long lists manageable, create listviews with inset formatting to make them more inviting and accessible, use split-button listviews that combine images and text, and provide two different links within a list item. You'll also learn to create links that open in dialogs, instead of browser windows, and how to create animated transitions to liven up the navigation experience.

Chapter 4: "Applying Data-Theme Styling." This chapter explains and explores how you customize the look and feel of jQuery Mobile styles. The default jQuery Mobile CSS file has within it a set of color swatches that can be applied with HTML coding. I walk you through how that works in this chapter. This chapter introduces you, as well, to some other styling techniques—how to use buttons to make links easier to tap in mobile devices, how to assign styling to those buttons, and how to make any element of a jQuery Mobile page smaller using the `mini` attribute.

Chapter 5: "Customizing Mobile Styles with ThemeRoller." This chapter introduces the key online resource for creating highly unique sites—jQuery Mobile ThemeRoller. The chapter covers these elements of custom theming mobile sites—the importance of mobile-friendly, high-contrast color schemes; the relationship between jQuery Mobile themes and color swatches; how to define custom site-wide style elements like fonts, rounded corners, icons, and box shadows; how to define up to 26 different custom color swatches; and how to save and apply custom CSS for a mobile site.

Chapter 6: "Creating Collapsible Blocks." The focus of this chapter is using collapsible blocks—boxes that open or close to reveal or hide content. Collapsible blocks provide a significant alternative to listviews for packing a set of options into the small space of a mobile device viewport. Beyond collapsible blocks, this chapter explains how to absolutely position footers at the bottom of a mobile page, which is a handy technique when you are paying close attention to maximizing the content you can pack into a smartphone viewport while keeping a page inviting.

Chapter 7: "Designing with Grids." As the world of mobile devices continues to expand, and as tablets and high-resolution, larger smart phones became dominant in web browsing, it is important to explore the option of designing multicolumn layouts with grids. In this chapter I show you how to do that using HTML5 grids—blocks formed by the intersection of (horizontal) rows and (vertical) columns that provide an option for designing multicolumn page layouts for mobile devices.

Chapter 8: "Providing Native Video." Video has evolved from a peripheral element of the mobile web browsing experience to an expectation. In this chapter, I explain step-by-step how to implement *native* video—video that plays without plug-in software and works in every mobile device.

Chapter 9: "Providing Audio for Mobile." Mobile audio, including downloaded audio files and Internet radio stations, makes up a substantial chunk of all mobile web usage. While Internet radio and commercial music downloads are mainly dominated by massive commercial entities (like Pandora, Spotify, and iTunes), smaller projects and institutions—commercial and non-commercial—can make effective use of online audio. In this chapter, I teach you how to both produce and distribute mobile-ready native audio that runs without plug-ins.

Chapter 10: "Scaling Images for Mobile Devices." Designing images for mobile still requires finding ways to package a "one-size-fits-all" image into a multi-sized viewport world. I show you how to do that in this chapter, using CSS3 media queries to produce images that rescale to display properly in different viewports (browser windows).

Chapter 11: "Building Mobile-Friendly Forms." In this chapter you learn to use HTML5 to validate and prompt form data, how to send collected data to a server, and most of all, how to design dynamic, inviting forms that make it easy for mobile users to interact with your site, your product, your mission, and your organization.

Chapter 12: "Deploying Mobile Widgets." Widgets allow designers to add animation and interactivity to mobile sites without much, or even any, coding skills in JavaScript. And templates can greatly aid productivity in building sites. In this chapter, I show you how to integrate and customize widgets from jQuery Mobile's library. I focus on a couple particularly useful widgets—popups and buttons.

Chapter 13: "Building a Complete Mobile Presence." This chapter explains how to integrate a mobile site with a laptop/desktop site—how to handle and optimize search engine results when you have similar content on multiple pages, and how to tell search engines which page is the one to display in search results. This chapter also explains how to detect and divert users with mobile devices, sending them automatically from a laptop/desktop site to a mobile-friendly site. This chapter also covers features like caching (storing) page content in devices, implanting a live chat, and geolocation, all used to provide an app-like experience with a mobile site.

Chapter 14: "Using Templates." Templates are not just for beginners. They allow designers at any level to get a quick start on projects. And good templates provide reliable, tested code. In this chapter, you learn to use a jQuery Mobile template to build pages, forms, navbars, buttons, and other useful elements in a mobile website.

About the Website

The website for this book is located at http://dk-mobile.uphero.com. There you will find code for many of the projects explored in this book. (You may also download the companion website files from http://www.cengageptr.com/downloads.) Look for tips within most chapters directing you straight to the page at the website from which you can copy code.

You'll find it easier to copy-and-paste code from the website, since code copied and pasted from e-books tends to get corrupted. The book's website also provides a few examples and demonstration models of the projects in this book.

I've provided a way to submit issues, error reports, and suggestions at the book's site, and I invite you to use that as well.

Please use the book's website, at http://dk-mobile.uphero.com, to get help with book-related issues. But you can learn more about me and keep up with my various projects at davidkarlins.com.

Looking forward to "seeing" you online!

PART I

BUILDING ANIMATED, INTERACTIVE WEBSITES WITH HTML5

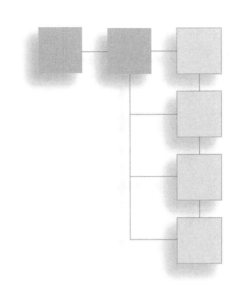

CHAPTER 1

SOLVING MOBILE DESIGN CHALLENGES WITH HTML5

If you've picked up this book on a shelf, or are checking it out via your preferred online book distributor, you already know that a mobile presence is essential to connect your online content with an increasingly mobile-focused online community. If that's your perception, you are correct! This first chapter addresses that idea—breaking down and identifying specific features of a website that make it inviting and accessible to tablet and smartphone visitors.

What might be more mystifying—and understandably so—is *how* to build a mobile-friendly website.

Answering that question requires identifying the discrete elements that make a website mobile-friendly. But here's the short answer: The widest range of approaches to building mobile-friendly websites are based on creating sites in HTML5. With that foundation, other tools, specifically CSS3 styling and JavaScript animation, can be plugged into mobile sites easily. How that works is, in one sense, the point of this book.

BUILDING MOBILE-FRIENDLY SITES WITH HTML5

Before learning *how* to build mobile-friendly sites, it will be helpful to identify the specific features that make a website mobile-friendly. In other words, to get philosophical for a moment, before deciding that the *answers* lie in HTML5-based mobile development, you need to identify the *questions*.

3

On that basis, you can survey the different approaches to building mobile-friendly websites, including how they solve (or don't solve) different aspects of designing and implementing a successful mobile-web presence.

Elements of a Mobile-Friendly Design

When users enjoy a positive experience at a mobile-friendly website, they are unlikely to say, "Wow, I really appreciated the lighting-appropriate color scheme, the unit of measurement applied to fonts, the compressed, fast-loading images, the hassle-free video, and the engaging animation and interactivity." But even if a user isn't consciously itemizing all the factors that make the visit to a site a favorable one, unconsciously, or subconsciously, the visit to a really mobile-friendly should *feel* inviting, intuitive, and hassle-free.

On the other hand, if any of those elements are *missing*, users might simply tap the home button on their mobile devices, and move on to another website in search of a more hassle-free, inviting experience.

So, what are the basic features that make a website mobile-friendly? Design and technical creative innovations are part of the pathway on which current mobile design standards and technology evolved. But those innovations emerged in response to specific *challenges* involved in building mobile sites. There are, in short, elements of the mobile web experience that are qualitatively different than the desktop/laptop world which, for a couple of decades, has defined the web experience.

What elements distinguish the mobile browsing experience? They include:

- **Size:** Obvious perhaps, but mobile viewports (the size of the browser window) are qualitatively smaller than those in desktops and laptops. This has implications for accessibility and design that you need to consciously identify and address.

- **Lighting:** Mobile devices tend not to have as powerful back-lighting as desktop and laptop screens. They are much more frequently viewed in outdoor lighting conditions that render many color schemes frustrating or worse. Serious mobile design takes these issues into account with color schemes that work under extreme lighting conditions.

- **Speed:** Mobile devices tend to have slower processors than desktop and laptop computers. Mobile users frequently depend on slower WiFi connections, and even slower 3G, 4G or LTE connections. Mobile content has to be created and deployed to take that into account.

- **Touch screens:** Mobile devices overwhelmingly rely on touch screens for navigation and other user input, as opposed to desktop and laptop computers that still, to a large degree, rely on keyboards and mouse input. This has profound implications for designing mobile sites.

These four elements don't exhaust the specific challenges of building effective mobile sites. In the course of this book, I'll address a number of other dimensions to building mobile sites, ranging from embedding mobile-accessible video to making forms easy to use in a smartphone or tablet. But this list is a good basis to begin to explore the essential challenges in developing mobile-friendly sites.

To get a sense of just how different mobile design is, compared to desktop/laptop website design, compare the desktop/laptop presence of the highly successful eBay site with its mobile sibling.

The eBay full-sized site (see Figure 1.1) includes very substantial drop-down menu elements activated by links in the top navigation bar. Users are "clued in" that the navigation bar text provides links with underlining that is triggered when they hover over the menu item.

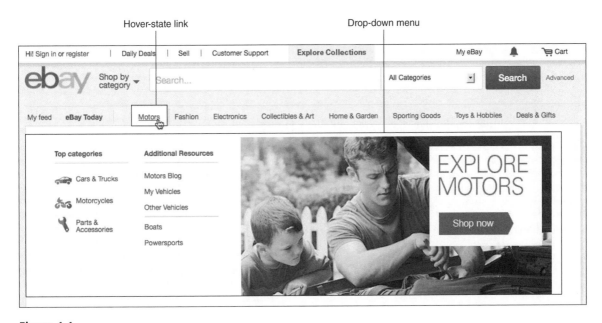

Figure 1.1
The eBay desktop/laptop website includes hover-state link display, drop-down menus, and other design elements that won't work in mobile devices.

Source: eBay™ Inc.

On the other hand, eBay's mobile site (see Figure 1.2) provides an immediately accessible, prominent search box, and a few thumbnail images to guide buyers to product categories.

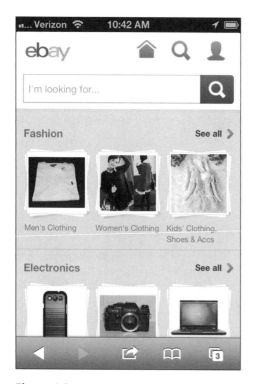

Figure 1.2
eBay's mobile website features a navigation design that relies on a small number of thumbnail images that are easy to access in mobile devices.
Source: eBay™ Inc.

There are different "levels" of lessons you can draw from comparing the desktop/laptop and mobile versions of eBay's site. On one level, you can see that mobile navigation "plays by different rules." Developers can't rely on hover-states, pop-out menus, and other design techniques that require a mouse and a functioning hover-state (there is no hovering in mobile devices because there is no mouse to point at an object to trigger a hover-state response).

So, that's one lesson: Navigation is completely different in mobile devices. But on another level, you can see that eBay's mobile presence is not a quantitative adaptation of the full-sized site. It is not the full-sized site with resized images and text, nor is it the full-sized site with some added animation, nor the full sized site with easier-to-click links. It is all those things, but beyond that, it is a *completely different* design.

Although it's not so apparent, eBay's mobile site uses different technologies and relies on new HTML5 elements that enable mobile-friendly animation and interactivity.

Before you dive into how to implement those exciting HTML5 elements, zoom in for a moment on some of the specific challenges you have to solve to create mobile sites that will really engage your users.

One Size Does Not Fit All

The smaller size of the viewport in mobile devices (compared to desktop and laptop monitors) has *qualitative* implications. You saw, in the eBay example, how links are much bigger on the mobile site—they are thumbnail images as opposed to small text.

And page layout is handled differently in mobile design. Typically, full-sized sites are framed by two- or three-column layouts (each column, in turn, can be broken into smaller columns). If I'm shopping for an iPhone 5 on eBay, for example, I see a three-column page on my laptop that includes an image on the left, details in the middle, and an ad—among other elements—on the right (see Figure 1.3).

Figure 1.3

The full-sized eBay website is designed with a three-column layout.

Source: eBay™ Inc.

The same information is presented to a smartphone user in a one-column layout, as shown in Figure 1.4.

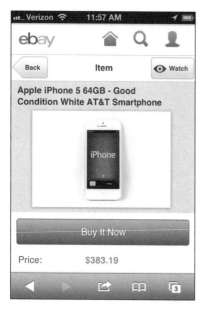

Figure 1.4
Smartphone page designs typically present content in a single column, as shown here at the eBay site.
Source: eBay™ Inc.

Another dimension to the size challenge is presenting text in a readable size on mobile devices. Among other shortcomings, the website of *The New York Times* does not adjust type size when viewed in a mobile device (see Figure 1.5).

Tip

The New York Times does distribute an effective app, including a minimalist free version, and a pay version that provides users with much of the content of the paper in an inviting and accessible form. The section called "Approaches to Mobile Development," later in this chapter, explores the relationship between proprietary apps and web apps (which run on any device, free).

Figure 1.5
The smaller viewport in mobile devices requires different font sizing technique to make text readable—without applying those techniques, users have to rely on their fingertips to zoom in on text to read it.
Source: *The New York Times* Company.

There are other implications to the size differential between desktop/laptop viewports, and those in mobile devices, particularly smartphones. This section is attempting to show you how the size difference requires a radically different approach to developing mobile page designs.

Lighting

One of the more under-appreciated differences between desktop/laptop browsing, and mobile web browsing, is lighting. It's highly unlikely that a desktop user will be browsing to your website outdoors on the kind of bright sun-shiny day that Johnny Nash and Jimmy Cliff used to sing about ("I Can See Clearly Now"). On the other hand, even with all the power modern technology can pack into a lightweight, thin tablet, the backlighting in those tablets (let alone a low-priced smartphone) can't compete with the sun.

The solution? Well, in part it is for mobile users to find a shady spot to search for a coffee shop or do their online surfing. But even with that, effective mobile sites use higher contrast color schemes that work better in bright lighting conditions. Tan text on a beige background might be a subtle, even classy, look on a laptop indoors. But it will be highly unreadable outdoors on a smartphone.

The Orbitz travel site, for example, has blue links on a black background for folks booking flights and hotels on their laptops. That's an effective, aesthetic look, as you can see in Figure 1.6.

Figure 1.6
Low-contrast color schemes, like blue type on a black background, are appropriate for viewing on powerfully back-lit desktop monitors and laptops.
Source: Orbitz® Worldwide Inc.

For travelers booking their trips as they wait outside for a cab, Orbitz presents a higher-contrast set of colors—white type on a dark blue background, as shown in Figure 1.7.

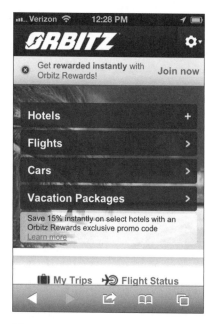

Figure 1.7
High-contrast color schemes, like the white type on a dark blue background at the Orbitz mobile site, make text easier to read in less-than-optimal lighting conditions.
Source: Orbitz® Worldwide Inc.

Speed

Another underrated difference between mobile and full-sized web page design is speed. Mobile users are at the mercy of wildly inconsistent, but often frustratingly slow, connections when they are untethered from their WiFi connections. Even the most high-powered, expensive tablets can't come close to matching the processing power of a low-budget laptop.

This speed gap has profound implications for developing mobile sites. It impacts the size of photos presented in mobile sites and the amount of video (or audio) data streamed into the site, and it calls for a very different approach to presenting multipage content.

By a "very different approach" to multipage content, I mean this: Traditional websites are constructed with multiple HTML pages that open and close as users navigate through the site. But forcing mobile users to wait for pages to open can be frustrating and tedious, since the process takes longer on mobile devices for the reasons I just identified. The solution is to build mobile websites that download *all at once* into a user's mobile device, so that navigation from page to page is seamless and quick. HTML5 provides solutions to this challenge, and I spend a significant part of this book walking through how to implement them.

Developing for Touch Screen Interaction

As you saw with the eBay site, navigation is very different in mobile devices, compared to devices with external inputs in the form of keyboards and pointing devices. Drop-down menus, triggered when a user hovers over a link at the top (or left side) of a page, are generally ineffective in mobile devices. In part, that is a product of the smaller viewport in mobile devices. But even more fundamentally, the difference is in how users interact with the site.

Mobile users use their fingers to tap, swipe, squeeze, and expand their way around a site. Mobile design has to take that into account.

And even beyond that, mobile users expect forms of interactivity and animation that are intuitive and correspond to the ways in which they interact with a website. When users tap a button pointing to the right, they expect some kind of animated transition that makes it feel like they have moved "to the right" of the viewing area. You and I (designers and developers that we are) know that these users aren't actually moving off the right edge of the page, but we can and should provide them with transition effects and animation so that it *feels* like they have moved to the right. The right-pointing navigation icons at the right edge in the BBC website in Figure 1.8 is a nice, clean example of providing that feel.

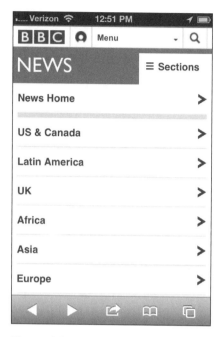

Figure 1.8
Many mobile sites use navigation structures that invoke a feeling of moving to a page to the right of the current screen, like the right-pointing navigation symbols at the BBC site.
Source: © BBC™.

Mobile Design and Implementation Solutions

Now that you have a feel for the different challenges involved in building mobile-friendly websites, this section surveys the available solutions, and explains where HTML5-based techniques fit into the picture.

Mobile development solutions can be broken into five possible approaches. Some of these approaches overlap. Some are alternate pathways to solving the same problems. But they do, generally, comprise specific development tracks.

From simple to complex, they are:

- No mobile design
- Fluid design

- Responsive design
- Web apps
- Native apps

Approaches to Mobile Development

The following sections explore the pros and cons of each of these approaches.

No Mobile Design

This approach refers to websites that are built for laptop/desktop displays, and do not adapt to mobile devices. Most often, this approach is adopted simply because the design and development team for a website has not yet appreciated the need for an effective mobile presence.

In other situations, the nature of the site, and its intended audience, is such that it is not necessary or appropriate to develop a mobile presence. For example, some galleries that I've worked with have eschewed a mobile presence on the basis that the presentation of art on a mobile device inevitably degrades the viewing experience.

There is also a cost factor. Your company may determine that developing a mobile presence is just not cost effective at a particular moment.

But aside from specific and relatively rare scenarios, the approach of ignoring mobile design generally has the effect of turning away a large and growing potential set of users.

Fluid Design

The concept of fluid design emerged in the desktop/laptop era, when great disparity emerged in the viewports in which users viewed websites. Designers used huge monitors measuring in the range of 2,500 pixels wide, whereas the emerging (at the time) notebook market was producing laptops with screen widths around 1,000 pixels.

In an attempt to create sites that adjusted to this variation in width, fluid design relied on elements sized in relative units of measurement—generally percentages—instead of fixed units of measurement (like pixels). So, to take a very simple example, a designer might define the width of the box that held page content to be "66 percent" of the width of the viewport (the browser window in which the page was displayed).

Elements of the fluid design approach remain applicable to modern design for mobile challenges. For example, an image might be sized to fill half the width of a viewport. But fluid design alone cannot provide the range of mobile-specific features—things like alternate color schemes, mobile-accessible navigation, and so on, that are required for a fully mobile-enabled site.

Responsive Design

Responsive design rises to the level of providing a more-or-less satisfactory mobile experience. Beyond simply *resizing* different elements for full-sized and mobile devices, responsive design makes possible different color schemes, different navigation devices, and even different content.

Technically, responsive design is applied by creating alternate CSS (Cascading Style Sheet) files. Responsive design uses HTML to identify a visitor's viewport width, and then invokes different CSS style sheet files or style definitions depending on the viewport.

Here's how this works. In short, you define *breakpoints* that invoke different styles. So, for example, you might define a breakpoint at 480 pixels. Any viewport of 480 pixels or fewer (like most smart phones) triggers one set of styles. Those styles might have smaller images, higher contrast colors, and a single column of content.

Alternately, if someone views your site in a viewport larger than 480 pixels, but narrower than, say, 1,040 pixels (here I am defining the widths of larger smart phones and tablets), they would see a different set of styles that would present larger images, more nuanced colors, and perhaps two columns of content.

Finally, in this scenario, a third set of styles might be defined for viewports wider than 1,040 pixels. This set of styles would apply to larger laptop and desktop displays. It might present even larger images, even more subtle color schemes, and multiple columns of content.

You'll explore responsive design to a limited extent in this book. A really fully implemented responsive design approach relies on very extensive CSS style sheet coding, beyond the scope of this book. But more to the point, the HTML5-based mobile app pathway that I focus on in this book provides a very inviting, mobile-specific approach to user interactivity. In short, designing specifically for mobile allows you to build in features like animation and interactivity that aren't available through responsive design.

Mobile Apps

What users think of as "apps" are actually divided into two categories. *Native* apps, which are discussed next, run without a web browser. *Web* apps run with a browser. Web apps and native apps look and feel pretty much the same to their users. They offer the same sets of animation and interactive features. They rely on similar navigation devices, and present the same content.

Mobile apps have the flexibility to present relatively straight-forward, no frills content, making booking an airline flight, for example, a hassle-free experience for a frazzled user rerouting a business trip (see Figure 1.9).

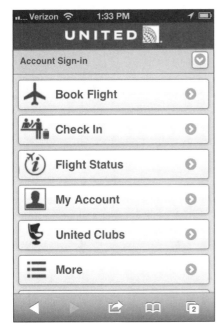

Figure 1.9
The United Airlines mobile site emphasizes clean, easy navigation.
Source: United Airlines™ Inc.

Mobile apps can also be highly animated, with rich media, as shown in Figure 1.10. These kinds of sites stretch the limits of design options in the limited space available in a mobile device.

Figure 1.10
The Walt Disney World mobile site is packed with images and animation.
Source: The Walt Disney Company.

The technical basis for mobile apps is (drum roll please) HTML5! As mobile apps are the most cost-effective approach to providing a fully animated, interactive mobile experience, this approach is the focus of this book.

Native Apps

The difference between native and web apps is that native apps run in mobile devices without a browser. That means they are full-fledged applications, computer programs, created in a high-level programming language like Objective-C. It also means that developers have to program separate apps for the iOS (Apple) and Android mobile operating systems. And, if they want to reach the entire spectrum of mobile users, they have to program even more apps for Blackberry devices, Windows Mobile devices, and other operating systems.

The cost of developing native apps is exponentially more than that of developing web apps for two reasons. One is the level of skill and work that goes into building a native app. The other, as noted, is the need to build separate apps for every mobile operating system (and in some cases, for different versions of different operating systems).

What, then, is the advantage of a native app over a mobile app? Promoters of native apps make an argument that the user experience is better because there is no browser interface. The counter-argument here is that mobile browser interfaces are so minimalist—disappearing in many cases once a user has navigated to a site—that this is not an issue. Native apps can run without Internet connections, but so can correctly deployed web apps. The gap between control over the user experience with web apps and native apps is small—to the point that it is rarely noticeable by users. But there are interface options available to native app designers that are not available in mobile apps, including the freedom to design pages that display with no browser interface navigation elements visible at the bottom of the screen (see Figure 1.11).

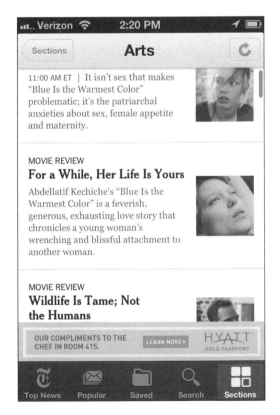

Figure 1.11
The New York Times native app displays without browser navigation icons at the bottom of the screen.
Source: *The New York Times* Company.

There is one, indisputable advantage to native apps: you can sell them. Developers who create native apps can register to be certified Apple mobile app developers (a process roughly equivalent in time and cost to getting a driver's license), and can sell apps through iTunes, Google Play and other proprietary app stores for Microsoft, Blackberry, and others.

Mobile apps can still require users to register to access content, and to pay for that access. But only native apps can be sold.

What if you're not sure you want to sell an app, or simply make your site content accessible in a highly mobile-friendly form? In that case, you can start with a web app, and later shop for development teams who will convert your web app into a native one.

Tip

This comparison of web and native apps is necessarily simplified and compressed. For one thoughtful, objective comparison of the advantages and disadvantages of the two paths to a mobile presence, see the Lionsbridge whitepaper entitled "Mobile Web Apps vs. Mobile Native Apps: How to Make the Right Choice" (http://www .lionbridge.com/files/2012/11/Lionbridge-WP_MobileApps2.pdf).

Everything You Wanted to Know About Developing Mobile Apps with HTML5, But Were Afraid to Ask

Everything you have surveyed to this point—the requirements for a successful mobile presence, and the possible technical approaches to building that presence—have pointed to the real advantages of an HTML5-based web app approach.

HTML5 is the foundation for building web apps, and it is how the *content* for those apps—text, images, media, input forms, navigation elements, and more—is created and embedded in pages.

But HTML5 cannot provide styling needed for everything from rounded-corner buttons to gradient blend background fills. For that, you need CSS3.

And HTML5 cannot provide the animation you need for dynamic effects, transitions, and interactivity. For that, you need JavaScript.

Allow me, for a moment, to switch places with you and pose (and then answer) some questions I anticipate you having at this point!

Q: *Whoa! I thought I was getting a book that would walk me through everything I need to build mobile apps in HTML!*

A: You are!

Q: *But, are you telling me I also need to learn CSS3 and JavaScript!?*

A: No.

Q: *OK, then, where will we get the CSS3 and JavaScript needed to "complete the package" and put together a really great mobile site?*

A: The CSS and JavaScript coding required for web apps is generated through different free, online resources. The framework you use in this book is jQuery Mobile, an extension of the popular jQuery library of JavaScript widgets built with JavaScript.

Q: *That was a lot of terminology. JavaScript? jQuery? Library? Widget?*

A: JavaScript is the programming language used to build animated and interactive elements in web pages. jQuery is a set of packaged modules built with JavaScript that are accessible to non-developers. A jQuery widget is a specific useful tool built with jQuery, like a slideshow, a calendar, or a drop-down menu, that is relatively easy to embed into an HTML5 website. And a library—in this context—is a combination of jQuery and CSS files that mesh together.

Q: *So why isn't this book called "Building Websites with jQuery Mobile?"*

A: Because HTML5 is the dynamic factor in building web apps. The jQuery Mobile part is all pre-built. You "plug into" it. But you customize the content of the mobile site and define the animation and interactivity with HTML5.

Q: *OK, what about styling. I know some CSS3; can I use it to style the mobile web apps I build using what I learn in this book?*

A: Yes, to a limited degree. But even if you didn't know any CSS3, there are online tools to generate unique, custom styling for jQuery Mobile pages built with CSS3.

Q: *Will this book show me how to use those tools?*

A: You betcha!

Q: *So, it sounds like the main technical skill I need to build mobile apps is a command of HTML5?*

A: Right!

Q: *I'm kind of familiar with HTML5; will that help?*

A: It will help. But some of that HTML5 is very specific to mobile apps, so it might be new to you. Even you're not familiar with HTML5, this book can help. I walk through all the HTML5 required to build mobile apps.

Q: *OK, so can I get started on that HTML5?*

A: Coming right up!

An HTML Refresher

Here's the basic workflow you'll traverse in this book to build mobile web apps with HTML5:

- You'll define your pages as HTML5 pages, so that browsers will recognize all the HTML5 elements you use (some of which are new to HTML5, and not available in older versions of HTML). What about browsers that don't recognize HTML5? All mobile browsers recognize HTML5 (although not all of them recognize all elements in HTML5—I address those issues as they emerge).

- You will link to JavaScript and CSS files at jQuery Mobile that enable some (but not all) of the elements you'll build into your pages.

- You will generate customized CSS styling to replace the default styles provided by jQuery Mobile.

- The bulk of the book's project will be defining mobile app content in HTML5, including headings, content areas, footers, text, images, links, video, audio, animation, page transitions, forms, and more.

You'll start with the basic page structure for an HTML5 page.

Preparing to Build a Mobile App with HTML5

It's important to pause and survey the tools and knowledge you need to build a mobile app with HTML5.

What Don't You Need to Buy

Some good news first: You don't need to buy anything. Assuming you have access to a computer, you've spent all the cash you need to spend to build and launch a mobile app with HTML5. HTML5, of course, is free. So is jQuery Mobile and CSS.

You do need a code editor, but you can get good ones for free.

Tip

Edit your code in a code editor, not a text editor. Text editors (like WordPad) tend to corrupt HTML and other code. If you have a favorite code editor already, use it. If not, I recommend NotePad++ for Windows (http://notepad-plus-plus.org/) and TextWrangler (http://www.barebones.com/products/textwrangler/) for Macs. These are not the most high-powered code editors, but I find they're more manageable for people new to coding.

If you use a text editor that supports or uses RTF (Rich Text Formatting), make sure to save your HTML and/or CSS coding in plain text UTF-8. Do *not* save files in RTF format. Avoid using dedicated word processors like Microsoft Word of Google Docs for coding. These applications have features that are very useful for creating formatted text documents (like smart quotes for example) that will invalidate HTML5 code.

Organizing Files

You should create a folder on your desktop that will hold all the files you create as you build a mobile app with HTML5. I'm calling mine `website`.

That folder will end up full of files. But if you keep all the files you need in *one folder* none of them will get lost or disconnected from each other.

By the way, stick to lowercase filenames, with no spaces or punctuation or special characters. You *can* use dashes (-) or underscores (_) to separate sets of characters in file names, but again, avoid using spaces. That will prevent confusion and corruption of your files.

Maintaining an Online Connection

You can work through the process of building a mobile app with HTML5 without an Internet connection, but you can't actually test your site in a browser without that connection. That's because the JavaScript and CSS you need to make your HTML5 web apps function is contained in online files hosted by a CDN (a content delivery network).

Technically, it is possible to build and test mobile apps without an Internet connection, but that's a problematic approach, especially for people new to the process. So the one condition for working through this book is that you'll need an Internet connection. Not all of the time. But when it comes time to test your site, you'll need that connection.

Do You Need a Remote Hosting Server?

Remote hosting servers make your site available to the world. They also include programs that allow some back-end scripts to work, like the scripts that manage data submitted in forms.

You do not need a remote hosting server to build or test HTML5 web apps that use jQuery Mobile.

Tip

There are features of advanced websites that require a hosting server—either one you install on your own computer, or one you contract for online. But the HTML5 mobile sites you learn to build in this book do not require those features.

That said, to launch a real, live mobile website, you need to upload it to a server. If you haven't contracted for a remote server before, I cover the process of shopping for and choosing a hosting server in my book *Building Websites All-in-One For Dummies* (co-authored with Doug Sahlin).

How Much HTML5 Do You Need to Know?

To answer the question: none. You can take on this project without any exposure to HTML5, or HTML period for that matter. That said, the more comfortable you are with HTML, and specifically HTML5, the better.

In the remainder of this chapter, I provide a crash course in the essential HTML5 required to build the foundation of an HTML5 mobile web app. And then, in the remaining chapters of this book, you'll explore a range of HTML5 elements used to add content to your sites.

Tip

Here are a few accessible resources for HTML5 tutorials, definitions, and syntax:

The w3schools site (http://www.w3schools.com) is a commercial site with what I find to be very useful tutorials and examples, all free.

The W3C site is a non-commercial, official depository for HTML5 documentation. The site is frequently updated but at this writing, HTML5 documentation is found at (http://www.w3.org/html/wg/drafts/html/master/).

And I provide links to a range of HTML5 resources at my own site at davidkarlins.com.

What about CSS3? CSS3, with major new features (compared to CSS2), provides the styling tools required to build vibrant, dynamic, inviting mobile websites. But you don't need to know how it works. As I noted earlier, if you do, that will be of some help. However, to be candid, the CSS required to style the pages you're going to be building is too complex for anyone to try to edit by hand. Instead, you'll generate the massive CSS files needed to customize the look and feel of your mobile sites using graphical interface online tools.

Which graphical interface online tool? I cover that in Chapter 5, but the tool is called ThemeRoller. Don't experiment with it too much until you get the basic site built, because I want to walk you through the process in a way that avoids pitfalls and hassles. But the short story is that you'll generate the CSS3 style sheet code in ThemeRoller.

Building an HTML5 Page Template

Time for your crash course in building an HTML5 page template. You'll use that template to add all the cool features in your mobile app.

Quick reminder: To avoid unnecessary trauma and stress, be sure you have a) created a folder on your desktop (I suggest calling it `website`) in which you will save all your files, and b) you're using a dedicated code editor like NotePad++ or TextWrangler, and *not* a text editor or word processor to create your code.

Okay then, here you go! There are three main parts to an HTML5 document:

- The `<doctype>` declaration tells browsers that this is an HTML5 file.
- The `<head>` element holds content that does not display in the page.
- The `<body>` element holds content that does display in the page.

Here's the code you'll use to start building your HTML5 mobile app:

```
<!doctype HTML>
<html>
<head>
</head>
<body>
</body>
</html>
```

Note that the `html`, `head`, and `body` elements have open tags (`<html>`, `<head>`, and `<body>`) and closing tags (`</html>`, `</head>`, and `</body>`).

Most elements in HTML do have open and closing tags.

Tip

While a "standard" HTML course might emphasize that not all HTML elements have open and closing tags (line breaks, for instance, are simply `<br>` or `<br/>`, but not both), I'm going to emphasize the opposite point.

Why? Because as you start building HTML5 elements to design mobile web apps, there are going to be a lot of elements. No sense sugar-coating this—there are going to be a *lot* of elements. If you haven't closed an element after opening it, the page can fall apart, become corrupted, and not display correctly. Of course, I'll walk through how to avoid that happening, and provide techniques for trouble-shooting when it does. But it's worth emphasizing here the importance of being vigilant about closing tags.

If you want to test your page in a browser now, here's how you do it:

1. Edit your code to include a test line of content:

```
<!doctype HTML>
<html>
<head>
</head>
<body>
Hello world!
</body>
</html>
```

2. Save the file in your code editor as `index.html`.

3. Use the File > Open option in your browser to open the file and view it. The result should be an uber-minimalist web page with no styling, but with the content displaying in the browser, such as the one shown in Firefox in Figure 1.12.

Figure 1.12
Testing a basic HTML5 template in a browser.
© 2014 Cengage Learning. Source: Mozilla FireFox.

Summary

In the next chapter, you learn all about the content of the `<head>` element to "plug in" to jQuery Mobile, and you begin to build mobile app content with HTML5. I introduce and walk through each element as you add it to your page, and contextualize it in the larger picture of building mobile pages with HTML5.

There are a few "take home" points from this chapter that will make the rest of your journey smoother:

■ You are building HTML5 pages. They require the template elements built in this chapter, simple as those were. Without the `<doctype>` declaration, and open and closing `<head>` and `<body>` elements, nothing will work. (The `<html>` element is necessary to make some scripts work and should be used to enclose all the HTML on the page.)

■ Keep in mind where you're headed. You're building a mobile app so that users feel as if they are navigating from page to page, when in reality, they are staying within a single HTML page the entire visit. That will speed download time, make links open quickly, and even allow the users to continue to access all the site content when they are not connected. Again, I walk through that process in Chapter 2, but I wanted to emphasize the importance of the very simple page template you just built. *All* your site content is going on that page. You'll see how this works starting in the next chapter!

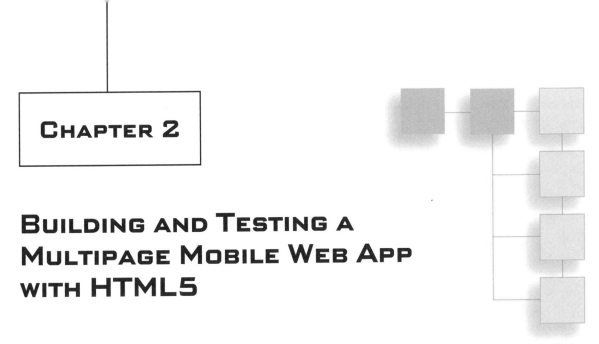

CHAPTER 2

BUILDING AND TESTING A MULTIPAGE MOBILE WEB APP WITH HTML5

In this chapter, you'll begin to build and test HTML5-based pages that look and feel like mobile apps—web apps for short. You'll start by surveying approaches to testing mobile sites. And once I've walked you through how to set up a testing environment, you will build a basic mobile-friendly page in HTML5!

If you're new to building mobile websites, here's a basic challenge: You are going to be creating websites in desktop or laptop computers for the most part. There are emerging apps for building websites in some tablets, but they're not robust enough to do the kind of website development you'll be doing, at least at this stage of the game.

But given that you will develop the mobile sites on laptop or desktop computers, there are serious limitations to how much you can *test* your sites on laptops or desktops. Obviously the size factor comes into play. Your sites are being built to display optimally on much narrower mobile devices. In addition, most laptop/desktop development environments do not have touch screen capability, so you can't test touch screen interactivity in the development environment.

DEALING WITH MOBILE RESOLUTIONS

Mobile devices have much higher pixel resolutions than laptop/desktop devices. The pixel resolution of different mobile devices varies greatly, but as a ballpark figure, it tends to be three or four times that of a laptop/desktop screen.

Wikipedia maintains as updated a list as is publicly available of the screen resolutions of mobile devices. The article is called "List of Displays by Pixel Density." At this writing, it can be found at https://en.wikipedia.org/wiki/List_of_displays_by_pixel_density.

Note that pixel resolution values for mobile devices can be deceiving. iPhone 5's, for example, boast a pixel width of 1,136 pixels in landscape (sideways) mode and 640 pixels in portrait (normal) mode.

However, those dimensions are very similar to the pixel width of a 2012 Macbook laptop. The specs for that 13-inch laptop are 1280 pixels by 800 pixels. How can a 4-inch (or so) wide iPhone have a screen that is about the same width in pixels as a 13-inch laptop? Maybe you've figured out where I'm going here: the pixels on the iPhone are much smaller than the pixels on a Macbook. And while numbers vary, this comparison typifies the gulf between pixel sizes on laptops and desktops on the one hand, and mobile devices on the other hand.

I'm walking through this in detail because the implications are great for designing mobile-friendly websites. Let's take an example: A 12-pixel high font size that displays at an accessible 1/6 of an inch or so height on a laptop/desktop computer will display at much less inviting 1/18th or 1/24th of an inch on a mobile device.

Let me illustrate. Figure 2.1 shows the default paragraph text, with no styling defined, in a laptop browser.

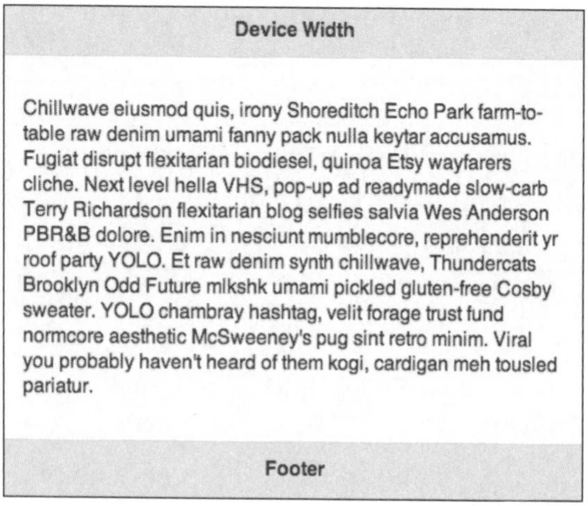

Figure 2.1
Previewing default paragraph text on a laptop browser.

The text is readable. But if I open this page in a mobile device (for example, an iPhone), the default display for paragraph text (generally 16 pixels high) is uninviting if not down-right unreadable. It's too small.

Figure 2.2 shows the same page, but this time viewed on an iPhone instead of on a laptop.

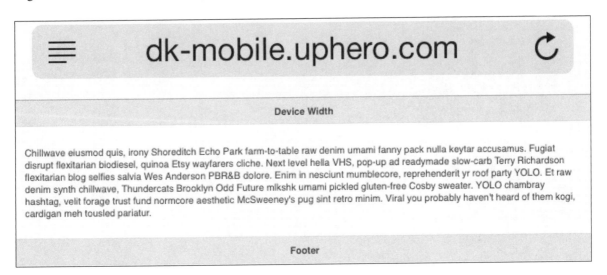

Figure 2.2
Previewing default paragraph text on an iPhone.
© 2014 Cengage Learning.

Those of you who are conversant with defining styles with CSS might be thinking, "I've got the answer, larger fonts for mobile devices." Interestingly, the basic solution to appropriately sizing text is found in HTML, not in CSS. There is an HTML *meta-tag* (a tag that has overarching impact on a page) that "resets" the resolution of a mobile device to more realistically reflect the size fonts should display. With that meta-tag implemented, the iPhone page displays the same text at a readable size, as shown in Figure 2.3.

Figure 2.3
Previewing default paragraph text with an adjusted mobile resolution.
© 2014 Cengage Learning.

Later in this chapter, in the section called "Building a Basic Multipage Site with jQuery Mobile," I'll show you how to implement the HTML meta-tag that adjusts screen width But if you're curious now, it looks like this:

```
<meta name="viewport" content="width=device-width, initial-scale=1">
```

Find the Code...

Later in this chapter, I organize all the HTML I introduce into a template you can use. You can find that code at the website I've set up to share the code used in this book. That site is http://dk-mobile.uphero.com. If you want to navigate directly to the page containing the code for this chapter, that link is http://dk-mobile.uphero .com#ch02.

TESTING WITH EMULATION

Perhaps you're wondering how on earth a mobile developer can begin to test a site in the dozens, or hundreds, of popular devices? If so, you're right to be thinking about that. After all, even the most gadget-obsessed designer can only own so many mobile devices!

So, before you start *building* mobile pages, you'll need a technique for *testing* those pages in as realistic an environment as possible. You'll review different options for doing that, but here's a preview of what I'm going to recommend: I'll show you how to set up a free, real-live remote website that you can use to test your pages, either on your own mobile device (if you have one), or using an online-simulation resource. All of these resources are free.

I'll also share some suggestions for a coding environment for the laptop/desktop setup that you are using to build your mobile pages. If you have one you like already, you're set. If not, I'll recommend options for PC and Mac users.

Then, with coding and testing environments established, you'll start building mobile pages! By the end of this chapter, you'll understand how to create a mobile-friendly page, and test it.

PREVIEWING AND TESTING MOBILE WEBSITES

Because users experience websites very differently in mobile devices, you'll need to *test* mobile web pages differently than you would if you were testing pages designed for laptop or desktop users.

There are three basic approaches to testing.

You can just preview a mobile page in a desktop/laptop browser. Figure 2.4 shows *The Boston Globe*'s website, previewed in Google's Chrome browser, with the browser width set to 480 pixels.

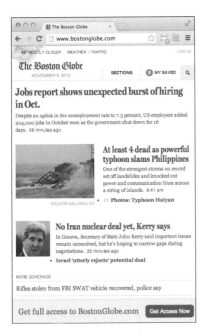

Figure 2.4
Previewing a mobile website in a laptop browser.
Source: *The Boston Globe*™ Inc.

Or, you can preview the page using simulation applications. These are online resources that emulate or simulate (create an approximation of) the experience of using a site in a mobile device. Figure 2.5 shows *The Boston Globe* site, displayed in a simulation of how it will look in an Android Operating System mobile device.

Figure 2.5
Previewing a mobile website with an online emulation resource.
Sources: *The Boston Globe*™ Inc and Sauce Labs, Inc.

Finally, you can preview using a real mobile device. This is the most accurate way to test how your mobile website will look and feel in a mobile device, as shown in Figure 2.6.

Figure 2.6
Viewing the *The Boston Globe* site in an iPhone.
Source: *The Boston Globe*™ Inc.

Let's preview these three basic approaches in a bit more detail:

- Test mobile pages in a regular laptop/desktop browser (like the current versions of Firefox, Chrome, Safari or Internet Explorer). This is the easiest testing environment to set up since you already have one or more of these browsers installed on your laptop or desktop. I'll walk through how to overcome the limitations of testing in a regular laptop/desktop browser to the greatest degree possible.

- Use simulation applications, either installed on your computer, or at a remote site. Simulation apps provide a closer-to-real testing environment, compared to simply testing in a laptop/desktop browser. They are a hassle to install and set up on your laptop or desktop, so, as you'll see, I'll recommend you avail yourself of online simulation resources.

- Finally, the best way to test a mobile site is to open it in an actual mobile device.

The second and third options in this list—using simulation resources and testing in an actual mobile device—are most easily accomplished if you have a remote testing server. There are other approaches and workarounds to creating "real-life" testing environments, but they're quite complicated and tedious to set up.

Tip

There are also paid on-line services that give you access to virtual machines with different operating systems and browsers, but they are usually rather expensive. This option is worth considering if you end up doing a lot of cross-platform development. I contract with a service called Sauce Labs (https://saucelabs.com/) for commercial development.

In the following sections of this chapter, I'll walk you through three alternative workflows: testing in your computer, testing with online simulator resources, and testing in your own mobile device.

The first option is quite simple. You don't have to do anything to set it up. And you don't need an active Internet connection to use it. It involves testing your mobile pages as you build them, in a laptop/desktop window sized to match typical smartphone and tablet viewports (screen widths).

The more advanced workflows involve uploading your pages as you build them to a remote server, and then either testing them in your own mobile device, or using online simulation resources. For this option, you need to have a remote server. Perhaps you already have one. If not, I'll walk you through how to get and set one up free, next.

Defining a Local Development Folder

Regardless of which technique you use to test your mobile site, there is one essential element that has to be carefully set up before you can build or test a local site. Is that a ready cup of hot coffee or tea? Probably a good idea to have that prepared, but technically speaking that's not an essential requirement for building a mobile site.

The essential technical foundation for any website, and for mobile sites in particular, is to define *a single folder* that will hold all your files. I emphasized this point in the section "Organizing Files," in Chapter 1, but I'm redundantly emphasizing it here for two reasons.

One is that you might have skipped Chapter 1. The other is that keeping all your website files in a single folder (it can include subfolders) is even more important as you define a remote testing server. Keep in mind that this remote server has to be *synchronized* with the local development environment.

In other words, you'll *build* your site on your own local computer, but you'll *test* it, and ultimately *publish it* for the world to see, on a remote server. And if your files are scattered about your local computer, it will be unnecessarily difficult to transfer them to the remote server without corrupting them.

Tip

> As I noted, the single folder in which you organize all your website files can include subfolders. If your site is large (hundreds of files), it is good practice to organize files into subfolders. For example, you can put images in a folder named images, scripts in a folder named assets, custom fonts in a folder called fonts, and so on. But remember, keep all these subfolders *within a single main folder* so your files don't go "astray," corrupting your site.

Preparing a Test File

Let's build a very simple web page and preview it in a desktop or laptop browser. Using your code editor, create a new HTML file. Save it as test01.html. Use the following as a very simple, basic, starter code:

```
<!doctype html>
<html>
<head>
<meta charset="UTF-8">
<title>Mobile Test Site</title>
</head>
<body>
<h1>Welcome!</h1>
<h2>This is a Test</h2>
<p><a href="http://www.wikipedia.org">This is a link to Wikipedia</a></p>
</body>
</html>
```

Save the page with this code as test01.html.

Tip

> You'll find the final code for this chapter in easy to copy-and-paste form at http://dk-mobile.uphero.com/#ch02.

Establishing a Remote Hosting Server

Testing websites on a server is part of the workflow for all serious web development projects. The essential element in a web server is software that provides tools that aren't normally available on your own computer. For example, you cannot test scripts written in the PHP programming language to manage data unless your site is hosted on a server.

For laptop/desktop website development, one option is to install server software on your own computer. MAMP (for Macs), WAMP (for Windows), and LAMP (for Linux) servers are used by developers to test websites that will collect and distribute data from server-hosted databases.

That approach doesn't solve the problems you face designing for mobile devices. Your challenge is to find a hosting environment that allows you to see—and to the greatest extent possible—*feel* how a site will work in a mobile device. As noted earlier, the two most effective, accessible options for that are testing with online simulation resources, and testing in a real mobile device. And, again as noted earlier, doing either of those without a remote hosting server is tricky at best.

On the other hand, setting up a remote server is not a hassle. If you have one already, you've solved that challenge. If not, you can follow these steps to acquire and begin to use a free remote server-hosted website from 000webhost.com. Here's how:

1. Go to 000webhost.com.

2. Scroll down the page to compare options for free and paid hosting (see Figure 2.7). Paid hosting is reasonably priced, and provides extra features. You don't need those features to build and test a mobile site, but don't let me discourage those of you with the financial resources to do so from signing up for a paid site. That said, the free site option will work fine for testing mobile sites. Select an option.

Free or paid hosting? Compare our plans:		
	» Free Hosting	» Premium Hosting
Price	$0.00	$4.84 / month
Disk Space	1500 MB	Unlimited Disk Space!
Data Transfer	100 GB / month	Unlimited Data Transfer!
Add-on Domains	5	Unlimited
Sub-domains	5	Unlimited
E-mail Addresses	5	Unlimited
MySQL Databases	2	Unlimited
Free domain yourname.COM, .NET, .ORG, .INFO, .CO.UK	✗	✓
Control Panel	Custom Panel	cPanel Pro, see demo
Reseller Hosting Feature	✗	✓
	Order Now	Order Now

Figure 2.7
Selecting the free option for hosting at 000webhost.com.
Source: First Class Web Hosting™.

3. After you complete the signup process, you'll receive username and password information in an email. And a URL! That URL is the address where your website will be found on the Internet. Note it. When you want to see how your site looks, open that URL in your browser.

4. Click on the link at the 000webhost.com home page to the Members Area, and use your username and password to log in to your site. The domain management page opens. Of course your domain management page will look a bit different than mine (in Figure 2.8), since you and I have different domain names.

5. Click on the link to the CPanel for your website. This opens the control panel, where you can manage your site.

» Domain	» Status	» Action
dk-mobile.uphero.com	Active	Go to CPanel Build Website

Figure 2.8
Opening the control panel at 000webhost.com.
Source: First Class Web Hosting™.

6. Scroll down the Control Panel page to the Files section. Click the File Manager icon (see Figure 2.9). This opens the File Manager module that you'll use to upload files to the remote server as you build your remote site.

Figure 2.9
Navigating to the File Manager at 000webhost.com.
Source: First Class Web Hosting™.

7. Files accessible to the public (and that can be opened with a browser) are saved to the public_html subdirectory. When you are ready to upload files to the server, select that subdirectory, as shown in Figure 2.10.

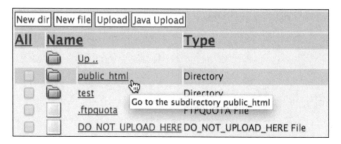

Figure 2.10
Selecting the `public_html` subdirectory.
Source: First Class Web Hosting™.

8. With the `public_html` subdirectory selected, you use the Upload button to select and post files to your server (see Figure 2.11).

Figure 2.11
Selecting the Upload button.
Source: First Class Web Hosting™.

I expect some of you are familiar with uploading files to a server. However, if this is your first experience with remote web hosting servers, bookmark Steps 4–8. Refer to them whenever you're instructed to upload a file to the remote hosting server. If, on the other hand, you're an old pro at managing files with another file transfer application (like FileZilla), feel free to use that instead.

Tip

The 000webhost.com option I suggest in the previous steps is a remarkable deal; it's free, ad-free web hosting that supports all the features needed to build a modern mobile website with HTML. That said, paid hosting services provide more extensive support, fewer downtime issues, and are likely to be a bit less frustrating if you are new to interacting with hosting services. I generally find the options listed and reviewed at http://inexpensivewebhosting.co/ to be pretty reliable. These paid hosting services generally cost under $5/month.

I did promise that there is an even simpler way to test mobile pages, without establishing a remote server.

Previewing in a Desktop/Laptop Browser

There are dozens of free online resources, apps, and add-ins for previewing mobile pages in desktop and laptop browsers. You'll use one that is free, quick and easy to install, and works in any environment. It is an extension to the Google Chrome browser. So, for starters, if you don't have Chrome installed on your computer, go to www.google.com/chrome and install Chrome.

Next, install the Window Resizer extension. You can search for it in the Google Chrome store (https://chrome.google.com/webstore; see Figure 2.12). When the Window Resizer install window appears, click to Install it as an extension in Chrome.

Figure 2.12
Searching for the Window Resizer.
Source: Google Chrome™.

Now let's preview the mobile site. With Chrome open, choose File > Open File. In the dialog that opens, navigate to and double-click on the test01.html file you created for this experiment.

Click the Resize Window icon in the upper-right corner of the Chrome toolbar. You'll see options for viewport widths that match a wide variety of mobile devices, as shown in Figure 2.13.

Figure 2.13
Selecting a viewport size in Window Resizer.
Sources: Google Chrome™ and ionut-botizan.net.

Start by selecting the 480 × 800 pixel option. This provides a rough approximation of how your page will look in many smartphones.

Previewing mobile pages with a tool like Window Resizer provides a quick, functional way to get a rough sense of how pages will look in mobile devices. For a more developed preview, you'll post the page to a remote server and test it with a simulator.

Previewing with Simulation Resources

Previewing mobile pages in a simulator provides a significantly more accurate picture of how the page will look and feel to mobile users. The accessible mobile device simulators you're going to explore access your page from the web, not from your computer. Previewing your site in a mobile device simulator requires that your site be uploaded to a remote host. If you need some refreshing in how to set that up, jump back to the section called "Establishing a Remote Hosting Server" earlier in this chapter.

There are a number of valuable options for online emulation resources. The one you're going to use is Mobile Phone Emulator, which you can find at http://www .mobilephoneemulator.com.

Start by navigating to that website, mobilephoneemulator.com. With that site open, follow these steps to preview your page:

1. The first dialog asks you to specify your monitor size (see Figure 2.14). This helps the emulator more accurately "convert" your experience from your laptop or desktop to the mobile preview. If you don't know the width of your monitor, grab a ruler and do a quick measurement. Then enter that width in the dialog and click OK.

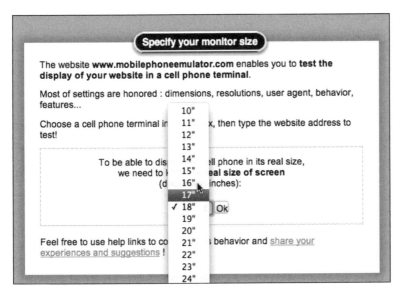

Figure 2.14
Entering your monitor width in the Mobile Phone Emulator.
Source: COWEMO SAS.

2. Choose a cell phone terminal from the drop-down list on the right, as shown in Figure 2.15.

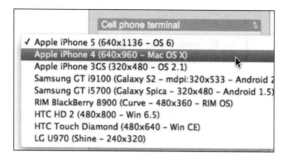

Figure 2.15
Choosing a cell phone to emulate.
Source: COWEMO SAS.

3. Next, enter the URL for your uploaded `test01.html` file in the website to emulate field. Click Go (see Figure 2.16).

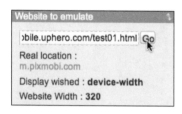

Figure 2.16
Choosing a website page to test in the emulator.
Source: COWEMO SAS.

4. You can now test your page in the emulator, including links (as you add them).

Testing in an emulator environment will provide more of a feel for how users experience the site in their mobile devices, including simulating the device interface.

There are more developed emulation resources for professional developers. I'm steering sharply toward free resources in this book, but the emulation site I use for myself is saucelabs.com.

In Sauce Labs (saucelabs.com), I can spin up an iOS or Android not only to see how a site looks, but also to take screenshots, interact with a mobile web app, record a video, and more. See Figure 2.17.

Figure 2.17
Testing a page in Sauce Labs.
Source: Sauce Labs, Inc.

Testing with Mobile Devices

The best way to test a mobile website is in a mobile device. Here, you get a feel for how dense the pixel resolution in mobile devices is, the touch-based elements of your page, the color, video, and sound, and other dimensions of the site that will be experienced by users.

The process is pretty simple: Open your page in a mobile device.

Which mobile device should you use, and how many do you need to use? Obviously, developers can't stock every mobile device their visitors might use. You should start with whatever mobile device you have. And then, as your resources expand, and as you get a better sense of your audience, you might invest in a few additional mobile devices. Personally, I have an iPhone, an Android mobile phone, and a Kindle Fire tablet, and I test sites in those three devices.

BUILDING A MULTIPAGE HTML5 MOBILE PAGE

In Chapter 1 of this book, I identified problems that need to be solved in order to build a mobile-friendly website. Earlier sections of this chapter walk through how to set up both a development environment on your computer, and a testing environment.

Now it's time to start building mobile-friendly, interactive web pages with HTML5!

In Chapter 1, you explored basic alternative approaches to building mobile-friendly sites, and identified the one you'll use in this book: HTML5 for content, combined with jQuery Mobile for animation and interactivity. You won't *program* jQuery Mobile, because it's already built and ready for you to use. But you'll definitely code HTML5. Using HTML5, you will define page content and style.

How will you define style with HTML, when normally CSS (Cascading Style Sheets) files are used to define styling in web pages? The answer is that you'll generate the CSS you need for a completely unique, customized look and feel for your pages, and you'll apply that generated CSS with HTML5 code. In short, for the bulk of the rest of this book, you'll be building and customizing the mobile site content and styling with HTML5.

Building a Basic Multipage Site with jQuery Mobile

The basic web page you build for your mobile-friendly site will have standard HTML5 <head> content, plus a few special elements.

The basic HTML5 page elements that are included in the <head> element are:

- A doctype declaration telling browsers this is an HTML5 page (this actually comes *before* the <head> element, but I'm including it in this discussion since the doctype declaration is part of the code that appears before the <body> element, and is part of the code that that does not define content visible in a browser window).

- A page title that will display in title bars of browsers.

Then, the page will have three lines of code that are specific to an interactive, animated mobile site:

- A metadata element that forces mobile devices to report their actual width to a browser.

- Links to the centrally distributed jQuery file, and the centrally distributed Mobile JavaScript file that enable dozens of animated, interactive, web-friendly widgets.

- A link to the centrally distributed CSS file that works with the jQuery Mobile JavaScript file to provide the animation and interactivity associated with widgets.

Let's break this all down in two ways. First, let's examine this code, and then let's zoom in a bit on what it means and how it works.

Here's the code you'll use to create a new HTML5 mobile page.

You can copy and paste it (or type it) into your code editor now, and save it as `index.html` if you wish to work through this section of the book as an annotated tutorial.

Tip

Remember, the final code for this chapter in easy to copy-and-paste form is at http://dk-mobile.uphero.com/ #ch02.

```
<head>
<meta charset="UTF-8">
<title>Page Title</title>
<meta name="viewport" content="width=device-width, initial-scale=1">
<link rel="stylesheet" href="http://code.jquery.com/mobile/1.4.1/
    jquery.mobile-1.4.1.min.css" />
<script src="http://code.jquery.com/jquery-1.10.2.min.js"></script>
<script src="http://code.jquery.com/mobile/1.4.1/
    jquery.mobile-1.4.1.min.js"></script>
</head>
```

Defining Viewport Scale

Let me expand briefly on why the viewport tag in the `<head>` element is necessary. Without it, there will be no consistency to the size of type and other elements when users visit your mobile site using different mobile devices. Here's the non-technical explanation: Pixel resolution on mobile devices is usually much higher than on laptops or desktops.

Roughly speaking, there are three to four times as many dots per inch (dpi) in a mobile device. So, a mobile device, even in portrait mode (as normally viewed, not turned sideways), might "report" to a browser that the device viewport is 960 pixels wide, or 1920 pixels wide. I'm picking values somewhat at random here since this is different in every device, but these are typical ballpark figures for how mobile devices report their viewport width to a browser.

But, in terms of how the page *looks* to a user, it's really a 480 pixel wide page. Again, I'm picking a value somewhat arbitrarily, but this is in the ballpark of what a typical smartphone viewport should be reported at.

This disparity between the technical viewport size, and the (much lower) real-world viewport size of mobile devices will skew how pages look in a mobile device. A web page designed for a 960-pixel wide screen will, for example, appear in most mobile devices with tiny, unreadable type and images about a quarter the size the designer intended them to be viewed at.

When you design pages for mobile devices, you will design them with page widths, fonts, images, videos, and so on meant to be viewed in "real-world" sizes, not scrunched up to a quarter of their size. So, the line of code:

```
<meta name="viewport" content="width=device-width, initial-scale=1">
```

in the head element will essentially revalue how a pixel is reported to a browser, so that your mobile-ready pages open as they should.

Note

Forcing devices to open mobile pages at the size they were designed to work at does *not* disable user's ability to zoom the pages with their fingers.

The links to the JavaScript and jQuery Mobile files connect the page to these two major libraries of code. The link to the CSS file plugs in CSS style definitions that sync with that code.

Linking to the JavaScript and CSS Files

You do not edit the JavaScript files used in mobile sites. If you're a JavaScript expert and you want to work on editing the centrally distributed JavaScript that makes mobile websites tick, you can join the editing community at jQuery Mobile and be part of that collective project, but these files are not editable by individual developers.

You *will* change the CSS file. But that is a massive file (about 800 different CSS style declarations), and, to emphasize the point, it is synchronized closely with the JavaScript that enables the animation and interactivity you'll be building into your pages. So, when it comes time to edit this, you'll use a special online resource, the jQuery Mobile ThemeRoller, to do that.

In most working developments, its best to link to the required JavaScript and CSS files. The Content Delivery Networks (CDNs) that host these files are powerful, reliable, and fast as any servers.

However, in development environments where you do not have Internet access, you can download these three files and link to them at your own site. The download links are found by going to the ever-changing jQuery Mobile home page (jquerymobile.com), clicking on the link to the latest stable version of jQuery Mobile, and then using the links to download the JavaScript and CSS files to your own computer. Save them in the root folder for your site. If you do that (and again, unless you're very comfortable with downloading and installing scripts, I'm not recommending this), your head content will look like this:

```
<head>
<meta charset="UTF-8">
<title>Page Title</title>
<meta name="viewport" content="width=device-width, initial-scale=1">
<link rel="stylesheet"jquery.mobile-1.4.1.min.css" />
<script src="jquery-1.10.2.min.js"></script>
<script src="jquery.mobile-1.4.2.min.js"></script>
</head>
```

An Important Note on jQuery Mobile Versions

jQuery Mobile is an open-source resource. It's free! And it's a very valuable tool for mobile web developers. But one issue I have with the team that maintains the files that make jQuery Mobile work with HTML5 is that they update the code too frequently. The template code I provide in this chapter links to the current versions of jQuery Mobile JavaScript and CSS as we go to press. But the team at jQuery Mobile may make tweaks to this code, and when you read this book, there may be a new version of some or all of these files.

What does that mean for you? It does not mean that the links in the template code in this chapter are bad, or wrong, or buggy, or problematic. But it does mean that the energetic team at jQuery Mobile has introduced some new tweaks or features, and provided a new set of files. Unfortunately, the team doesn't always make it easy to locate the updated links to the new files (available through Content Delivery Networks). But if you hunt around at jquerymobile.com, you can find them. Again, you don't *need* to update, and I generally don't recommend updating every time the team introduces a new version of jQuery Mobile. The version linked to in this template is stable, and will be supported for years to come.

EDITING A MULTIPAGE DOCUMENT

You've spent enough time previewing the process and exploring some of the theory behind building interactive, animated, mobile-friendly pages with HTML5. This included utilizing the jQuery Mobile library of widgets (which you will deploy with HTML5, and by linking to the CDN jQuery, and jQuery Mobile files).

Time to build a multipage site! If you're working along with me in this chapter, you can copy the following into your code editor (index.html), *replacing* anything in your open file to this point:

```
<!DOCTYPE html>
<html>
<head>
<meta charset="UTF-8">
<title>Page Title placeholder text</title>
<meta name="viewport" content="width=device-width, initial-scale=1">
<link rel="stylesheet" href="http://code.jquery.com/mobile/1.3.2/
    jquery.mobile-1.4.1.min.css" />
<script src="http://code.jquery.com/jquery-1.10.2.min.js"></script>
<script src="http://code.jquery.com/mobile/1.4.1/jquery.mobile-1.4.1.min.js"></script>
</head>
<body>
<div data-role="page" id="page01">
<div data-role="header">
<h1>HTML5 Mobile App</h1>
</div>
<div data-role="content">
<h1>Welcome!</h1>
<p>Home page placeholder text</p>
<ul>
<li><a href="#page02">Page 2</a></li>
<li><a href="#page03">Page 3</a></li>
<li><a href="#page04">Page 4</a></li>
</ul>
<p>This page built with HTML5 using jQuery Mobile</p>
<img src="http://view.jquerymobile.com/1.3.2/dist/demos/
    _assets/img/jquery-logo.png" width=240px">
</div>
<div data-role="footer">
<h4>Built with HTML5 using jQuery Mobile</h4>
</div>
</div>
<div data-role="page" id="page02">
<div data-role="header">
<h1>Page 2</h1>
</div>
<div data-role="content">
<p>Page 2 content</p>
</div>
<div data-role="footer">
<h4><a href="#page01">HOME</a></h4>
</div>
```

```
</div>
<div data-role="page" id="page03">
<div data-role="header">
<h1>Page 3</h1>
</div>
<div data-role="content">
<p>Page 3 content </p>
</div>
<div data-role="footer">
<h4><a href="#page01">HOME</a></h4>
</div>
</div>
<div data-role="page" id="page04">
<div data-role="header">
<h1>Page 4</h1>
</div>
<div data-role="content">
<p>Page 4 content</p>
</div>
<div data-role="footer">
<h4><a href="#page01">HOME</a></h4>
</div>
</div>
</body>
</html>
```

Tip

The final code for this chapter is in easy to copy-and-paste form at http://dk-mobile.uphero.com/#ch02.

Testing a Multipage Mobile Site

Before dissecting this code, test it. As discussed earlier in this chapter, you can do that three ways. First, you can simply open it in a browser window sized to match a 480-pixel wide smartphone, as shown in Chrome in Figure 2.18.

Figure 2.18
Testing a basic mobile HTML5 template in Chrome.
Source: The jQuery Foundation™.

You can see that testing the site in a regular browser, sized to 480 pixels wide, gives a *rough* approximation of the user experience. You can test links, and use the browser's Back button to test out navigation.

A more accurate test results when you upload the page to a server and open it in an emulation program, like Sauce Labs or Mobile Phone Emulator. The text size is more accurate, and you can get a feel for how the page will look and function in a mobile device, as shown in Figure 2.19.

Figure 2.19
Testing a basic mobile HTML5 template with Mobile Phone Emulator.
Source: COWEMO SAS.

Finally, the *most* accurate test is to upload your site to a remote server and open it in a mobile device, as shown in Figure 2.20.

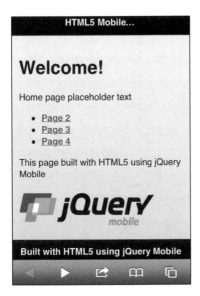

Figure 2.20
Testing a basic mobile HTML5 template in an iPhone.
Source: The jQuery Foundation™.

Examining and Editing Mobile HTML5 Elements

I'm confident that you can figure out, on your own, that the text and images in this template are editable. You can replace the text, images, and links with your own content.

What might not be so intuitive are the special `<data-role>` elements that populate this template. They include `<data-role="page">` elements that are *hidden* until they are selected. These data-role pages are the essence of navigation within a mobile site. They allow users to download a *single HTML document* and browse around within it, thus providing the appearance and feel of navigating from one page to another in a "normal" website.

Within each `<data-role="page">` element, you see `<data-role="header">`, `<data-role="content">`, and `<data-role="footer">`.

Notice that the headers and footers have built-in styling (white text centered on a black background). That is a result of the central CSS file being applied to these elements. I walk you through how to adjust that styling in a limited way a bit later in this chapter, and you'll return to custom styling throughout the remaining chapters in this book.

The data-role elements you've applied so far (for pages, headers, footers, and content) don't produce any interactivity. But other data-role elements do. One of the most widely applied is the `<data-role="listview">` element. Here's how that looks, applied to the navigation links in the first data-role page of the template:

```
<ul data-role="listview">
<li>
<a href="#page02">Page 2</a></li>
<li> <a href="#page03">Page 3</a></li>
<li> <a href="#page04">Page 4</a></li>
</ul>
```

The only change I've made here is to add `"data-role="listview"` to the opening `<ul>` tag in the navigation list. But this one little edit changes the appearance of the navigation list, and makes it interactive, as shown in Figure 2.21.

Figure 2.21
Testing an interactive listview.
Source: The jQuery Foundation™.

This example, adding `data-role="listview"` to a `<ul>` tag, provides a good model for how jQuery Mobile JavaScript interacts with the HTML5 coding you create to provide animation and interactivity. In the remaining chapters of this book, you'll explore how to further control and enhance that interactivity.

Editing Color Swatches

By applying a listview to an unordered list (a `<ul>` tag), you saw how HTML5 interacts with and enables animation and interactivity provided by jQuery Mobile. Before closing this chapter, I want to provide a taste of how HTML5 is also used to control styling provided by the central CSS file that makes jQuery Mobile sites tick.

You can change the appearance of any element by adding the code to that element:

```
data-theme="a" (or "b" or "c" or "d" or "e")
```

Here's an example:

```
<div data-role="header" data-theme="c">
```

Here, I've added `data-theme="c"` to a header. The result is black text on a gray background, which replaces the default white text on a black background, and is shown in Figure 2.22.

Figure 2.22
Applying a data-theme color swatch.
Source: The jQuery Foundation™

You can find demonstrations of each of the five data theme color swatch sets at the jQuery Mobile site. That site changes constantly, so I won't give you a specific link, but search for "jquery mobile themes" and you'll find links to pages that demonstrate how those data-theme color sets look. Figure 2.23 shows the results of my search.

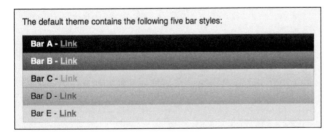

Figure 2.23
Surveying jQuery Mobile data-theme swatch color sets.
Source: The jQuery Foundation™.

Summary

In the next chapter, you learn to define and style a range of jQuery Mobile interactive and animated tools, including expanding the basic listview you learned to create in this chapter. You also learn to fine-tune how you apply data themes to control the appearance of every element in your site.

There are three "take home" points from this chapter that will make the rest of your journey more effective:

- You need to set up a testing environment since you are developing your site in a laptop or desktop computer, and it is going to be used in mobile devices. A window sizing plug-in for your browser is the easiest solution. Uploading your site to a hosting server and testing it using emulation resources is a more accurate gauge of how your site will look and feel in a mobile device. The ultimate testing environment is to actually test your remote site using one or more mobile devices.

- The `<head>` content provided in this chapter establishes the critical link between your web page and the magic of jQuery Mobile animation and interactivity. Every jQuery Mobile page has links to the JavaScript and CSS files required to make that page respond to user actions in mobile devices.

- The listview data-role converts a simple unordered list into a dynamic, animated navigation bar that responds to user touch in a mobile device screen. It is a good example of the kinds of interactive elements you can access with HTML5 in a page linked to the jQuery Mobile scripts.

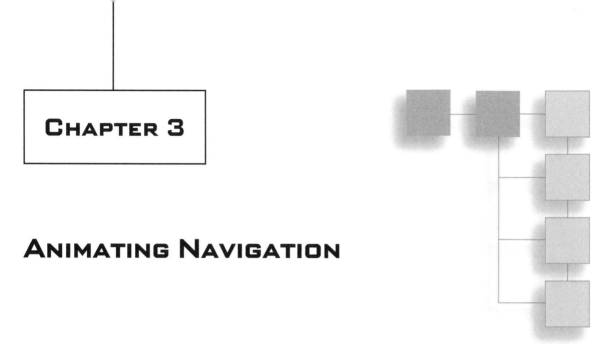

CHAPTER 3

ANIMATING NAVIGATION

Without a useful navigation system, any site is unusable. That applies doubly in mobile design, where space is at a premium, and where links need to stand out from the page.

In this chapter, you'll explore how to enhance navigation lists (*listviews*), and how to make the experience of navigating your mobile site a pleasant and inviting one for your users.

In the course of doing that, I'll walk you through when and how to define these navigation options:

- Listviews with filters to make long lists manageable.
- Listviews with inset formatting to make them more inviting and accessible.
- Split button listviews that combine images and text, and provide two different links within a list item.
- Links that open in dialogs, instead of in browser windows.
- Transitions to animate the navigation experience.

THE ROLE OF INTERACTIVE, ANIMATED NAVIGATION

There are two key concepts to wrap your head around when building navigation for mobile web apps with HTML5.

The first is that what *appears to the user* to be navigation between "pages" in your mobile app is really navigation between `<div data-role="page">` elements. These elements appear and disappear, giving the impression that different pages are opening and closing. The big advantage to this approach is that pages open and close quickly. If users have to wait for their 3G, 4G, or LTE connection to open your "click here now for fast, fast, fast, information" link, they might move on to another site.

The other advantage to having your entire mobile app download all at once is that, having opened a "page" at your site, users can navigate throughout your site when they are out of WiFi or mobile range. That's particularly handy if you're building mobile sites for users in Moscow, Tokyo, Mexico City, New York City, Paris, or Almatyor (Kazakhstan)—or anywhere else that mobile users travel by subway (where, for the most part, they are out of Internet range).

You activate jQuery Mobile's page navigation power with HTML5. And in this chapter, you'll see how that works. I'll show you how to build pages that pop, flip, and fade when they open or close. I'll show you how to open pages in dialogs—more or less "pop-up" elements that provide engaging navigation for photos and captions, videos, or other content that you want users to open and close. I'll also show you how to implement app-style swipe-driven navigation.

CUSTOMIZING LISTVIEWS

I introduced the *listview* in Chapter 2. You return here to explore them in depth because they are the universally applied way to provide navigation in a mobile site. Listviews can be simple, clean, and inviting, like the one from SiriusXM Radio shown in Figure 3.1.

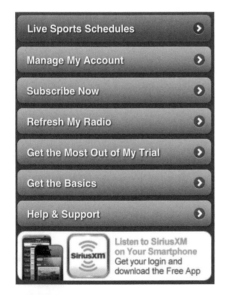

Figure 3.1
The SiriusXM Radio website.
Source: 2013 SiriusXM Radio Inc.™

Or they can be jazzed up, and still inviting, like the one from Sioux Falls, SD, shown in Figure 3.2.

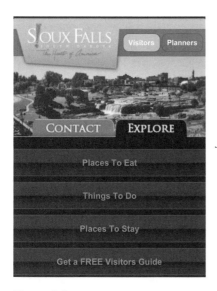

Figure 3.2
The Sioux Falls Convention and Visitor's Bureau site.
Source: Sioux Falls Convention and Visitors Bureau.

Given that listviews play such a central role in defining a user's experience at your mobile website, I'm going to spend some time walking through them in detail, including how to set them up to provide effective navigation, and how to apply available styling options.

Listviews: Behind the Curtain

Listviews are built in HTML5 as... *lists*. In other words, an HTML5 `data-role="listview"` is a way to *view* a *list*.

Using lists to build navigation is a widely applied technique in contemporary web design, even beyond mobile design. To put that another way, when designers build navigation structures in HTML, they do so using unordered list (`<ul>`) elements with `<li>` list elements within them. Then they use CSS to style those navigation links.

In the pre-mobile era of web design, for example, unordered list elements with individual list items were used to create drop-down menus. The animation and interactivity that made drop-down menus change color, change opacity (so the content behind them on the page was partially visible), and drop down the page was supplied by JavaScript and CSS styling.

Now, drop-down menus are not a good fit for mobile web design. Drop-down menus don't work well in touch screen environments, where there is no "hover-state" because there is no mouse. And drop-down menus take up too much precious real estate in tiny mobile viewports. But the basic technique of defining a menu with a bulleted list (or, to put it in HTML terms, as an unordered list), and then animating it with CSS and JavaScript is still applicable, in different forms.

Creating a Basic Listview

The most basic and most widely applied approach to mobile app navigation is the listview. The HTML5 syntax is as follows:

```
<ul data-role="listview">
<li><a href="link"> display text </a></li>
<li><a href="link"> display text </a></li>
<li><a href="link"> display text </a></li>
</ul>
```

Here's an example:

```
<ul data-role="listview">
<li><a href="http://www.afghanistan.com"> Afghanistan </a></li>
<li><a href="http://en.wikipedia.org/wiki/Albania">Albania</a></li>
<li><a href="http://www.algeria.com">Algeria </a></li> </ul>
</ul>
```

Tip

Don't forget that you can download the code built in each chapter of this book at http://dk-mobile.uphero.com. If you want to jump right to the copy-and-paste ready HTML created in this chapter, go to http://dk-mobile .uphero.com/#ch03.

Figure 3.3 shows how the example might look in a mobile viewport.

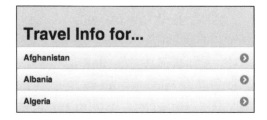

Figure 3.3
A basic listview.
© 2014 Cengage Learning.

Creating Split Button Lists

The simple, basic listview I just explained is the bread and butter of mobile navigation. You see it everywhere, and it's an effective, inviting, and intuitive way to let users navigate around your mobile site.

But sometimes a more complex listview is required. The *split button list* provides a clickable image, text, and an icon. Like many online retailers, Safeway, for example, uses a split button list at their mobile site to present both product category thumbnail images and text (see Figure 3.4).

Figure 3.4
Safeway's mobile site combines images (on the left) with text in a listview.
Source: Safeway™ Inc.

Listviews offer the option of having two separate link targets within a list item. One link is assigned to the image and text, the other is assigned to an icon on the right side of the list item.

For example, in the page shown in Figure 3.5, a user clicking on a map of Afghanistan will see a large map. But if the user clicks on the Information icon (the "i" in a circle), he goes to a page of information on Afghanistan.

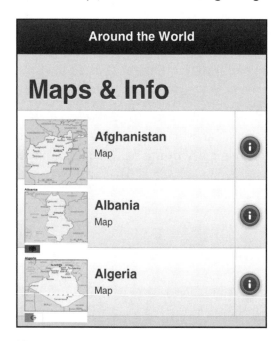

Figure 3.5
A split button list.

Data and map source: United States Department of State; design © 2014 Cengage Learning.

The syntax for a split button list is

```
<ul data-role="listview" data-split-icon="icon">
<li><a href="image link">
<img src="image" />
<h3>Top line of text</h3>
<p>Second line of text</p>
</a><a href="icon link">Text that displays when icon is hovered or clicked</a>
</li>
```

Again, the part that is a little counter-intuitive is that a split button list can have *two* different links, one associated with the image and text, and the other associated with the icon.

Split Button List Icons

You may have noted, in the syntax I provided for a split button list, the following line:

```
<ul data-role="listview" data-split-icon="icon">
```

This line defines that the unordered list (`<ul>`) that follows is a listview, that it is a *split button list*, and that an icon is required.

The icon options are outlined in Table 3.1.

Table 3.1   Options for Split Button List Icons

Code	Displays
data-icon="arrow-l"	Left Arrow
data-icon="arrow-r"	Right Arrow
data-icon="arrow-u"	Up Arrow
data-icon="arrow-d"	Down Arrow
data-icon="plus"	Plus
data-icon="minus"	Minus
data-icon="delete"	Delete
data-icon="check"	Check
data-icon="home"	Home
data-icon="info"	Information
data-icon="grid"	Grid
data-icon="gear"	Gear
data-icon="search"	Search
data-icon="back"	Back
data-icon="forward"	Forward
data-icon="refresh"	Refresh
data-icon="star"	Star
data-icon="alert"	Alert
data-icon="bars"	Bars
data-icon="edit"	Edit

© 2014 Cengage Learning. Source: David Karlins.

So, for example, if you want to display an information icon, you use this code:

```
<ul data-role="listview" data-split-icon="info">
```

Where Do Data-Icons Come From?

Among the great philosophical questions of our time (along with where did *we* come from?) is this: Where do *data-icons* come from? I pose this a bit flippantly, but among my clients and students, this is often a source of great confusion, and, correspondingly, great frustration.

If you rely on the Content Delivery Network (CDN) links to jQuery Mobile files–something I walk through in detail and strongly suggest in Chapter 2–you will link to, and rely on, the centrally distributed and maintained jQuery Mobile CSS style sheet files. Those CSS files, in turn, link to a set of several dozen icon image files. Those files are available in both PNG and SVG format in the version of jQuery Mobile being distributed as we go to press. So, the short answer is, you don't have to worry about where the icons come from, they are built into the linked files that make jQuery Mobile work and mesh with HTML5.

In Chapter 2, I briefly noted that those of you who are very (maybe I should add a second *very*) comfortable with managing file folder structures and linking to website files within subfolders can download the jQuery Mobile JavaScript and CSS files, save them to your own server, and rely on them instead of linking to the CDN versions of these files. If that's you, you can customize the icons by creating new PNG (and/or SVG) images, and replacing the image files in the `images` folder that is part of the downloaded jQuery Mobile set of files with your own custom images.

Split Button List: A Case Study

As I noted, split button lists are effective in a whole range of situations. They are basically the "illustrated" version of a simple listview. You might use a split button list to display products (or product categories); people (a head shot of department heads along with a link to their mobile pages); or enlargeable images.

Here's an example of a split button list—this creates the listview illustrated in Figure 3.5. In this example, a user clicking on a map or text will see an enlarged version of the country's map. If the user clicks on the info icon, he'll navigate to content about the selected country.

```
<ul data-role="listview" data-split-icon="info">
<li>
<a href="http://www.state.gov/img/10/40922/
afghanistan_map_201012worldfactbook_300_1.jpg">
<img src="http://www.state.gov/img/
10/40922/afghanistan_map_201012worldfactbook_300_1.jpg" />
<h3>Afghanistan</h3>
<p>Map</p>
</a>
<a href="http://www.state.gov/p/sca/ci/af/">U.S. State Department Information</a>
</li>
```

```
<li>
<a href="http://www.state.gov/cms_images/albania_map_2008.jpg">
<img src="http://www.state.gov/cms_images/albania_map_2008.jpg" />
<h3>Albania</h3>
<p>Map</p>
</a>
<a href="http://www.state.gov/p/eur/ci/al/">U.S. State Department Information</a>
</li>
<li>
<a href="http://www.state.gov/cms_images/map_algeria.jpg">
<img src="http://www.state.gov/cms_images/map_algeria.jpg" />
<h3>Algeria</h3>
<p>Map</p>
</a>
<a href="http://www.state.gov/p/nea/ci/ag/">
     U.S. State Department Information</a>
</li>
</ul>
```

Tip

You'll find the code for this case study at http://dk-mobile.uphero.com/#ch03.

Providing Search Filters

If the mantra for assigning value to real estate is "location, location, location," the mantra in identifying challenges in mobile web design might well be "size, size, size." As mobile designers, you and I are, and will always be, constantly battling to provide a lot of information in a small space.

Let's take the specific challenge of providing quick, easy access to a long list of options. There are close to two hundred countries in the world, and if your charge is to design and produce a useful listview for users to locate information about one of them, that's way more information than will fit in a smartphone screen!

A good solution: *filters*. A datalist filter acts something like a search box. As a user types in the filter, the set of options in the list is narrowed to match the characters typed into the filter. In the example shown in Figure 3.6, a list of countries is narrowed to only those with the letters "bah," in that order.

Figure 3.6
Narrowing list options with a filter.
Source: United States Department of State; design © 2014 Cengage Learning.

The basic syntax for adding a filter to a listview is as follows:

```
<ul data-role="listview" data-filter="true">
```

To break that down, you add `data-filter="true"` to an unordered list, `data-role="listview"` element.

Applying an Inset to a List

In the first part of this book, I am focusing on function, not form. You probably noticed that! Part II of this book focuses on making your mobile site *look good*, including adding color, styling fonts, and customizing how boxes, lines, backgrounds, and other elements appear to mobile users.

But here I do want to introduce adding an inset to a listview. Insets are basically dedicated style elements that apply specifically to lists. Insets give lists a more inviting look with rounded corners, and a bit of margin and padding spacing. Figure 3.7 shows the same list-view of countries I've been using as an example, but with an inset applied.

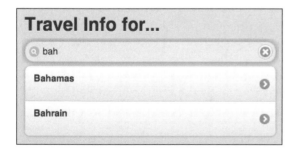

Figure 3.7
Inset styling applied to a listview.
Source: United States Department of State; design © 2014 Cengage Learning.

Note that the listview with the inset applied is indented, and displays with rounded corners.

The syntax is simply to add `data-inset="true"` to a listview element. For example:

```
<ul data-role="listview" data-filter="true" data-inset="true">
```

NAVIGATING WITH DIALOGS

An alternative way to provide navigation in a mobile site is to create pages that act as dialogs. Dialogs pop up in a mobile device, with a close button (an "x"), as shown in Figure 3.8.

Figure 3.8
Opening a page as a dialog.

Data and map source: United States Department of State; design © 2014 Cengage Learning.

By providing a close button, users can easily and intuitively return to the page from which they launched the dialog.

The syntax for a page that opens as a dialog is as follows:

```
<div data-role="page" id="name" data-dialog="true">
```

If, for example, you wanted a page named `dialog` to open as a dialog, you could use this code to create a link:

```
<div data-role="page" id="name" data-dialog="true">
```

By default, dialogs open with rounded corners, the close ("x") button in the upper left, and a background that creates the illusion for users that the dialog is suspended "on top of" the page from which it was opened.

You can move the close button to the right by adding a `data-close-btn="right"` parameter. You can turn off rounded corners with a `data-corners="false"` parameter.

So, for example, a dialog without rounded corners, and with the close button in the upper right corner, named `dialog`, would be defined with code like this:

```
<div data-role="page" id="dialog" data-dialog="true"
data-close-btn="right" data-corners="false">
```

Tip

You can further customize the appearance of dialog pages by applying custom themes, something I cover in Chapter 5 of this book.

When should you use a dialog, and when should you simply open a page using a regular link? That's a question of style, but here are some thoughts and suggestions:

- Use a dialog to present a small amount of information.
- Use a dialog when you want to ensure that a user will return to the page from which the dialog link is launched.
- Use dialogs to add dynamism and a more energetic, animated feel to the user experience.

DEFINING TRANSITIONS

You can add pizzazz to users' experiences at your mobile site by including jQuery Mobile page transitions. The turn transition creates the illusion that a user is turning a page in a print document. The pop transition—well, it makes pages appear to "pop" up. The default transition (if you don't specifically define one) is fade, which makes a page appear to fade in as it opens.

The syntax for a transition is:

```
data-transition="transition"
```

So, for example, a turn transition is applied with:

```
data-transition="turn"
```

Here's an example of that transition, applied to a dialog page, and opened with a link:

```
<a href="#page2" data-rel="dialog" data-transition="turn">
    Open Page 2 in a dialog - click "x" to close the page when you're done</a>
```

The available transitions are:

- Fade
- Pop
- Flip
- Turn
- Flow
- Slidefade
- Slide
- Slideup
- Slidedown
- None

The names are pretty descriptive of the animated transition effect. So instead of trying to create a narrative that describes them, I'll let you experiment with them.

Support for Transitions

What makes a transition work in a mobile device? Users don't need to worry about that, they just kick back and enjoy the inviting animation as new content slides, turns, fades, or pops onto their screens. But you should know what is "under the hood" (as they say in the car repair business) with transitions. They rely on CSS3 3D transforms. If you're interested in digging into the technical details of CSS3 transforms there are useful online resources, including a definitive article at W3C found at http://www.w3.org/TR/css-transforms-1. Of course, you don't need to create these 3D transform styles yourself; they come with the jQuery Mobile CSS. CSS3 3D transforms are supported by all *current-generation* mobile browsers except for Opera Mini. The main audience that won't see these animated effects are users of Internet Explorer 6-8, which of course is only desktop/laptop users, and an audience that mobile designers do not focus on.

Defining Reverse Transitions

By default, when a user presses the Back button in their device (not their browser, but their smartphone or tablet), the transition applies "in reverse." So, for example, a "turn" transition will appear to turn a page as if a reader was reading a book from beginning to end, but if that same user clicks the back button on their device, it will feel as if they are turning "back" a page in the book, from the end to the beginning.

What if you want to force a reversed transition? An example would be if you have pages you want a user to view in sequence, and you want reverse transitions when a user navigates, for instance, from page 3 back to page 2. To do that, add the `data-direction="reverse"` attribute to a link. In the following example, I am forcing a slide transition to take place from right-to-left instead of the default left-to-right:

```
<a href="#page2" data-transition="slide" data-direction="reverse">Page 2</a>
```

When to Use Transitions

The jQuery Mobile framework is a work in progress, and some features work more reliably than others. Transitions are in the process of being finalized and stabilized.

Right now, some browsers or devices display transitions with unintended flickers and flashes. As the months go by, the jQuery Mobile community will resolve that bug.

I noted earlier in this chapter that CSS3 3D transitions are supported in all current generation mobile browsers except Opera Mini. However, transitions also are inoperative on old mobile devices. Among my testing options is an old Android version 2.2 mobile phone, and transitions don't work on it. But this is not really a problem because users of these older devices still enjoy a satisfactory experience. Pages open smoothly for them. They just miss out on the full range of animated effects. In these older mobile environments, transitions default to fade on older devices. In short, the user's experience is not really negatively impacted.

Where does this leave you as you design for mobile? Even setting aside the temporary glitches (the flashes, which will be ironed out eventually), transitions are a high-impact navigation option. I've seen them used very effectively at sites that rely on a very distinct look and feel.

On the other hand, don't overdo it with transitions. Too many transitions can make a user's experience chaotic and distracting. In the vast majority of design situations, your goal will be to make transitions interactive and animated to create an inviting feel for the site, but not so animated and interactive that they overwhelm the site. In those cases, the default fade transition works fine.

So, store transitions in your mobile design skill set, but use them sparingly.

At the other end of the spectrum of mobile design, there are times when it is appropriate to dispense with *any* transition, even a fade.

And, by the way, you don't *need* to have transitions between pages. If your design mission is best served by a Spartan, no-frills look and feel, you can turn off transitions, including the default fade, with this syntax:

```
data-transition="none"
```

SUMMARY

Navigation is the nervous system of any website. But because mobile sites have such a small viewport to work with (especially on smartphones), there are special challenges involved in creating an engaging navigation structure.

You should avail yourself of special jQuery Mobile elements that facilitate providing inviting, accessible navigation. Listviews are the basic tool for mobile navigation, but you can enhance them with filters (for long lists) and split buttons (to provide images and alternate links), and you can animate links with transitions. In this chapter, you learned about the following navigational elements:

- Listviews with filters make long lists manageable.
- Listviews with inset formatting make them more inviting and accessible.
- Pages that open in dialogs, instead of in normal browser windows, work better in mobile settings.
- Transitions to animate the navigation experience make mobile browsing more enjoyable.

Here are a four "take home" points for presenting really inviting, dynamic navigation:

- You can make listviews more inviting with data-insets, which provide padding, margins, and rounded corners.
- You can add images and a second link (as well as an icon) to listviews by using the data-split property
- You can create dialog links, where users open a new page in a dialog.
- They're not appropriate everywhere, but when you need really dynamic links, experiment with transitions.

PART II

MOBILE DESIGN WITH HTML5

CHAPTER 4

APPLYING DATA-THEME STYLING

"Traditionally," if I can use that term in relation to the fast-evolving world of web design, web pages were built with HTML and CSS, with JavaScript sometimes added for animation and interactivity.

That's the same basic recipe used to build jQuery Mobile web pages. The JavaScript, in the main, is all written and distributed through the jQuery Mobile Content Delivery Network (CDN). You link to that JavaScript file in the <head> element of every jQuery Mobile site. The HTML, of course, you create yourself. That provides the unique content for your mobile website (text, images, video, and so on). But how is the CSS for jQuery Mobile sites managed?

The answer is that it is also centrally stored and distributed by the jQuery Mobile CDN. That CSS file (sometimes broken into two different CSS files) provides essential style definitions that make jQuery Mobile sites function properly. The CSS file required to make jQuery Mobile sites work is huge—defining nearly a thousand individual styles. As such, it is too big and complex to edit "by hand," even if you're an expert CSS coder.

So how, then, do you customize the look and feel of your jQuery Mobile styles? There are two answers to that question. One is that the default jQuery Mobile CSS file has within it a set of color *swatches* that can be applied with HTML coding. I'll walk you through how that works in this chapter.

Option two is to completely customize not only the color swatches in the jQuery Mobile style sheet, but to redefine other essential site-wide styling (like fonts and box corners).

I'll show you how to do that in Chapter 5, but I strongly recommend you work through this chapter first because the custom styling techniques covered in Chapter 5 build on basic styling that is explained in this chapter.

I'm going to introduce you, as well, to some other styling techniques in this chapter. I'll show you how to use buttons to make links easier to tap in mobile devices, and how to assign styling to those buttons. And, in this chapter, I'll show you how to make any element of a jQuery Mobile page smaller using the *mini* attribute.

Here's the basic plan for this chapter:

- Understanding themes and color swatches in jQuery Mobile.
- Applying data-theme color swatches.
- Providing and styling button links.
- Mini-sizing elements with the mini element.

Understanding Themes and Color Swatches

Before entering into an explanation of themes and color swatches in jQuery Mobile, I have to address a major change (not necessarily for the better) that took place with the introduction of jQuery Mobile 1.4.1. Version 1.4.1 is the version available as we go to press, and the version I link to in examples throughout this book, in general.

But as I've noted in previous chapters, the hard-working, creative team that makes it possible for us to connect HTML5 with jQuery Mobile and to create nicely animated mobile sites, updates the code too often, and too radically, without sufficient regard for the installed user base. Features that have been part of jQuery Mobile since its inception, like a set of color swatches that can be applied to elements, were abruptly removed.

In Chapter 5, I'll teach you to create your *own* themes and color swatches. And, as you build your own, professional-level mobile pages, you will want to design unique, custom themes. But the nice set of pre-set color swatches available before jQuery Mobile version 1.4.1 provided a convenient way to learn to *apply* color swatches. For that reason, I'll have you link to jQuery Mobile 1.3.2 for the code samples in this chapter.

As I mentioned briefly when introducing this chapter, a single style sheet (CSS file) provides styling for jQuery Mobile pages.

You must include a link in the `<head>` element of your jQuery Mobile page to an earlier version of jQuery Mobile's CSS file make that page work correctly. The entire `<head>` element code for jQuery Mobile 1.3.2 is

```
<head>
<title>Page Title</title>
<meta name="viewport" content="width=device-width, initial-scale=1">
<link rel="stylesheet"
    href="http://code.jquery.com/mobile/1.3.2/
    jquery.mobile-1.3.2.min.css" />
<script src="http://code.jquery.com/jquery-1.9.1.min.js"></script>
<script src="http://code.jquery.com/mobile/1.3.2/
    jquery.mobile-1.3.2.min.js"></script>
</head>
```

Tip

You'll find a copy-and-paste ready set of this `<head>` element, that links to jQuery Mobile 1.3.2, at http://dk-mobile.uphero.com/#ch04.

The line of code is updated frequently when new versions of jQuery Mobile are rolled out. Links to the latest version of this line of code can be found at http://jquerymobile.com/.

If you strip that code out of any jQuery Mobile page, you see a naked page indeed! I won't scare you with a picture of how that looks, but essentially you'll be looking at unformatted text, and that won't be an inviting experience for mobile users.

By default, that CSS file is distributed by the jQuery Mobile CDN. The CSS styles defined in that file mesh tightly and in complex ways with the JavaScript behind jQuery Mobile. That's one reason why you should not try to edit the CSS file that is supplied through the jQuery Mobile CDN (the other reason being the length and complexity of that file).

That jQuery Mobile CSS file includes CSS styles that mainly serve to make the animation and interactivity supplied by the JavaScript function. And, the CSS file includes styles that mainly serve to define styling—fonts, font colors, background colors, and so on—in jQuery Mobile pages.

In this chapter, I explain how to apply those color swatches. In Chapter 5, I explain how to customize both the jQuery Mobile theme and the color swatches associated with that theme. To do that, I'll show you how to generate two different CSS files, one with standard CSS that doesn't change, and the second with customized theme styling.

The reason I bring this up in this chapter is that you may encounter jQuery Mobile pages that have links to two different CSS files. Or, you might work with design applications (like Dreamweaver, for instance) that automatically generate two CSS files for jQuery Mobile sites. In this chapter, however, I refer to "the" CSS file for jQuery Mobile sites, in order to focus on the process of applying color swatches. Once you've wrapped your head around applying color swatches, the material in Chapter 5 for customizing jQuery Mobile CSS (and splitting the CSS file into two files) will make sense.

APPLYING COLOR SWATCHES

The styling component of the jQuery Mobile CSS file defines the page *theme*. As I noted, that theme includes *color swatches,* which are five different color schemes that can be applied to elements in a jQuery Mobile page.

Color swatches are applied with data-themes. A color swatch and a data-theme are the same thing. And color swatches are applied with HTML using one of five options:

```
data-theme="a"
data-theme="b"
data-theme="c"
data-theme="d"
data-theme="e"
```

There are limits to how much I can illustrate these themes in a black-and-white book. Actually, there are limits to how much data-theme can be previewed in a color book, since they include interactive color changes (for instance, a tapped button will change colors). But Figure 4.1 gives some sense of how the main data-themes look when applied to a button (data-theme b has a blue background and data-theme e has a yellow background).

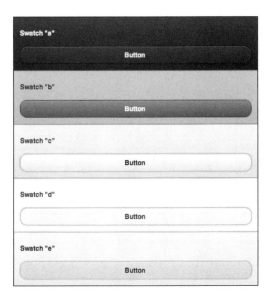

Figure 4.1
Applying the five data-themes (color swatches) in jQuery Mobile 1.3.2 to buttons.
Source: The jQuery Foundation™.

Data-themes alter their appearance depending on what element they are applied to. Figure 4.2 shows data-themes applied to a listview. They maintain the same basic colors that were applied to the buttons.

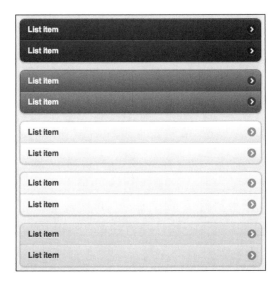

Figure 4.2
Applying data-themes to a listview.
Source: The jQuery Foundation™.

Applying Data-Themes to data-role="page"

The data-theme (color swatch) applied to a `data-role="page"` defines how that entire page appears. In other words, the color swatch you apply to a jQuery Mobile page applies to other elements in the page (like listviews) unless you apply a different data-theme specifically to those other elements.

Tip

> In Chapter 2, I explained how the `<div data-role="page">` element is used, in conjunction with jQuery Mobile, to create "pages" that look and feel (to the user) like web pages, but are actually elements within a single HTML file.

By default, `<div data-role="page">` elements have the c data-theme (color swatch) applied to their pages. To change that, you add a different data-theme to the `data-role="page"` element. In the following example, data-theme a is applied to a data-page:

```
<div data-role="page" id="page" data-theme="a">
```

That changes the page from the default, which is shown in Figure 4.3.

Figure 4.3
The jQuery Mobile 1.3.2 default data-theme c, applied to a page.

To the data-theme a, as shown in Figure 4.4.

Figure 4.4
Data-theme a, applied to a page.

Applying Data-Themes to Listviews

By default, listviews inherit the data-theme assigned to the `data-role="page"` element in which they are located. But you can, and often should, apply a distinct data-theme to a listview. A distinct data-theme makes a listview stand out, and sometimes makes it easier to read and use.

The following code example applies `data-theme="c"` to a listview.

```
<ul data-role="listview" data-theme="c">
```

Applied to a listview within a data-role page with the c data-theme applied, the listview in the example looks like Figure 4.5.

Figure 4.5
Data-theme c, in jQuery Mobile 1.3.2 applied to a listview.
© 2014 Cengage Learning. Source: The jQuery Foundation™. Image source: Brooklyn Botanical Garden.

Data-themes can be applied to individual list elements within a listview. For example, the following code applies separate data-themes to each list item in a listview:

```
<ul data-role="listview" data-inset="true">
<li data-theme="a"><a href="#">A</a></li>
<li data-theme="b"><a href="#">B</a></li>
<li data-theme="c"><a href="#">C</a></li>
<li data-theme="d"><a href="#">D</a></li>
<li data-theme="e"><a href="#">E</a></li>
</ul>
```

This code produces a listview that looks like the one shown in Figure 4.6.

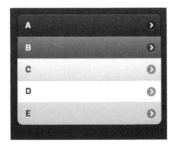

Figure 4.6
Data-themes applied to list elements.
© 2014 Cengage Learning. Source: The jQuery Foundation™. Image source: Brooklyn Botanical Garden.

Tip

You'll find a copy-and-paste ready set of this code at http://dk-mobile.uphero.com/#ch04.

Applying Data-Themes to Headers and Footers

By default, headers and footers adopt the `data-theme="a"` color swatch. That data-theme applies a very high contrast, white-on-black color scheme. The text is easy to read in almost any lighting condition.

To be clear, unlike listviews and most other elements, header and footer elements do *not* adopt the data-theme color swatch assigned to the data-page they are placed in.

But you can change the data-theme of a header or footer. The following code example shows `data-theme="e"` applied to a header.

```
<div data-role="header" data-theme="e">
```

And this code example shows `data-theme="e"` applied to a footer.

```
<div data-role="footer" data-theme="e">
```

STYLING WITH THEMED NAVIGATION BUTTONS

Links can be a hassle to tap in a mobile device. One of my pet peeves is when I'm trying to click on a link to read an article at one of the online publications to which I subscribe and end up missing the nano-sized link text and instead clicking a nearby link that opens a three-minute advertisement video.

You can make links easier to tap by assigning them to a button. The following syntax creates a button with text "Tap Here," and opens a link that you define by replacing the "#" code.

```
<a href="#" data-role="button">Tap Here</a>
```

That code converts a regular link that looks like the one shown in Figure 4.7 to an easier-to-tap button link, like the one shown in Figure 4.8.

Tap Here

Figure 4.7
A text link on a mobile page.
© 2014 Cengage Learning. Source: The jQuery Foundation™. Image source: Brooklyn Botanical Garden.

Figure 4.8
A button link.
© 2014 Cengage Learning. Source: The jQuery Foundation™. Image source: Brooklyn Botanical Garden.

You can theme link buttons. The following example code shows five different data-themes applied to a set of five buttons.

```
<a href="#" data-role="button" data-theme="a">data-theme="a"</a>
<a href="#" data-role="button" data-theme="b">data-theme="b"</a>
<a href="#" data-role="button" data-theme="c">data-theme="c"</a>
<a href="#" data-role="button" data-theme="d">data-theme="d"</a>
<a href="#" data-role="button" data-theme="e">data-theme="e"</a>
```

Figure 4.9 shows how that set of buttons looks.

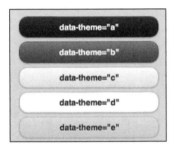

Figure 4.9
Button links with data-themes applied.
© 2014 Cengage Learning. Source: The jQuery Foundation™. Image source: Brooklyn Botanical Garden.

Building Navbars with Inline Buttons

Because buttons are so helpful in mobile navigation, I want to walk through in more detail how they can be deployed.

By default, link buttons are block elements, which means they each have their own row (line) in a page. But what if you want to have a row with multiple link buttons? In that case, you need to convert button links to inline, not block styles, so that line breaks are not forced between buttons.

You do that by adding this code to a button link:

```
data-inline="true"
```

Here's an example of inline buttons:

```
<a href="#" data-role="button" data-inline="true">A</a>
<a href="#" data-role="button" data-inline="true">B</a>
<a href="#" data-role="button" data-inline="true">C</a>
<a href="#" data-role="button" data-inline="true">D</a>
<a href="#" data-role="button" data-inline="true">E</a>
```

So, how about *theming* those buttons? Easy enough—you can apply data-themes to buttons. The following code applies five data-themes, one to each button:

```
<a href="#" data-role="button" data-theme="a" data-inline="true">A</a>
<a href="#" data-role="button" data-theme="b" data-inline="true">B</a>
<a href="#" data-role="button" data-theme="c" data-inline="true">C</a>
<a href="#" data-role="button" data-theme="d" data-inline="true">D</a>
<a href="#" data-role="button" data-theme="e" data-inline="true">E</a>
```

That code produces a set of buttons that looks like the ones shown in Figure 4.10.

Figure 4.10
Inline button links with data-themes applied.
© 2014 Cengage Learning. Source: The jQuery Foundation™. Image source: Brooklyn Botanical Garden.

Adding Icons to Themed Buttons

You can add icons to buttons to make them more intuitive navigation aids. Table 4.1 lists available icons, and the syntax used to add them to a button.

Table 4.1 Icons for Themed Buttons	
Icon	**Syntax**
Bars	data-icon="bars"
Edit	data-icon="edit"
Left arrow	data-icon="arrow-l"
Right arrow	data-icon="arrow-r"
Up arrow	data-icon="arrow-u"
	(Continued)

Table 4.1   Icons for Themed Buttons (*Continued*)

Icon	Syntax
Down arrow	data-icon="arrow-d"
Delete	data-icon="delete"
Plus	data-icon="plus"
Minus	data-icon="minus"
Check	data-icon="check"
Gear	data-icon="gear"
Refresh	data-icon="refresh"
Forward	data-icon="forward"
Back	data-icon="back"
Grid	data-icon="grid"
Star	data-icon="star"
Alert	data-icon="alert"
Info	data-icon="info"
Home	data-icon="home"
Search	data-icon="search"

© 2014 Cengage Learning. Source: David Karlins.

Figure 4.11 shows a left arrow data-icon, an up arrow data-icon, and a right arrow data-icon, all applied to a set of navigation buttons.

By default, all icons in buttons are placed to the left of the button text, but you can change that using the data-iconpos attribute to position the icon. The options are left, right, top, bottom, none, or notext (which shows only an icon, no text).

In Figure 4.11, for example, the right arrow icon is positioned to the right of the Next button, and the up arrow is positioned above the Home button.

Figure 4.11
Inline button links with data-themes and positioned arrows.
© 2014 Cengage Learning. Source: The jQuery Foundation™. Image source: Brooklyn Botanical Garden.

Here's the HTML to create the button list illustrated in Figure 4.11.

```
<a href="#" data-role="button" data-theme="a"
   data-icon="arrow-l" data-inline="true">Prev</a>
<a href="#" data-role="button" data-theme="b"
   data-icon="arrow-u" data-iconpos="top" data-inline="true">Home</a>
<a href="#" data-role="button" data-theme="a"
   data-icon="arrow-r" data-iconpos="right" data-inline="true">Next</a>
```

Tip

You'll find a copy-and-paste ready set of this code at http://dk-mobile.uphero.com/#ch04.

Grouping Themed Buttons with Control Groups

jQuery Mobile provides an option to group sets of navigation buttons in a control group. By wrapping a set of buttons in a `<div data-role="controlgroup"></div>` element, you remove all margins and drop shadows between buttons. Within a control group, only the left and right buttons display with rounded corners, which creates the feeling of a set of button options.

Figure 4.12 demonstrates three buttons wrapped in a control group.

Figure 4.12
Button links wrapped in a control group.
© 2014 Cengage Learning.

Here's the code to create the example illustrated in Figure 4.12:

```
<div data-role="controlgroup" data-type="horizontal">
<a href="#" data-role="button" data-theme="a" data-icon="arrow-l">Prev</a>
<a href="#" data-role="button" data-theme="a" data-icon="arrow-u">Home</a>
<a href="#" data-role="button" data-theme="a"
   data-icon="arrow-r" data-iconpos="right">Next</a>
</div>
```

Mini-Sizing Elements

Given how precious real estate is on a smartphone screen, mobile designers clamored for ways to downsize elements, and with the release of jQuery Mobile 1.1.0, the jQuery Mobile team responded with the data-mini attribute.

When you add a `data-mini="true"` parameter to many elements, including buttons and listviews, you shrink the size of the element. For example, the following code transforms a set of buttons within a control group to mini-sized:

```
<div data-role="controlgroup" data-mini="true">
```

The effect of adding a `data-mini="true"` parameter to an element varies depending on the element. But in general, this reduces an element's size by about 20 percent.

Figure 4.13 contrasts that mini-sized button control group to a full-sized set of buttons.

Figure 4.13
"Mini"-sizing a set of navigation buttons.
© 2014 Cengage Learning.

SUMMARY

In this chapter, you were introduced to basic elements of styling jQuery Mobile pages. The most essential styling technique is applying data-themes to different elements. Those data-themes are basically color swatches.

The data-themes built into almost all the jQuery Mobile CSS versions are high-contrast color schemes that work well in the wide range of lighting conditions that mobile users will encounter. And, by mixing and matching the five data-themes (a, b, c, d, and e), you can create a relatively unique color scheme for your mobile site.

That said, a really unique, professional looking mobile site requires custom theming. I'll show you how to do that in Chapter 5. But the skills you learned in this chapter—applying data-themes—will be required in order to apply the custom themes you create in the next chapter.

I also introduced you to themed navigation buttons. Along with listviews (covered in Chapter 3), sets of navigation buttons provide basic, highly functional, easy-to-access links in mobile sites.

And finally, I showed you how to "mini"-mize elements, to make them smaller.

Here are a four "take home" points for styling navigation and other elements:

- Data-themes can be applied to elements to provide a distinctive color scheme to that element.

- The data-theme you assign to a data-page element applies to most elements within that page, but not to the header and footer elements.

- Navigation buttons work better than text links in most cases for mobile navigation. They're easier to tap on a smartphone, and even on a tablet.

- Buttons and other navigation elements can have a `data-mini="true"` attribute that shrinks them by about 20 percent, making it possible to pack more content on a page.

CHAPTER 5

CUSTOMIZING MOBILE STYLES WITH THEMEROLLER

jQuery Mobile provides the juice that makes mobile websites snap, crackle, and pop. It enables animated transitions between pages and pop-up dialogs that appear as semi-transparent boxes "over" a page (this book explores transitions and dialogs in Chapter 3), and many other animated and interactive effects.

The downside to this, in a sense, is that in order for jQuery Mobile to do its thing, mobile websites built with it need to apply a centrally distributed CSS. That style sheet is so long and complex (defining nearly a thousand styles), and so integral to the functioning of jQuery Mobile, that even CSS3 experts are best advised to avoid tinkering with it by hand.

Does that mean, then, that you are stuck with the default site-wide settings in that CSS? Or with the limited color palettes available in the five jQuery Mobile color swatches (applying those swatches is the focus of Chapter 4 in this book)?

No!

There are effective online resources for creating highly unique styles and color schemes for jQuery Mobile pages. The most widely used and powerful is jQuery Mobile *Theme-Roller*, which is a powerful tool for customizing the CSS that goes with jQuery Mobile. I'll walk you through how to use that in this chapter.

In the course of doing that, I'll explain these elements of custom-theming mobile sites:

- The importance of mobile-friendly, high-contrast color schemes.
- The relationship between jQuery Mobile themes and color swatches.
- How to define custom site-wide style elements like fonts, rounded corners, icons, and box shadows.
- How to define up to 26 different custom color swatches.
- How to save and apply custom CSS for a mobile site.

USING ACCESSIBLE STYLES FOR MOBILE

I'm not focusing on the aesthetics of mobile website design in this book, but when it comes to color scheming, there is a point where aesthetics meets functionality. That is to say, if you're not careful about choosing appropriate colors, fonts, and other elements, users won't be able to, or won't want to, access your mobile content.

Professional designers understand this. An example I like to use with clients and students is the Brooks Brothers' website. Brooks Brothers relies on a lot of gray for branding, but white on gray is too low contrast to be visible for this upscale clothing retailer's clients to read on their iPads while yachting in bright sunlight or skiing in Aspen.

Figure 5.1 gives you a sense of the low-contrast color scheme the store uses in its full-sized site.

Figure 5.1
Brooks Brothers' low-contrast color scheme is consistent with their branding colors in a laptop.
Source: Brooks Brothers.

On the other hand, Figure 5.2 gives you a sense of the website color scheme changes for the mobile version—with a higher contrast gray-text-on-white color scheme.

Figure 5.2
Brooks Brothers uses a higher-contrast color scheme in its mobile site.
Source: Brooks Brothers.

While Brooks Brothers has a particular challenge, this example highlights how important it is to provide a *mobile accessible* combination of colors when you design mobile sites with HTML5.

The most succinct way to identify things to avoid is to provide a list of things to avoid. They fall into four categories, which I explain in more detail shortly:

- Avoid low-contrast color schemes.
- Avoid italics and overly intricate fonts.
- Avoid image backgrounds.
- Avoid absolute values for type. Size type in ems, not absolute values.

Avoiding Low-Contrast Color Schemes

One of the biggest, and perhaps most under-appreciated, differences between designing for mobile and designing for laptop/desktop use is how differently these two categories of devices present color. In the introduction to this chapter, I used the example of Brooks Brothers' website, and how the mobile site uses a color scheme that works better outdoors.

And I emphasized this is a general challenge, not specific to any particular website. Placing light-colored text on a light-colored background might work just fine when viewed in a laptop or desktop environment. But a navigation list like the one shown in Figure 5.3 is going to be illegible in bright sun on a low-budget mobile phone.

Figure 5.3
Low-contrast color schemes are hard to read on mobile devices.
© 2014 Cengage Learning.

It's better to use a simpler, high-contrast color scheme, like the one shown in Figure 5.4.

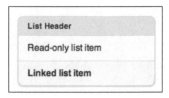

Figure 5.4
High-contrast color schemes are much more accessible on mobile devices.
© 2014 Cengage Learning.

Why are there such great differences in appropriate color schemes for laptop/desktop environments on the one hand, and mobile devices on the other?

The first difference is in the technology of the devices. While mobile devices are getting increasingly powerful and sophisticated, for a wide range of reasons, they do not support the same range and depth of color that laptop/desktop devices do. They do not have as powerful backlighting. And, in most cases, they do not support the same range of colors.

Mobile Color

I can't go into a detailed survey of the state of color support on mobile devices here, both because it would be too great a tangent from the topic of the book, and because the situation is in constant transition. But to give you an overall sense of the differences, most mobile devices have what is called "16-bit" color support, which means they display 4,096 different colors. By contrast, most desktop/laptop environments provide 24-bit color, which supports over 16 million colors. Some high-end mobile devices also support 24-bit color, but even older iPhones and Samsung Galaxy models, Kindles, and other devices support 16-bit color.

And 16-bit color does not provide the same support for the gradations of transparency available in a laptop or desktop environment.

The second difference between laptop/desktop color and mobile color scheming is environment. Mobile devices are much more likely to be viewed outdoors, in a very wide range of lighting, including bright sunlight.

That means that even when designing for the most expensive, high-powered tablets like the Kindle Fire, Nook, and iPad, which have some (if not full) support for 24-bit color, you'll want to stick to high-contrast color schemes.

How do you know if you have a high-contrast color scheme? On one level, that's kind of intuitive—light gray on white is a low-contrast color scheme, black on yellow is high-contrast. But there are resources that can quantify color contrast. Some of these have been developed to help web designers evaluate color schemes for how accessible they are to color-blind users (a significant element of the online audience). These tools also quantify *luminosity* (brightness) contrast, which is the key factor in making sites readable on mobile devices.

One of my favorites resources for checking color contrast is the Colour Contrast Analyser, which is a free download for Mac and Windows machines. It provides a color-contrast ratio between two different colors. You'll find it at http://www.paciellogroup.com/resources/contrastAnalyser. The Luminosity option provides a quantitative measure of color scheme contrast, as shown in Figure 5.5.

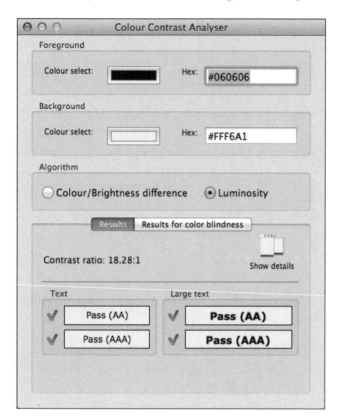

Figure 5.5
Testing color contrast with the Colour Contrast Analyser.
Source: The Paciello Group, licensed under a Creative Commons License.

Avoiding Overly Intricate Fonts

Customized web fonts are a useful element in your web design toolbox. I don't focus on the technology or how to use them in this book, but there are a number of online sources for fonts, some free, some not. You'll find easy-to-follow directions for choosing and embedding free custom fonts from Google at www.google.com/fonts.

Here, I simply want to caution you to use judicious common sense in applying custom fonts in a mobile website design. Avoid esoteric fonts that rely on extreme detail in mobile design. I don't want to step on the toes of the folks at Web Pages That Suck (http://www .webpagesthatsuck.com)—who use poor design examples to teach good web design—but I will caution against really compressed fonts.

For example, you're best to avoid fonts like the one shown in Figure 5.6.

Figure 5.6
Highly compressed fonts don't display well in mobile devices.
© 2014 Cengage Learning.

Sizing Your Type in Ems, Not Absolute Values

While I'm on the thread of readable type, in addition to using high-contrast color differences between text and background colors, the other key point to keep in mind is to size type in ems, not absolute units (like pixels).

When you size type in ems, the size of the type is essentially defined by the browsing environment. What then, is an *em*? It is a default font size for "normal" type defined by the browser.

Doesn't sizing font in ems give a designer less control over type size? In a sense, it does. But that's a good thing. Mobile devices "count" pixels so differently, and with such little consistency, that sizing type in pixels (or any other absolute unit of measurement) produces highly unpredictable and often unpleasant results.

Let's take an example. An iPhone 3GS (I know, an older model, but a good example and there are still many in use) has a screen width of 320 pixels in portrait (up and down, not sideways) mode. An iPhone 4S is the same size, but has a width of 960 pixels. That means if a designer defines a style for paragraph text that is 14 pixels, that text will appear about three times as big on 3GS as it does on the 4S if you rely on pixel sizing.

Another way to put this is that newer and more expensive mobile devices tend to have higher screen resolutions than older, cheaper devices. So a pixel on a lower-resolution device is going to be much bigger than a pixel on a higher-resolution device.

This is why designers should use ems as a unit of measurement for sizing fonts. A value of 1 em will be defined by a device as an appropriate size for normal (paragraph) text. And the actual size of an em adjusts, depending on the browsing environment.

In addition to sizing in ems, you want to make sure to force browsers to report a "real" viewport size. You do this by including the following line of code in the `<head>` element of every mobile site you build:

```
<meta name="viewport" content="width=device-width, initial-scale=1">
```

This line forces devices to report their viewport (screen) width in a standardized way. A very high-resolution mobile device will have its resolution adjusted down to reflect a user's actual experience.

Let me illustrate the concept using the two iPhones I used to discuss font sizing with ems. On the iPhone 3GS, a 320 pixel-wide image will fill the entire width of the viewport. But on a 4S, a 320 pixel-wide image will fill only a third of the screen.

A viewer on an iPhone 4S will have a very unsatisfactory experience. Her image will be tiny.

The previous line of code forces mobile devices to display elements at a scale more consistent with the actual appearance of their viewport, regardless of how many pixels they pack into the screen.

As I walk you through generating custom CSS for your mobile site shortly, I'll reinforce these points about using relative font sizes, and forcing devices to report actual screen width. And I will show you how this is done in ThemeRoller.

Avoiding Image Backgrounds

Throughout this book, I've tried to emphasize that one of the distinct features of mobile design is that pages should download quickly. Remember, mobile users do not always have access to WiFi, and are often at the mercy of slow connections.

This means, among other things, avoiding background image files as much as possible. Background image files—images that appear as the background for a mobile page or box—can enhance users' experiences by making pages more interesting and inviting. But they add seconds, sometimes many seconds, to the time it takes for a mobile page to appear. And that delay can make users' experiences unacceptably slow and frustrating.

The CSS you will generate using jQuery Mobile's ThemeRoller eschews (avoids) using image backgrounds.

CREATING CUSTOM THEMES AND SWATCHES

Having read about a few pitfalls you should avoid in styling mobile web pages, it's time to walk through the nuts and bolts of generating customized CSS with ThemeRoller.

Before you start walking through that process step-by-step, I want to introduce a caveat, and break down a couple concepts.

The caveat is that ThemeRoller is in a constant state of flux. I'll explain what that means specifically, but I also have written the following sections of this chapter in such a way that you should be able to navigate through ThemeRoller even as it evolves past the state it is in as this book goes to press.

The concepts I want to break down a bit involve how themes and swatches relate to each other.

ThemeRoller Is a Work-in-Progress

ThemeRoller is very valuable tool. It is also a work-in-progress. In many ways, the state of jQuery Mobile overall, and ThemeRoller in particular, parallels the ongoing evolution of WordPress. Yesterday's features have been replaced by a new set of features, and in a few months those features will be updated, eliminated, or enhanced.

Here I must editorialize for moment to provide you with some perspective on this, since as a mobile designer, you'll be working with a moving target in terms of available resources. In ancient times—measuring in web design years (the early 2010s)—design tools were mainly published by proprietary distributors (like the Adobe Corporation). They were revised periodically, say every 18 months or every year. Revisions were made judiciously, taking into account the installed user base, the interfaces they were used to working with, and features they relied on or built into their projects.

Lest I wax nostalgic, those tools were expensive! And there was a definite downside to the slow revision cycles.

But today's online, open source (and usually free!) design tools—like WordPress and jQuery Mobile ThemeRoller—are, frankly, *too* easily revised. One of the problems with this approach is that features or elements that you use and count on in one version might suddenly disappear in the next.

For example, in a recent upgrade, jQuery Mobile changed the default theme so that instead of providing five default color scheme swatches, it now provides only two variations of grayscale color swatches.

And, in a recent upgrade, ThemeRoller dropped support for gradient backgrounds behind boxes, buttons, and other elements. In the following section, I'll show you how to choose the best version of ThemeRoller for your styling needs, even if that is not the latest version.

Gradient Backgrounds: Here... Then Gone

Let me illustrate these changes I'm discussing by going a bit more into the example of the missing gradient background. Until version 1.4, jQuery Mobile ThemeRoller made it easy to define and apply gradient backgrounds to pages, boxes, buttons, and other elements. Gradient backgrounds can add texture to pages and elements and make them inviting to users.

With version 1.4 of jQuery Mobile ThemeRoller (and jQuery Mobile's default themes as well), the ability to create gradients has been removed by the collective that makes such decisions. Why? Well, a representative of the jQuery Mobile team explained that this was done "to give it [jQuery Mobile theming] a more modern look."

And so, with that "logic," the *option* of defining gradient backgrounds was removed from ThemeRoller with version 1.4.

Supported Browsers

The technical documentation for ThemeRoller states:

> *"This is a beta version of a developer tool so we're committing to supporting the latest versions of popular desktop browsers: Chrome, Firefox, Safari. Even though the tool works in IE9, it doesn't support CSS gradients so we don't recommend using this browser to create themes."*

In short, don't use IE9 with ThemeRoller. Use current versions of Chrome, Firefox, or Safari.

An Invaluable Tool

Before closing this section of the discussion of ThemeRoller, let me emphasize that it's the only tool that allows you to fully customize the look and feel of jQuery Mobile sites. It's easy (and fun!) to use. It adds real value to what you as a designer can do with mobile websites.

And, it's free!

Themes and Swatches

Most people refer to the five jQuery Mobile Themes (a, b, c, d, and e) as themes. It's easy to see why. You use the property `data-theme="a"` (or b, c, and so on) to assign colors to elements, and that code uses the term *theme.*

But when you start actually defining *themes,* it is necessary to understand that a *theme* in jQuery Mobile is actually the *entire CSS* that defines *everything* about page styling, while *color swatches* define the color schemes applied by the `data-theme` property.

Global Theme Elements

The elements defined by a *theme* for an entire mobile site include:

- **Font family:** The font (and backup fonts for when a user's environment does not support the first font) applied throughout the site.

- **Corner radii:** The roundness (or lack of) applied to the corners of boxes and other elements.

- **Icons:** As applied to elements (like those in a listview).

- **Box shadows:** The color, opacity, and size of drop-shadows applied to elements.

If you think about it, it makes sense that these elements are styled site-wide. It would be stylistically cacophonous (messy and chaotic), for example, if different elements in your mobile site had different border radii.

Swatch Elements

Swatches (like a, b, c, d, and e) define the colors for different data-themes. Here, you have a lot of freedom to define, in detail, the colors of different elements. For pages (`data-role="page"` elements), for example, you can define a text color, a text shadow color (helpful to make text more readable), a background color, and a border color.

That same set of color options is available for other elements, like headers and footers, and the body (content) of a page.

You can also define custom link colors for specific swatches.

You're not limited, by the way, to just customizing the five default swatches that come with jQuery Mobile sites (a, b, c, d, and e). You can define up to 26 swatches (a-z). That's plenty of swatch color sets for any site.

CREATING A CUSTOM THEME WITH THEMEROLLER

I've explained how ThemeRoller works, pointed to some potential pitfalls in mobile design, and hopefully enthused sufficiently about how useful and powerful a tool this is. So, it's time to get rolling!

To create a custom theme in ThemeRoller, go to http://jquerymobile.com/themeroller/ to access the latest version of ThemeRoller for jQuery Mobile. The opening screen is shown in Figure 5.7.

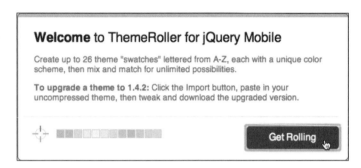

Figure 5.7
The opening screen in ThemeRoller.
Source: jQuery Mobile™.

Click the Get Rolling button. That launches ThemeRoller.

Define Global Elements

Theme elements that apply to all swatches are defined on the Global tab, shown in Figure 5.8.

Figure 5.8
Defining global elements in ThemeRoller.
Source: jQuery Mobile™.

Each of the five panels in the Global section can be expanded by clicking on the triangle to the left of the category. Doing this opens the panel, and you can see and edit settings for that category.

You preview any styling you apply in the Global tab by looking at the preview area for different swatches on the right side of the ThemeRoller window.

Defining Fonts

To define a site-wide font, enter a series of font faces separated by commas. For example, if you want to assign Arial as your font, but want to make Helvetica the backup for users who don't have Arial, enter Arial, Helvetica, as shown in Figure 5.9.

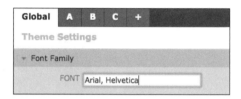

Figure 5.9
Defining fonts in ThemeRoller.
Source: jQuery Mobile™.

If your font has spaces in the name, enclose it in quotes, and place the separator comma *outside* of the quotes. For example:

`"Times New Roman", Times, serif`

The most widely supported fonts (and backups) in mobile devices are:

- Arial
- Times New Roman
- Courier New

Other widely supported fonts (grouped as font families) include:

- Arial, Helvetica, sans-serif
- Comic Sans MS, cursive, sans-serif
- Lucida Sans Unicode, Lucida Grande, sans-serif
- Tahoma, Geneva, sans-serif

- Trebuchet MS, Helvetica, sans-serif

- Verdana, Geneva, sans-serif

- Courier New, Courier, monospace

- Lucida Console, Monaco, monospace

You can see how your fonts will look in mobile devices by observing the effect in the preview area for different swatches, as shown in Figure 5.10.

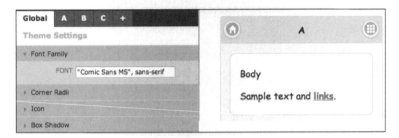

Figure 5.10
Previewing fonts in ThemeRoller.
Source: jQuery Mobile™.

The Native Font Option

Another option for choosing fonts is to use *native* system fonts, which are fonts built into different mobile devices. I won't go into this option in depth since it is relatively complex and requires different fonts for different devices. But for those of you with the need and capacity to explore this option (working in design environments with the personnel and resources to create many versions of a mobile site), there are advantages to native fonts. The main one is that they consume less bandwidth and download faster.

Here are some links to system fonts:

- iOS: http://iosfonts.com/

- Android: ver. 1-3 Droid ver. 4 Roboto http://www.granneman.com/webdev/coding/css/fonts-and-formatting/default-fonts/#android https://developer.android.com/design/style/typography.html

- Blackberry: https://en.wikipedia.org/wiki/BlackBerry_OS#BlackBerry_Fonts

- Windows: Segoe WP http://blogs.msdn.com/b/iemobile/archive/2010/11/10/supported-fonts-on-ie-for-windows-phone-7.aspx

- Kindle: http://wiki.mobileread.com/wiki/List_of_fonts_included_with_each_device

- Nook: http://nookdevs.com/Font_Changes

Styling Corner Radii

You can define roundness (corner radii) for both boxes and buttons in the Corner Radii panel. This is one of the expandable panels in the Global tab on the left side of the ThemeRoller window (see Figure 5.11).

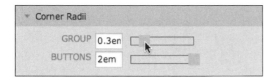

Figure 5.11
Defining corner radii for groups interactively.
Source: jQuery Mobile™.

To define the roundness of corners in boxes (like listviews), enter a value in the Group area. For buttons, enter a value in the Button area.

If you want to define border radii interactively, drag on a slider, as shown in Figure 5.11.

Defining Icon Appearance

You assign icons to lists with HTML, not by customizing CSS for a mobile site in ThemeRoller. For an exploration of available icons and how to apply them, see the section called "Adding Icons to Themed Buttons" in Chapter 4.

But you can customize the *appearance* of icons in ThemeRoller. You do that by choosing an icon color (black or white), with or without a disc around the icon, disc color (applicable only if you apply a disc), and disc opacity (also only applicable if you define a disc) in the Icon tab. The Icon tab is one of the expandable panels in the Global tab on the left side of the ThemeRoller window (shown in Figure 5.12).

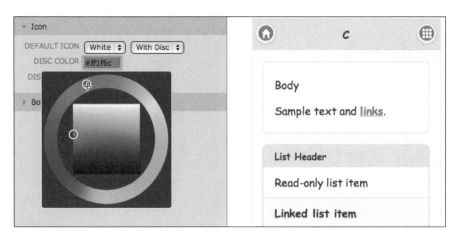

Figure 5.12
Defining an icon disc color.
Source: jQuery Mobile™.

Defining Box Shadow

Box shadows apply to every box in a site.

In the Box Shadow area, which is one of the expandable panels in the Global tab on the left side of the ThemeRoller window, choose a shadow color in the Color box; an opacity percentage in the Opacity box (100% is the darkest shadow; 0% is no shadow); and a size (in ems) in the Size box.

Figure 5.13 shows a pretty intense box shadow setting—a dark gray color, 90% opacity, and a thick 3em width.

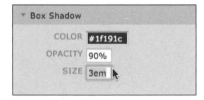

Figure 5.13
Applying a thick box shadow.
Source: jQuery Mobile™.

How does that look in a mobile page? You can tell by looking at any of the preview swatches, as shown in Figure 5.14.

Figure 5.14
Previewing a thick box shadow.
Source: jQuery Mobile™.

Defining Colors

Be warned, defining colors in ThemeRoller can be a bit counter-intuitive.

When you click a color swatch, the next step is to click the outer ring to click a color close to the one you want to apply to text in headers and footers, and use the inner gradient to fine-tune your selection.

The color you click will translate into a hexadecimal value in the Text Color box, as shown in Figure 5.15.

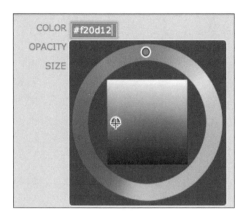

Figure 5.15
Choosing colors in ThemeRoller.
Source: jQuery Mobile™.

Defining Color Swatches

Once you have defined the theme-wide style elements (like font and border radius), you can define specific custom swatches.

You define colors for each swatch separately. To edit the colors (and other attributes) for a specific swatch, you first select that swatch from the set of tabs in the upper-left corner of the ThemeRoller page. Figure 5.16 shows Swatch A being formatted.

Figure 5.16
Styling Swatch A in a theme.
Source: jQuery Mobile™.

As with global formatting, you access the style options for any element in a swatch by expanding the panel (clicking the triangle to the left of the panel).

Defining Swatch Attributes

Having walked you through defining Global settings in detail, I'll avoid redundancy here.

You can hover over any input box for detailed tips on what it does, as shown in Figure 5.17.

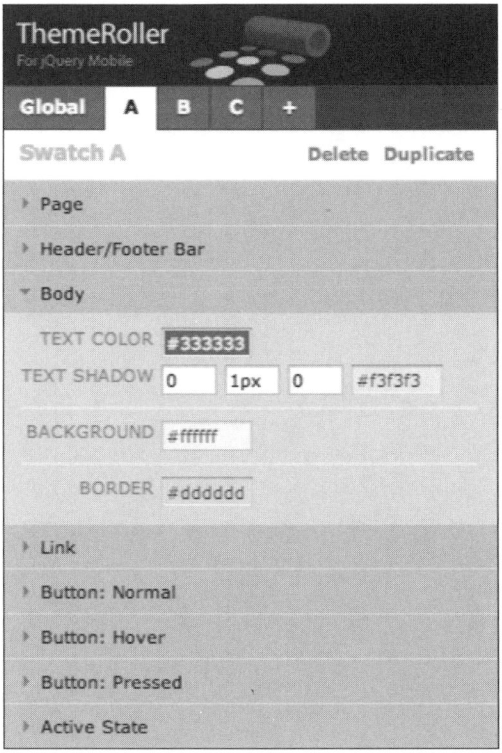

Figure 5.17
Getting a tip on defining text shadow attributes.
Source: jQuery Mobile™.

Here's what you need to know to customize header, footer, and content styles as well as button state styles for each swatch:

- Use the boxes in the Page area to customize the colors in pages, as shown in Figure 5.18. These settings apply to data-role="page" elements. The colors you define here apply to content in a page that is not inside the header, the footer, or the content area of the page, or that is not overridden by colors assigned to those elements within the page.

Figure 5.18
Defining colors for data-role="page" elements.

Source: jQuery Mobile™.

■ Customize header and footer colors (they will be the same) in the Header/Footer Bar
area, as shown in Figure 5.19.

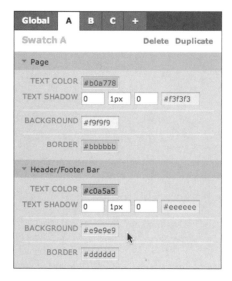

Figure 5.19
Defining colors for headers and footers.

Source: jQuery Mobile™.

- Customize body colors (content in pages defined by the `<data-role="content">` parameter). Note that if you leave text color, background color, or other settings blank (delete the default values and don't replace them with anything), the body styling will reflect the style you applied to pages (as shown in Figure 5.20).

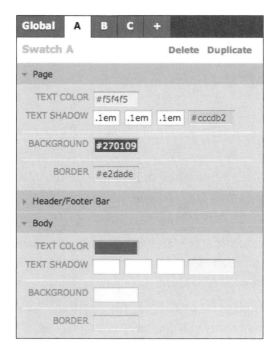

Figure 5.20
Leaving body styles undefined and applying page styles to body content.
Source: jQuery Mobile™.

- To define link state colors, click the + button next to Link Color to expand the options, and choose text color (and shadow), background color, and border color for three button states. Normal displays when a button isn't hovered over or pressed. (Of course, mouse-less mobile devices don't really take advantage of a hover state.)
- Define button state colors for normal, hover, pressed, and active states.

As you define styling, preview your theme colors in the selected swatch in the preview area.

Tip

Turn on the Inspector in the top, as shown in Figure 5.21. With the Inspector on, you can click an element in the preview area and the panel that provides settings for that element will open automatically and other open element settings will collapse.

Figure 5.21
Turning on the Inspector in jQuery Mobile ThemeRoller.
Source: jQuery Mobile™.

Creating Multiple Swatches

One color swatch might be enough for your site. Remember that with ThemeRoller 1.4, swatch a is the default. So, if you define styling for swatch a, and don't assign any data-themes to your page with HTML, swatch a will apply globally.

But for larger sites, or ones where you want more variety in styling in pages and elements, you can create up to 26 swatches! I haven't seen an environment yet where that many swatches were necessary, but the potential is there if you need it.

You can duplicate a swatch, and use it as a "template," so-to-speak, for additional swatches by clicking Duplicate next to a selected swatch, as shown in Figure 5.22.

Figure 5.22
Duplicating a swatch.
Source: jQuery Mobile™.

If you need more than three swatches, click the Add Swatch box to the right of swatch c to add more.

Downloading and Applying a Theme

After you define theme and swatch settings, you need to save your custom theme, download a new CSS file that will replace the default, and apply your new theme and swatches to your site.

There are three basic phases to this process:

- Download a new CSS file to your computer, and save it in the folder in which the rest of your website files are saved.

- Un-link your jQuery Mobile links and re-link them to new CSS files that work with the custom CSS you created in ThemeRoller.

- Apply your customized swatches with HTML.

I cover each of these steps in more detail next.

Downloading a Theme

I'll start with the process for saving and downloading the theme.

To do that, follow these steps:

1. Click the Download button at the top of the ThemeRoller screen. The Download Theme dialog opens.

2. Enter a custom theme name in the Theme Name field of the Download Theme dialog box. If you're feeling a bit uneasy about the process so far, you can use the suggested filename, which is my-custom-theme.

3. You can look over the rest of the instructions in the Download Theme dialog box, but I'll get back to them in the next step.

4. Click the Download Zip button, as shown in Figure 5.23.

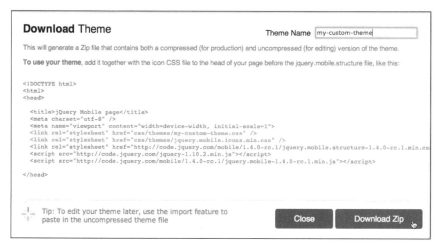

Figure 5.23
Downloading a custom theme.
Source: jQuery Mobile™.

5. Your browser's download dialog box will appear. This will be different depending on your browser, operating system, and other environmental factors. But I'll assume that you can figure out how to save the downloaded ZIP file to your website's root folder, or to copy it there after you download it.

6. Unzip the files. All the files you need will be extracted to a themes folder that gets created.

7. Use your operating system's file manager to rename the folder into which the files were extracted to .css. The file structure of the folder in which your website files are saved should look something like the one shown in Figure 5.24.

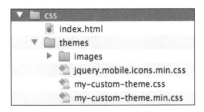

Figure 5.24
Downloaded files from ThemeRoller.
Source: jQuery Mobile™.

You're now ready to apply your theme. But don't close your browser window, I'll be sending you back to the download dialog shortly.

Changing the jQuery Mobile Links

Having downloaded the custom CSS file generated from ThemeRoller, the next step in the process is to change the default jQuery Mobile links from the centrally distributed CSS to your own custom CSS.

To do that, follow these steps:

1. Jump back to your browser, and again click the Download button to open the Download Theme dialog.

2. The safest way to be sure you are linking to all the files required to make your custom theme work is to copy all the code in the dialog <head> element, as shown in Figure 5.25.

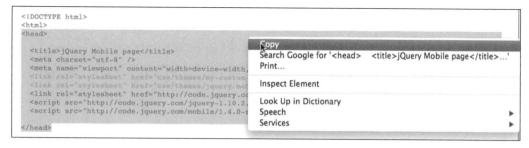

Figure 5.25
Copying code from ThemeRoller.
Source: jQuery Mobile™.

3. Open your mobile site in your code editor and select all the code in the `<head>` element.

4. Paste the copied `<head>` element with all the copied content, replacing your previous `<head>` element.

5. You can customize the `<title>` element (the content that appears in a browser title bar) by editing the "jQuery Mobile page" placeholder text.

6. With links to your custom CSS in place, test your page in a browser!

Troubleshooting and Understanding ThemeRoller Themes

Did your custom theme work? If so, don't skip ahead. I'll start with a bit of excavation into what you accomplished. And then I'll provide some tips in case your theme didn't work.

The basic concept behind ThemeRoller is this: the massive CSS file that makes jQuery Mobile work is split. Essential CSS that makes jQuery Mobile sites work is linked to a file saved to the CDN (central distribution network). If you look at the code you copied into your `<head>` element, you'll see one of the CSS files that's linked to is at the jQuery Mobile site. That's the file that has the *non*-customized CSS for your site.

But what you downloaded from ThemeRoller were one, two, or more CSS files that have the *rest* of the CSS required for your site. This is the *custom* CSS that defines the colors, fonts, icons, border radii, and other custom styling you created in ThemeRoller.

What if your custom styling isn't visible when you preview your site in a browser? The first troubleshooting step is to make sure the links in your `<head>` element to the CSS files *at your site* are correct. Make sure you used your operating system's file manager to rename the folder into which the files were extracted to .css, and that your CSS link is to a file in the css/themes folder. Your filenames may differ from those shown here, depending on the version of jQuery Mobile you used, and the features you chose for your custom theme. However, in most cases, the link code to your custom CSS files in your <head> element should be:

```
<link rel="stylesheet" href="css/themes/my-custom-theme.css" />
<link rel="stylesheet" href="css/themes/jquery.mobile.icons.min.css" />
```

Here's another possible issue: Remember that by default, the a swatch is applied to everything in your site. So you might need to apply other swatches to see some of the custom styling you created in ThemeRoller. I'll show you how to do that next.

Applying Custom Swatches

You can apply any swatch that you defined in ThemeRoller to elements in your jQuery Mobile page. I'll show you a few examples.

This code demonstrates applying swatch b to a page:

```
<div data-role="page" id="page" data-theme="b">
```

This code applies custom swatch c to a listview:

```
<ul data-role="listview" data-theme="c">
```

And this code applies swatch d to a header:

```
<div data-role="header" data-theme="d">
```

You get the concept. After you define data-themes, test your newly applied swatch by saving your edited code and opening the HTML file in your browser.

SUMMARY

jQuery Mobile ThemeRoller is the pivotal resource in creating custom CSS for jQuery Mobile-based mobile websites.

Here's the problem ThemeRoller solves: The CSS required to make jQuery Mobile's animation and interactivity click is too complex, and too long, to customize "by hand."

Here's how ThemeRoller solves that problem: It creates custom CSS for *customized* parts of the CSS required to make jQuery Mobile pages work, and provides a link to a CSS file at the jQuery Mobile CDN (content delivery network) that supplies the remaining CSS.

The key to understanding how to define custom styling in ThemeRoller is that some styling is applied to an entire mobile site (like font families), while other styling (like colors) is defined by swatches. The swatches you define in ThemeRoller are then applied in your mobile site by editing the HTML5 code to add `data-theme="a"` (or b, c, d, and so on) to apply swatches to different elements.

Finally, let's briefly review what ThemeRoller does for you. It creates new jQuery Mobile CSS files that replace the default theme color swatches (a, b, c, and so on) with custom swatches. You can create up to 26 of these color swatches—but again, three to six swatches should be sufficient for most sites.

It is important to pay attention to detail in the steps in this lesson for generating and applying custom themes with ThemeRoller. But the following points summarize the main steps in using ThemeRoller to create custom themes:

- At the jQuery Mobile ThemeRoller website, define site-wide elements in the Global tab.

- After defining global styling, you can define up to 26 separate swatches (a-z) that apply colors, shading, and other attributes to specific elements like pages, headers, footers, and listviews.

- After you define both global and swatch styles, use jQuery Mobile ThemeRoller's Download Theme dialog to download customized files. Unzip those files and save them to the folder in which your website files are saved.

- Copy and paste the `<head>` element content supplied by ThemeRoller, replacing the `<head>` code in your site.

- Apply swatches to page elements with HTML5 `data-theme` parameters.

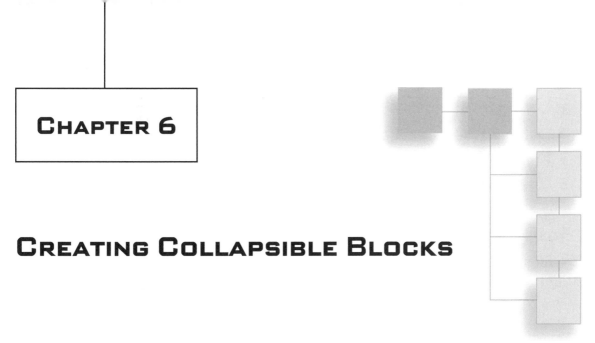

CHAPTER 6

CREATING COLLAPSIBLE BLOCKS

The focus of this chapter is *collapsible blocks,* which are boxes that open or close to reveal or hide content. Collapsible blocks and panels provide a significant alternative to listviews for packing a set of options into the small space of a mobile device viewport (listviews are explored in Chapter 2 of this book).

You can combine listviews with collapsible blocks to present a large set of navigation options on a mobile site's home page. You learn to do that in this chapter as well.

Beyond collapsible panels, this chapter explains how to absolutely position footers at the bottom of a mobile page, which is a handy technique when you are paying close attention to maximizing how much content you can pack into a smartphone viewport while keeping a page inviting.

Finally, this chapter introduces and explains how the "mini" feature can be used to downsize (shrink the size of) different mobile page elements.

You accomplish all of these tasks with HTML5, in pages linked to the jQuery Mobile JavaScript and CSS files that enable the animation and interactivity required to make panels expand and collapse, footers stay where they are supposed to stay, and content to shrink.

In the course of doing that, I'll walk you through when and how to define these design options:

- Creating collapsible (and expandable) blocks.
- Combining collapsible blocks with listviews.
- Positioning footers absolutely.
- Going "mini" to provide more content in a page.

USING COLLAPSIBLE BLOCKS

The humble listview—a set of reasonably attractive navigation options combined with an inviting set of animated effects—is the basic navigation tool for building mobile site home pages. Rather that force you to flip or scroll back to Chapter 2 for a visceral reminder of how they work, Figure 6.1 shows a set of links, styled as a listview.

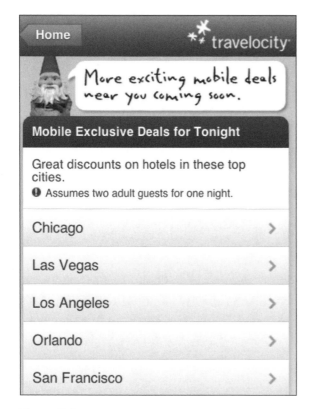

Figure 6.1
An inviting listview at Travelocity's mobile site.
Source: Travelocity, Inc.

But there are times when users need something in between a list of options and a full-blown new page (or, in HTML5 and jQuery Mobile, a new `data-role="page"` that looks and feels like a web page). For example, news sites like Google News often allow users to see a bit of a preview of a story before deciding whether to click a link and wait for the news story to load in their mobile devices. In Figure 6.2, note the (small) "Show More" text with the down-pointing symbol.

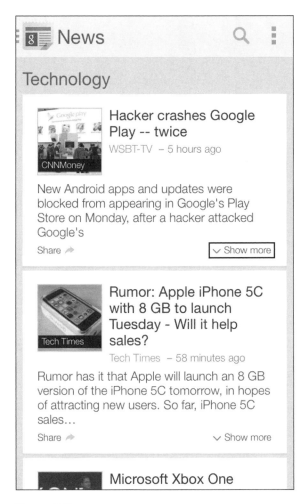

Figure 6.2
A collapsed expandable block.
Source: Google Chrome™.

If users are thinking about following a link to a story (and enduring whatever time it takes to open a page at an external news source), they can expand the block to see more about the story. They then have the option of collapsing the block (in this case by clicking the "Show Less" text), as shown in Figure 6.3.

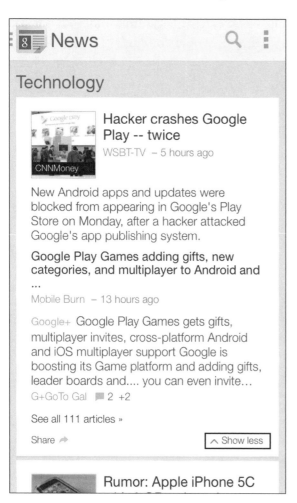

Figure 6.3
An expanded block.
Source: Google Chrome™.

Defining Collapsible Blocks

The basic syntax for a collapsible block is as follows:

```
<div data-role="collapsible">
<h3>Collapsible title goes here</h3>
<p> Collapsible content goes here.</p>
</div>
```

By default, a collapsible block is collapsed when the page in which it is embedded opens. So, the collapsible block defined by the previous code looks like Figure 6.4.

Figure 6.4
A collapsed block.
© 2014 Cengage Learning.

When a user taps on the + (plus) symbol or on the visible text, the block expands, as shown in Figure 6.5. Users can collapse the block again by tapping the - (minus) symbol or the visible text.

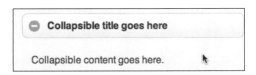

Figure 6.5
An expanded block with placeholder text.
© 2014 Cengage Learning.

Here's a bit of code with a real-life example that you can use as a template and adapt. It includes some text, an image, and a link for users who want to explore the subject at an external site.

```
<div data-role="collapsible">
<h3>NPBG</h3>
<img src="http://www.npbotanicgarden.com/gallery/
    getslideshowimage.aspx?image_id=4" width="320"
    alt="Northern Plain Botanical Gardens">
<p>The Northern Plains Botanic Garden
    located at 1201 28th Ave N in Fargo, ND.
    When developed, it will feature a 52 acre
    botanic garden for the entire Fargo / Moorhead metropolitan region.</p>
<p><a href="http://www.npbotanicgarden.com/"
    target="blank">Visit the NPBG site</a></p>
</div>
```

Grouped with other collapsible panels, the previous code looks like Figure 6.6 in a mobile device.

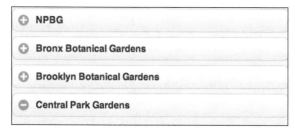

Figure 6.6
A collapsed block with other collapsed blocks.
© 2014 Cengage Learning.

When it's expanded, the code presents a picture, a short description, and a link to the external site, as shown in Figure 6.7.

Figure 6.7
Expanding a block with an image, text, and a link.
© 2014 Cengage Learning. Image source: Northern Plains Botanical Garden.

Grouping Collapsible Blocks in Sets

When you group collapsible blocks in a set, only one of the blocks expands at a time. If a user expands one block within the set, all the other blocks collapse. This technique is useful, for example, when you have three expandable blocks on a page, and you want all three to be visible in either expanded or collapsed mode at all times, as shown in Figure 6.8.

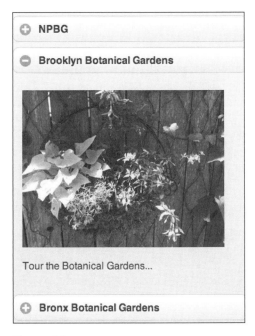

Figure 6.8
A set of collapsible blocks, with the middle block expanded.
© 2014 Cengage Learning. Image source: Brooklyn Botanical Garden.

Here is the template code for a set of three collapsible blocks:

```
<div data-role="collapsible-set">
<div data-role="collapsible">
<h1>Block 1 title</h1>
<p> Block 1 expanded content.</p>
</div>
<div data-role="collapsible">
<h1>Block 2 title</h1>
<p> Block 2 expanded content.</p>
</div>
<div data-role="collapsible">
```

```
<h1>Block 3 title</h1>
<p> Block 3 expanded content.</p>
</div>
</div>
```

Nesting Collapsible Blocks

You can provide rather complex navigation options by nesting collapsible blocks—that is, placing one or more collapsible blocks inside another collapsible block.

There's no special trick to doing this. You create a collapsible block, and then put another one inside of it. The challenge is to keep your HTML5 coding straight, as this involves a bunch of open and closed <div> tags.

Here's an example of how you might use embedded collapsible blocks: In the project I threw together for this chapter, I built a mobile site that is a guide to New York City's various botanical gardens, with photos from each. But if I wanted to provide access to different areas at, for instance, the Brooklyn Botanical Gardens, I might have expandable blocks for the Shakespeare Garden, the Cherry Esplanade, the Children's Garden, and the Herb Garden. In that case, I could create embedded collapsible blocks to provide easy access to any of these areas of the mobile site.

Here's the template code for two collapsible blocks, each with two collapsible blocks nested inside of them:

```
<div data-role="collapsible">
<h1>Main collapsible block title</h1>
<p>Main content.</p>
<div data-role="collapsible">
<h1>Nested title 1a </h1>
<p>Content 1a.</p>
</div>
<div data-role="collapsible">
<h1> Nested title 1b</h1>
<p> Content 1b.</p>
</div>
</div>
```

Tip

You can find copy-and-paste ready code for this example at http://www.dk-mobile.uphero.com/#ch06.

Figure 6.9 shows this template with all blocks expanded.

Figure 6.9
Nested expandable blocks.
© 2014 Cengage Learning.

Expanding Blocks by Default

What if you want a collapsible block to be *open* when a user opens a page? By default, collapsible blocks are closed when a page opens. But you can override that with this parameter:

```
data-collapsed="false"
```

Here's an example of that syntax applied to a collapsible block:

```
<div data-role="collapsible" data-collapsed="false">
```

Tip

This technique of defining a collapsed state of `false` (to show a collapsible block expanded when a page opens) also works for nested collapsible blocks, so when you expand the main block, one or more nested blocks are expanded by default.

Why would you want to do this? After all, the point of a collapsible block, in general, is to provide a hint of the content in the block, to give a user the option of expanding the block to see the rest of the content.

But there are times when you want to feature the content in one block in particular. That might be a lead story at a news site or blog. It might be a featured product at a retail site.

Figure 6.10 provides an example of one collapsible block that appears expanded when the page opens.

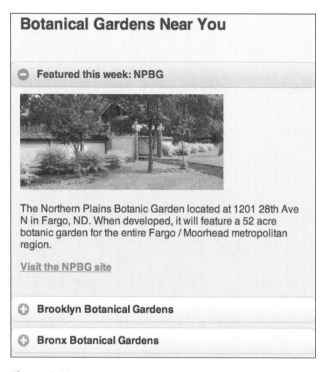

Figure 6.10
A collapsible block open by default.
© 2014 Cengage Learning. Image source: Northern Plains Botanical Garden.

Styling Collapsible Blocks

You can customize the colors in any element of a collapsible block by defining a data-theme. Chapter 4 explains how to apply data-themes and Chapter 5 explains how to customize those data-themes, so I won't rehash that all here. But it might be helpful to walk through a couple examples of how data-themes apply colors to the different elements that make up a collapsible block.

The following syntax applies data-theme e to a collapsible block:

```
<div data-role="collapsible" data-theme="e">
```

And this syntax applies data-theme e to an entire collapsible set:

```
<div data-role="collapsible-set" data-theme="e">
```

If you apply a data-theme to a collapsible set, and separate data-themes to collapsibles within that set, the separate data-themes applied to each collapsible will trump the data-theme applied to the set.

Tip

> Remember, almost all styling for jQuery Mobile-based mobile sites is applied with data-theme parameters. I'm including this example of how to apply a data-theme to a collapsible block so you don't stress trying to figure out how to customize the colors, fonts, boxes, shadows, and other styling elements associated with a collapsible block.

FIXING HEADER OR FOOTER POSITION

While on the topic of managing the position and size of elements on a mobile page, it's helpful to know that you can fix headers at the top of a page, and/or footers at the bottom of a page.

What this means is that as a user scrolls down (or up) a page, the header and/or footer remains in view. This is useful when you want a page title, a home link, or some other content inside either a header or footer to be visible all the time, no matter where a user scrolls on the page.

To take a negative example, where this is not done, one of my favorite news sites requires me to scroll up, and up, and up, and up... to the top of the list of articles, before I can change topic areas (such as from Sports to Entertainment). It would be nice if they locked either the header or footer on the screen with fixed positioning, so I could jump back to the home page without all that scrolling.

The syntax to fix a header at the top of the mobile screen is as follows:

```
<div data-role="header" data-position="fixed">
```

And the syntax to fix a footer at the bottom of a user's mobile screen is as follows:

```
<div data-role="footer" data-position="fixed">
```

It's hard to convey the impact of this in a static screen capture, but Figure 6.11 gives a sense of a fixed header remaining at the top of a page as a user scrolls down that page. No matter how far down the page users scroll, they can always see the "Flowers" header, reminding them what section of the website they are located in.

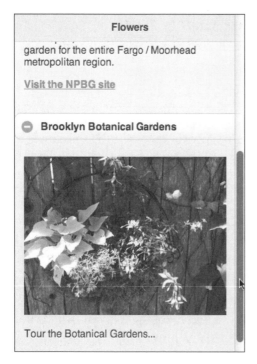

Figure 6.11
A fixed header ("Flowers") on a page of collapsible blocks.
© 2014 Cengage Learning. Image source: Northern Plains Botanical Garden.

Tip

Like any good thing, collapsible blocks can be overused. But the bigger danger is not using them when you should. Remember, in mobile devices—especially with smartphones—screen real estate is at a premium. The more you can unclutter a mobile page by hiding content a user might not need, the more inviting that page will be.

Going Mini

On the general theme of compacting a lot of accessible content onto a page… you can add a mini parameter to make elements smaller. That mini element goes well with collapsible blocks, since as a designer, you are likely employing collapsible blocks to squeeze a lot of content onto a mobile page without making the page feel cramped.

Before I show you how to do this, let's put the "mini" idea in perspective. After all, there is a challenge with mobile web pages to keep content large enough to read and navigate. But the mini parameter in jQuery Mobile doesn't reduce elements so much that they become inaccessible. Figure 6.12 compares the sizes of a normal-sized listview (on the left) and a mini-sized listview (on the right).

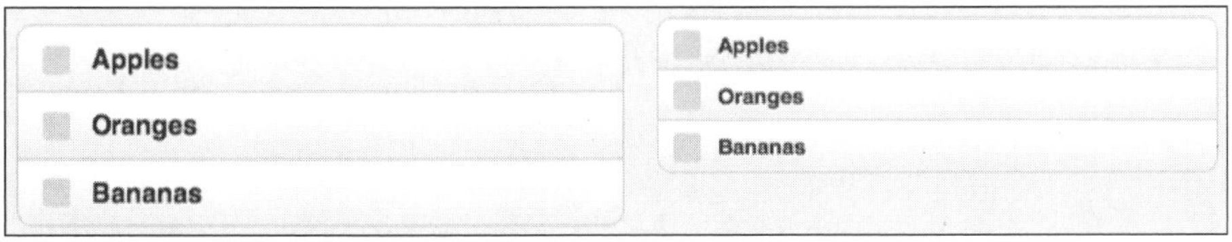

Figure 6.12
Comparing a normal listview (left) with a mini-sized one (right).
Source: jQuery Mobile™.

The syntax to add a `mini` parameter to a collapsible set is as follows:

```
<div data-role="collapsible-set" data-mini="true">
```

And the syntax to add a `mini` parameter to a single collapsible block is as follows:

```
<div data-role="collapsible" data-mini="true">
```

Normally, you'll want to apply the `mini` parameter to an entire set of collapsible blocks—mix-matching mini and non-mini blocks would create an odd, cluttered look.

Tip

If you add `mini` to a `collapsible-set`, all the nested collapsible blocks within that set will inherit the mini styling. But if you add a `mini` parameter to a collapsible block, it affects only that block and not the nested blocks.

Summary

In so many ways, the challenge of building accessible, inviting mobile websites revolves around making a lot of content available in a small space. Collapsible blocks provide a very effective technique for doing that.

Essentially, collapsible blocks allow you to provide a taste of a larger bite of content, which can be revealed by a user who expands the block. Collapsible blocks can be:

- Grouped into sets, so that when one block opens, the other blocks close.

- Set to open by default when a page loads (normally collapsible blocks are closed when a page opens).

- Custom styled with data-themes.

- Made more compact with `data-mini` parameters.

Here are three "take home" points for making effective use of collapsible blocks:

- Collapsible blocks are a powerful way to pack a lot of content onto a tiny mobile device viewport.

- You will often want to group collapsible blocks in sets, so that users engage with a relatively compact, compressed page environment as they explore different block content.

- You will often want to apply the `data-mini="true"` parameter to pack more collapsible block options onto a page.

- Since sets of collapsible blocks will tend to push content "below the fold" on mobile devices, consider fixing header and/or footer locations to keep those orientation elements on the screen as users explore content.

CHAPTER 7

DESIGNING WITH GRIDS

As the world of mobile devices continues to expand, and as tablets and high-resolution, larger smartphones became dominant in web browsing, it is important to explore the option of designing multicolumn layouts with grids.

Grids, which are blocks formed by the intersection of (horizontal) rows and (vertical) columns, provide an option for designing multicolumn page layouts for mobile devices using HTML5 (backed up with jQuery Mobile).

Readers with a long history of involvement in web design might be thinking, "Designing with rows and columns… isn't that something like designing web pages with *tables*?"

Yes, it is. Tables were originally implemented in HTML as a tool for sharing rows and columns of data. Creative designers started using tables for page design, with cells (the intersections of rows and columns) serving as boxes holding content.

As web design evolved, tables fell out of favor as a tool for page design, replaced by ⟨div⟩ tags and later by HTML5 semantic elements (like ⟨header⟩, ⟨article⟩, ⟨footer⟩, and so on), combined with CSS styling. You'll see in this chapter that grids are not simply the "return of tables." They are built with HTML5 ⟨div⟩ tags that interact with jQuery Mobile's set of class styles. But the concept, from a design perspective, is similar.

In this chapter, I show you how to use grids for mobile design, and how to implement them. Along the way, I'll walk you through:

- Defining two- and three-column layout grids.
- Populating layout grids with text and images.

- Customizing the size and style of layout grids.
- Customizing styling for specific blocks within a grid.

The Role of Grid Design

The dominant approach to designing pages for mobile devices, particularly for smartphones, is a list. Let's face it, as big as smartphones are getting, they're still *small*. And there isn't room for a lot of material on any one page. Listviews (introduced in Chapter 2) and collapsible elements (introduced in Chapter 6) allow designers to pack long lists of links onto a smartphone's small screen.

But there is a time and place—particularly as smartphone screens expand—for page layouts that present at least two columns of layout. You can see this done effectively in news media websites, retail websites, and in other places.

For example, the online retailer Boozt does a nice job of presenting different clothing departments (men, women, and kids) with the grid design shown in Figure 7.1.

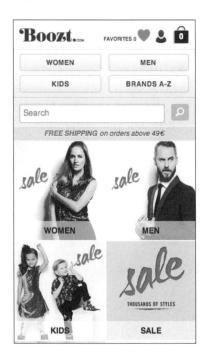

Figure 7.1
A two-column grid design.
Source: Boozt™.

Likewise, OpenView Venture Partners uses a three-column grid to effectively present services and resources to smartphone users, as shown in Figure 7.2.

Figure 7.2
A three-column grid design.
Source: OpenView Venture Partners™.

You can even push the limits of design for smartphone viewports with creative use of grids. Figure 7.3 is from the home page of Random House's Weekly Lizard imprint.

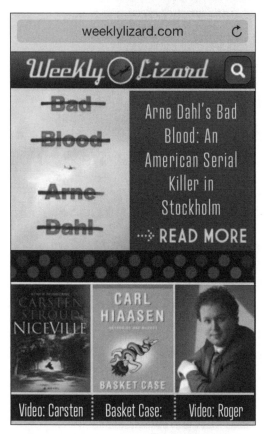

Figure 7.3
Using grids for a creative smartphone page design.
Source: Random House™.

DEFINING TWO-COLUMN GRIDS

The most useful, widely applicable grid-based design is a two-column layout. The HTML5 code that defines a two-column grid is as follows:

```
<div class="ui-grid-a">
<div class="ui-block-a">left content placeholder text</div>
<div class="ui-block-b">right content placeholder text</div>
</div>
```

The basic syntax here is that the `"ui-grid-a"` class invokes a style in the jQuery Mobile style sheet that creates a two-column grid (if you replace that with `"ui-grid-b"`, you get a three-column grid, and if you use `"ui-grid-c"`, you create a four-column grid).

Within the grid, the `"ui-block-a"` class style defines a left-side block, and the `"ui-block-b"` class style defines a right-side block.

I walk you through how this works, step-by-step. Later, I deconstruct the elements involved, and show you how to customize the content.

The Rapidly Evolving World of jQuery Mobile

I've noted in earlier chapters in this book that jQuery Mobile's centrally distributed files (the JavaScript and CSS that make jQuery Mobile pages work) are updated frequently.

When you build a jQuery Mobile page, you generally link to the centrally distributed network (CDN) files in the `<head>` element of every jQuery Mobile page.

At this stage of its life, jQuery Mobile is mature and stable enough so that updates tend not to be prompted by significant flaws or bugs. Many of the updates tweak styling and effects in jQuery Mobile.

Books (like this one) and even online resources don't, couldn't and probably shouldn't attempt to keep pace with the updates at jQuery Mobile. Even the documentation at jQuery Mobile is often a version or two or three behind the latest links.

The versions of jQuery Mobile CSS and JavaScript in any code example you read in this book, or anywhere else (including the overwhelming majority of the documentation at the jQuery Mobile website), reflect the version of jQuery Mobile in use at the time of writing. *Those links will work fine.* They don't go away when a new version of jQuery Mobile files is released. But if you want to update those links to the latest versions, you can go to the website jquerymobile.com, search for updated links to the latest versions, and replace the version numbers in the examples I use in the book with those versions.

For example, if I use a link to:

```
//code.jquery.com/mobile/1.4.0/jquery.mobile-1.4.0.min.css
```

And the links at jquerymobile.com show that the current version is 1.4.1, you would change the code to:

```
//code.jquery.com/mobile/1.4.1/jquery.mobile-1.4.1.min.css
```

Building a Grid

The first step in building a grid-based page using jQuery Mobile is to create the basic HTML5 to connect to the current jQuery Mobile scripts and style sheets, and generate a data-page. Then, you include a basic grid.

Here is the code to do that:

```
<!DOCTYPE html>
<html>
<head>
<title>Page Title</title>
<meta name="viewport"content="width=device-width, initial-scale=1">
<link rel="stylesheet" href="http://code.jquery.com/
    mobile/1.4.0/jquery.mobile-1.4.0.min.css"/>
<script src="http://code.jquery.com/jquery-1.10.2.min.js"></script>
<script src="http://code.jquery.com/
    mobile/1.4.0/jquery.mobile-1.4.0.min.js"></script>
</head>
<body>
<div data-role="page" id="page">
<div data-role="header">
<h1>Heading</h1>
</div>
<div data-role="content">
<div class="ui-grid-a">
<div class="ui-block-a">left column content</div>
<div class="ui-block-b">right column content </div>
</div>
</div>
<div data-role="footer">
<h1>Footer</h1>
</div>
</div>
</body>
</html>
```

Customizing Grid Content

The grid—to zoom in—is defined by this section of the code:

```
<div class="ui-grid-a">
<div class="ui-block-a"> left column content</div>
<div class="ui-block-b"> right column content </div>
</div>
```

The result is not particularly dramatic. By default, grid blocks have no styling; they simply present content side-by-side. But this basic code provides the starting point for side-by-side content in mobile devices, as shown in Figure 7.4.

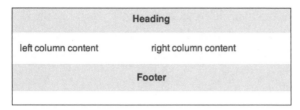

Figure 7.4
A basic two-column grid with placeholder text.
© 2014 Cengage Learning.

But if you add some real text and images, and the basic grid becomes a framework for a simple two-column display, as shown in Figure 7.5.

Figure 7.5
A basic two-column grid with images and text.
© 2014 Cengage Learning. Image source: Brooklyn Botanical Garden.

Embedding Video in Grids

In Chapter 8, I'll walk you through the ins and outs of providing accessible, fast-downloading video in mobile pages. The code you learn there for embedding video works just fine inside a grid.

I don't want to be too redundant on using video in mobile devices, given I wrote a chapter on that. So I refer you to Chapter 8 for a full exploration of how to embed video. But here's an example of how you could embed a video in one column (the right) and a description in the other (left) column:

```
<div class="ui-grid-a">
<div class="ui-block-a"> video description here</div>
<div class="ui-block-b"> right column content
<video controls>
<source src="name.mp4" type="video/mp4">
<source src="name.ogv" type="video/ogg">
Your browser doesn't support the video tag.
</video>
</div>
</div>
```

When I pop in a real video (replacing *name* with a real video file), and add a bit of real text to the left column, this code produces a grid like the one shown in Figure 7.6.

Figure 7.6
A basic two-column grid with a video in the right column.
© 2014 Cengage Learning.

Adding Rows to Two-Column Grids

If you want to repeat rows of two-column blocks within a grid, you can copy and paste the code for another left and right block. So, for example, the following code produces a three-row, two-column grid.

```
<div class="ui-grid-a">
<div class="ui-block-a"> left column content</div>
<div class="ui-block-b"> right column content</div>
<div class="ui-block-a"> left column content</div>
<div class="ui-block-b"> right column content </div>
```

```
<div class="ui-block-a"> left column content</div>
<div class="ui-block-b"> right column content </div>
</div>
```

And this code produces a grid like the one shown in Figure 7.7.

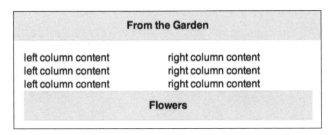

From the Garden	
left column content	right column content
left column content	right column content
left column content	right column content
Flowers	

Figure 7.7
A basic two-column grid extended to three rows.
© 2014 Cengage Learning.

Of course you can populate these blocks with images, text, or even video. You might want to jump back here to the three examples I provided early in this chapter of commercial sites. They do nice jobs of using grids for visual mobile home pages.

STYLING GRID BLOCKS

The easiest way to style grid blocks (with properties like background color, height, width, margin, and padding) is to create a `<style>` element in the `<head>` element of your mobile page, and define styles for it.

Here's an example that applies background colors, widths, margin and padding to both the a and b blocks:

```
<style>
.ui-grid-a .ui-block-a {
width: 60%; height:150px;
background-color:orange;
padding:5px;
margin:5px;
}
.ui-grid-a .ui-block-b {
width: 30%;
height:150px;
background-color:aqua;
padding:5px; margin:5px;
}
</style>
```

To deconstruct the previous code a bit, I define a compound style that applies to the .ui-block-a class style *when it is embedded in* a .ui-grid-a class style.

That style (with width, height, background color, padding, and margins) is applied to every *a* (left side) block in the grid.

The second line of the style code defines a compound style that applies to the .ui-block-a class style *when it is embedded in* a .ui-grid-b class style. That style (again, with width, height, background color, padding, and margins) is applied to every *b* (right side) block in the grid.

The result produces a grid like the one shown in Figure 7.8.

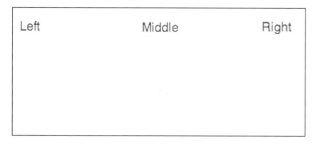

Figure 7.8
A basic two-column grid extended to three rows with styling applied.
© 2014 Cengage Learning.

Page Layout with Multicolumn Grids

Up to this point I have focused on two-column grids, but grids can be three, four, or even five columns wide. This is particularly effective as a design tool for tablets, where more than two-columns might be appropriate.

Grids are designed to wrap to multiple rows of items. For example, if you specify a three-column grid (ui-grid-b) on a container that has nine child blocks, it will wrap to three rows of three items each. A CSS rule in the "master" CSS file for jQuery Mobile that clears floats and starts a new row when class="ui-block-a" is applied.

The following code creates a three-column, one-row grid with placeholder text that identifies each block.

```
<div class="ui-grid-b">
<div class="ui-block-a">Left</div>
<div class="ui-block-b">Middle</div>
<div class="ui-block-c">Right</div>
</div>
```

This code creates a set of blocks like the one shown in Figure 7.9.

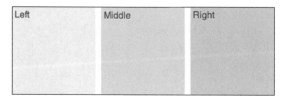

Figure 7.9
A three-column grid extended to three rows with placeholder text.
© 2014 Cengage Learning.

Styling Multicolumn Grids

You might be wondering whether you can you apply styling to a three-column grid the same way I explained how to create styling for a two-column grid. If you guessed yes, you're right.

The difference between the styling defined in the previous section for a two-column grid, and creating styling for a three-column grid, is that instead of defining compound class styles for `.ui-grid-a .ui-block-a`, you need to define styles for the compound class style `.ui-grid-b .ui-block-a`, as well as for `.ui-grid-b .ui-block-b` and `.ui-grid-b .ui-block-c`.

Here's an example that applies styles to the three blocks in a three-column grid:

```
.ui-grid-b .ui-block-a {
width: 30%;
height:150px;
background-color:beige;
padding:5px;
margin:5px;
}
.ui-grid-b .ui-block-b {
width: 30%;
height:150px;
```

```
background-color:lightgray;
padding:5px;
margin:5px;
}
.ui-grid-b .ui-block-c {
width: 30%;
height:150px;
background-color:silver;
padding:5px;
margin:5px;
}
```

Figure 7.10 shows how that styling looks when applied to a three-column grid.

Figure 7.10
A three-column grid with width, height, background color, padding, and margins defined.
© 2014 Cengage Learning.

Grids as Navigation Bars

As I mentioned, you can technically extend grids to five columns. That's not a design technique you'll use often given the constrained viewports of mobile devices. And that's true even if you're designing for a tablet. But there are times and places where a five-column grid is applicable. For example, you might create a five-column grid for a page targeted to an audience of tablet users. Or you might use a five-column grid for a horizontal navigation bar.

Here's the basic syntax for a five-column grid, with numbers as placeholders for each column content:

```
<div class="ui-grid-d">
<div class="ui-block-a">1</div>
<div class="ui-block-b">2</div>
<div class="ui-block-c">3</div>
<div class="ui-block-d">4</div>
<div class="ui-block-e">5</div>
</div>
```

When might you use a configuration like this? One scenario is a tabbed menubar. The following code creates a template link bar.

```
<div class="ui-grid-d">
<div class="ui-block-a"><a href="#">Link 1</a></div>
<div class="ui-block-b"><a href="#">Link 2</a></div>
<div class="ui-block-c"><a href="#">Link 3</a></div>
<div class="ui-block-d"><a href="#">Link 4</a></div>
<div class="ui-block-e"><a href="#">Link 5</a></div>
</div>
```

Here's an easy-to-customize example of a CSS style definition for one of the five tabs. You could easily duplicate this example and customize it to create your own:

```
.ui-grid-d .ui-block-a {
width: 19%;
height: 35;
background-color: #BFBFBF;
padding: 7px;
margin: 3px;
border-radius: 12px 12px 0px 0px;
-webkit-border-radius: 12px 12px 0px 0px;
-moz-border-radius: 15px 15px 0px 0px;
border-top: thin black solid;
}
```

In this example, I defined just a bit short of 1/5 of the width of the viewport for each tab (19%), and I defined background color, height, padding, and margin. I added a bit of a border radius (with proprietary prefixes for different browsers), and finally a top border. With slightly different background colors for blocks b, c, and d, this produces a tab bar like the one shown in Figure 7.11.

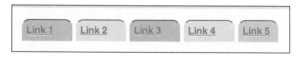

Figure 7.11
A five-column grid styled to serve as a tabbed link bar.
© 2014 Cengage Learning.

Five-column grids are kind of a hassle to code. And, that five-column grid example I just explained is stretching the limits of design with grids and blocks.

Much more typically, you'll use a two- or maybe three-column grid to provide a couple (or three) columns of text and images for page layout. A two-column grid is easily coded and provides a convenient way to design two-column layouts for smartphones and tablets.

Summary

As mobile devices command more and more of the browsing environment, designers face ongoing challenges to present content in creative and inviting ways. Listviews, which I introduced in Chapter 2, are probably going to remain the dominant way of offering users a set of options when they arrive at a mobile website. But a second approach is to provide a grid of choices.

Grids allow more freedom for larger thumbnail images, more colorful and dynamic links, and combinations of text, images, and even video. Of course, they take up more space than a listview, but they are often more fun for users to engage with.

Grids are divided into blocks. Blocks can have styles created for them that define the width, height, border, border-radius, margin, padding, and other properties. And any specific block can be individually styled, with unique background colors, for example.

There are four choices for grids:

- `<div class="ui-grid-a">` class styles create a two-column grid.
- `<div class="ui-grid-b">` class styles create a three-column grid.
- `<div class="ui-grid-c">` class styles create a four-column grid.
- `<div class="ui-grid-d">` class styles create a five-column grid.

Here are a four "take home" points for designing with grids:

- Don't overdo it! Generally a two-column grid is about as many columns as a smartphone can display effectively.
- You can include images, text, or video in a grid block.
- By default, grids evenly divide a page (so for example, two-column grids create two columns that take half the page each). But you can customize widths with CSS.
- One effective use of three-, four-, or five-column grids is in creating navigation bars.

Part III

Using HTML5 to Deploy Mobile-Friendly Content

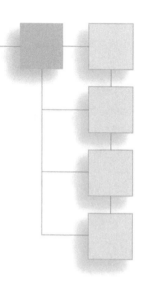

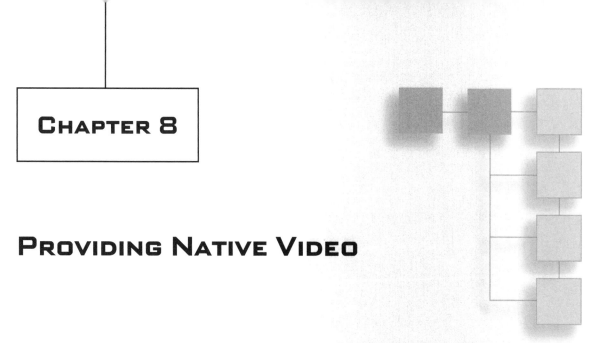

CHAPTER 8

PROVIDING NATIVE VIDEO

Today's mobile web designer—that is, you and I—do our work framed by two converging trends. One is the mass migration from desktop/laptop usage to web browsing with mobile devices. Around the moment this book goes to press (and is available for download), the statistical bridge will have been crossed: more people will visit websites on mobile devices than on laptops and desktops.

The second trend is the degree to which video is evolving from a peripheral element of the web browsing experience to an expected element in that experience. For example, the Hulu website reports that about half of those watching video through their Hulu Plus service were using tablets and smartphones in 2013. As the mobile generation comes to dominate web browsing, as the audio and video quality of mobile devices improves, and as more and more video content is available online, video will continue to be an increasingly important part of the mobile browsing experience. Figure 8.1 shows an episode of *Ellen* on my iPhone at Hulu.

Figure 8.1
Online video in a smartphone.
Source: Hulu™.

And video is integral to all kinds of mobile-focused websites. Online publications of all types integrate video into many of their stories, like the feature shown in Figure 8.2, from *USA Today* on a new tech gadget, accompanied by a video demonstration.

Figure 8.2
Online video enhancing a news story.
Source: *USA Today*™.

There are many specific challenges in presenting video for mobile devices. For example, mobile devices cannot be expected to have proprietary video players (like Flash Player, QuickTime Player, or Windows Media Player) installed. They have slower 3G, 4G, or LTE connections. And of course the screens are smaller than those on laptops or desktops.

In this chapter, I'll walk you through how to understand and solve these challenges using HTML5.

Mobile Video Is Native Video

I noted in the introduction to this chapter that mobile devices cannot be expected to support proprietary media players.

Instead, mobile devices overwhelmingly provide access to video through *native* video, which is video that plays in browsers *without* the need for proprietary player software like Flash, Windows Media Player, or QuickTime.

Before walking you through how to solve this issue and provide native video with HTML5, let me explain the substantial differences between how access has historically been provided for video for laptop/desktop users, and the *different* way accessible video is created for mobile devices.

The Evolution of Mobile Video

Until the advent of HTML5, in order to watch video on a computer or device of any kind that device needed to have a media player application. That wasn't a huge problem for most users. Macs came with the QuickTime Player installed. Windows computers came with Windows Media Player installed. And most browsers either came with the Flash Player installed, or strongly prompted users to download the Flash player.

While users experienced hassles when they tried to watch a video with a format that wasn't supported by their installed player software, those hassles were generally surmountable. They might be prompted to download and install a different player, or their player might include options or add-ins that supported different formats.

Those days are not entirely gone, but the player-dependent method of providing access to online video is not reliably functional for mobile viewing. Fewer and fewer mobile devices support the Flash player, and proprietary player software is a bad fit for the multiplicity of devices, operating systems, and browsers that populate the mobile viewing environment.

HTML5 and Native Video

One of the most significant changes in HTML5, compared to previous versions of HTML, is support for native video, which plays in a browser without plug-in software.

With native video, users do not rely on proprietary software or plug-ins like Flash, Windows Media Player, or QuickTime.

To be clear, native video is supported by nearly all modern browsers, *including laptop/ desktop* browsers. So, you can reach an overwhelming majority of users with current generation browsers (well over 90%) with native video. You do not have to create and make available different sets of video for mobile devices and laptop/desktop devices.

As we go to press, the current versions of the following browsers *do* support HTML5 native video:

- Android browser
- Blackberry browser
- Chrome
- Chrome for Android
- Firefox
- Firefox for Android
- IE Mobile
- Internet Explorer
- iOS Safari
- Opera
- Opera Mobile
- Safari

Opera Mini does not support HTML5 video.

Different Browsers Support Different Native Video Formats

There are essentially three different native video formats:

- Theora (files with the `.ogg` or `.ogv` filename extensions)
- H.264 (usually files with `.mp4` or `.m4v` filename extensions)
- WebM (files with `.webm` filename extensions)

There are complex economic, property-rights, and competitive factors behind why different browsers support different native video formats, and understanding what those are isn't critical for designers. Here's the bottom line: *Every* browser that supports HTML5 native video supports Theora or H.264 video, or both. H.264 is the dominant video format, but it is not fully supported in many recent versions of Firefox or Opera, and many versions of Android's native browser still in use.

So, you can reach a large majority of users with H.264 video alone, but to provide support for many Firefox and Android smartphone users, you should also provide Theora video.

Tip

About WebM. I'm focusing on H.264 and Theora OGG video formats in this chapter, because if you create video in both of those formats, your video is supported in all mobile devices. But the third option, WebM, is supported on Android devices. WebM is an open-source software project. Learn more at http://www .webmproject.org/.

Support for HTML5 Video

A good resource for tracking support for HTML5 on different devices is caniuse.com. You can find their table listing which browsers support which native video formats at http://caniuse.com/video.

Native Video Looks Different in Different Browsers

With native video, the player looks different in different browsers. Not radically different, but the controls and frame are slightly different. Let me illustrate with examples. Figure 8.3 shows a video I directed in Chrome.

Figure 8.3
Native HTML5 video in Chrome.
© 2014 Cengage Learning.

Figure 8.4 shows that same video in Firefox.

Figure 8.4
Native HTML5 video in Firefox.
© 2014 Cengage Learning.

Note that the play/pause buttons on the far left, the scrubber bar, the time indicator, the volume control, and the full-screen button are all styled differently in the Chrome and Firefox video players.

And, as you can see in Figure 8.5, the video player in Safari for mobile (iOS) has a different display as well.

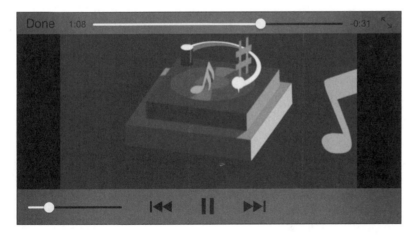

Figure 8.5
Native HTML5 video in Safari for mobile.
© 2014 Cengage Learning.

With native video, designers sacrifice some control over video display to browsers. In the old model of plug-in dependent video, a designer could create a custom player in Flash, for example, and impose that player with defined controls on any browsing environment. That freedom was part of what Apple originally objected to, insisting on the need to define a user experience on its mobile devices including video player design.

Hosted Video vs. YouTube

One option for providing access to video at your site is to embed video hosted at YouTube, Vimeo, or other video-hosting services. This is an appropriate solution for beginning-level web hosting. If you host your videos at YouTube, there's no coding involved. You simply copy and paste code from YouTube, and the YouTube video displays within your site.

However, relying on YouTube or other non-commercial video hosting sites has its problems. When I refer to non-commercial video hosting, I'm referring to hosting services (like YouTube) that do not specialize in hosting professionally distributed video. When you use YouTube, you don't control the video, the rights to the video, or how the hosting site presents it. The hosting site harvests your visitor data and uses it for marketing. Your viewers will have the chance to see and perhaps be distracted by other videos. Those can include videos about or by a competing brand, band, resource, or product.

For these reasons, advanced web designers either contract with a paid, commercial video hosting site or host their own videos. Hosting services are useful in some circumstances. Every video-hosting service allows you to generate an iFrame tag. This tag embeds content from another web page within your page. You can think of it as a "window" into another page. The site from which you're embedding content determines the content of the iFrame element. But you define the size and location of the iFrame tag itself—the element that holds the embedded content.

Generating Mobile-Ready Video Files

Professional video producers can export video to the H.264 and Theora formats, and provide you with both files to use in building mobile-friendly websites with HTML5.

And, it is relatively easy to convert existing video files created using amateur or semi-professional tools into Theora files. When you record video on a digital camera, you typically generate files in non-compressed formats, like MOV (QuickTime) or WMV (Windows Media).

You can then convert those video files to HTML5-ready, compressed formats—Theora or H.264. The online-convert website provides an online resource where you can upload a file (or provide a URL for an online video), and convert it to Theora. That site is at http://video.online-convert.com/convert-to-ogg. If you're comfortable with video compression and editing, you can adjust things like audio quality, frame rate, and size, as shown in Figure 8.6.

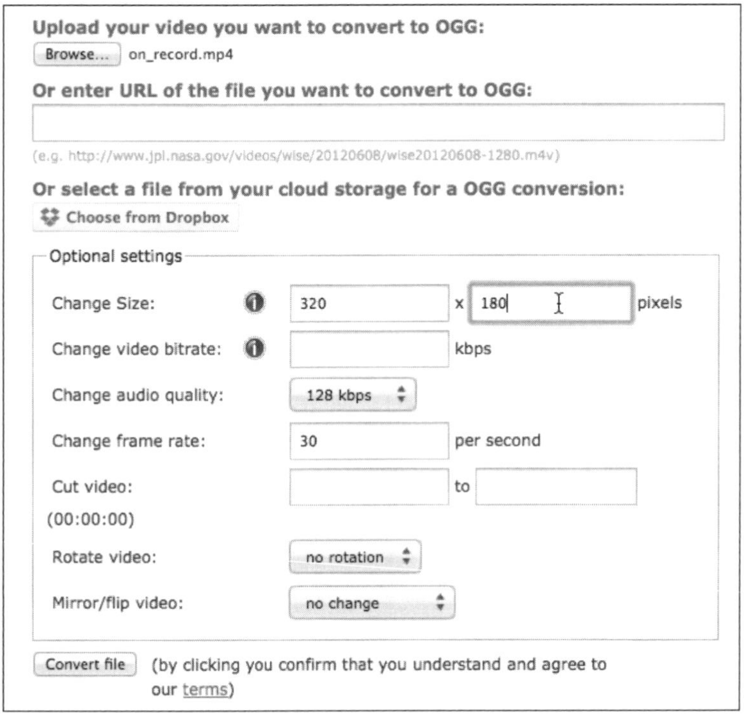

Figure 8.6
Converting an H.264 video to Theora.
Source: Online-Convert.com.

Since the H.264 format is proprietary rather than open source, tools for generating H.264 video tend to be available through commercial video-editing software. In other words you have to pay for them. You might have software that generates H.264 with your digital camera or video recorder. Professional video compression tools are part of many video-editing programs. For instance, Adobe Premiere, Apple Final Cut Pro, iMovie, and the current version of Windows Movie Maker all export or convert video to H.264 format. If you have almost any version of Adobe Creative Suite, it includes a utility (currently called Media Encoder) that produces H.264 video.

Tip

H.264 Conversion Resources. Aside from commercial H.264 export utilities provided with Adobe Creative Suite, there are some online options for converting video to H.264 format. One option for free open-source H.264 encoding is provided by the VideoLAN organization. At the VideoLAN website (https://www.videolan.org/developers/x264.html), you can download x264, a free software library and application for encoding video streams into the H.264/MPEG-4 AVC compression format.

USING HTML5 FOR MOBILE-READY VIDEO

I know. I spent quite a bit of time explaining what native video is, how to get it, and when to use it. Sorry about that, but native video is new, it's confusing, and it is one of the more radical changes in HTML5.

I wanted to be sure you were clear that you need to provide *both* H.264 and Theora video files to address all contemporary browsers. And that you understood what those files are, and how you get them.

But now it's time to walk through *how* to embed native video in your HTML5 mobile-friendly pages!

Embedding HTML5 Video

Here is the basic syntax to embed a native HTML5 video in a page:

```
<video>
  <source src="file.mp4" type="video/mp4">
  <source src="file.ogv" type="video/ogg">
</video>
```

The example code above provides both an H.264 option (the `.mp4` file) and a Theora option (the `.ogv` file). Between the two, this covers the bases for all contemporary browsers.

Note

When you provide video sources, list the H.264 (.mp4) option first, and the Theora option second. Some versions of Apple's mobile browser will not detect H.264 video if it is not listed as the first source.

What About Older Browsers?

All contemporary browsers (except Opera Mini, which is a very niche community) support HTML5 native video. But what about *non*-contemporary browsers? Specifically, what about Internet Explorer versions 6-8 that, at least as of this writing, are still entrenched in some large institutions deeply invested in Microsoft Windows XP for their network technology?

Where support for the IE 6-8 audience is still an issue (and this is the call of the stakeholders behind any website), you can provide an option to watch Flash video. I'll explain how to do that later in this chapter.

Note that in the previous template syntax, the `<source>` element is embedded in the `<video>` element. The `<video>` element parameters apply to all the sources in the element.

For example, if you elect to display controls for the video (which I'll explain shortly), you do that for all the sources.

Video Options

The `src` parameter is the only required parameter for HTML5 video. But to display controls (like play, pause, and volume buttons and sliders—which I illustrated with examples in different browsers in Figures 8.3, 8.4, and 8.5), you need to add the `controls` parameter.

You can also define a set size using `height` and `width` parameters for the `<video>` element. And you can define autoplay, which starts a video playing as soon as a page opens. That option should come with a "use with care!" warning. Some users will resent it if a loud audio track on a video begins playing when they open a page.

Defining Controls, Autoplay, Size, and Looping

The basic options for a video include controls, autoplay, size and looping.

Controls are the start/pause button, scrubber bar, volume control, full-screen button, and other options (as noted earlier, how these display is defined by the browser).

Size can be defined in height and width, usually in pixels. Autoplay launches a video even without a user clicking the play button. A nice accompanying option is the mute parameter, which at least begins the video with the audio muted. And looping repeats a video.

Here is the syntax for a video element that displays controls:

```
<video controls>
```

Here is the syntax that defines a width of 320 pixels and a height of 240 pixels (a common size for online videos):

```
<video width="320" height="240">
```

And the following syntax turns on autoplay:

```
<video autoplay>
```

When (and if) you turn on autoplay, you can mute the audio track. Here's the syntax for a `video` element with both autoplay and mute enabled:

```
<video autoplay muted>
```

Caution

Safari, Firefox, Chrome, and Opera all support the muted parameter, but Internet Explorer 10 doesn't.

Here's the syntax to loop a video to play repeatedly:

```
<video loop>
```

You can combine any or all of these parameters. The following example defines a video element with height, width, controls, and loop:

```
<video width="320" height="240" controls loop>
```

Video files are large, and mobile designers are up against the challenge of reducing the wait time for users who are watching videos on their mobile devices tied to 3G, 4G, or LTE connections. One option is to add a preload parameter to the video tag that downloads a video when the page opens, even before a user plays the video. Here's the syntax to do that:

```
<video preload>
```

Internet Explorer 9 and 10 don't support the preload parameter, and support is spotty for mobile devices. But this option will help some mobile users.

Caution

Preload can slow down the opening of a page. A good rule of thumb is to use preload only when a video is the sole element or the main element on your page.

Adding Posters

Native video players (in both mobile and desktop/laptop browsers) support the display of a *poster*—that is, an image file that displays in the video player when the video isn't playing.

The following syntax is used to define a poster image for a video:

```
<video poster="file.png">
```

The poster file can be a still captured from a video. Or, you can use another image file you create specifically to display while a video downloads.

Given the importance of keeping users engaged while a video downloads (sometimes slowly) into their mobile device, an attractive poster image is often an important part of making HTML5 mobile video friendly and inviting.

Styling Video Elements

The easiest way to customize the display of a video player is to define a style for the `<video>` element in CSS. Here's a template that can be added to the `<style>` element of an HTML5 web page, or a CSS style sheet:

```
video {
width: 320px;
padding: 5px;
margin: 5px;
background-color:darkgray;
border:2px lightgray solid;
box-shadow: 10px 10px 5px black;
}
```

The result looks something like Figure 8.7.

Figure 8.7
Applying CSS styling to the `<video>` element.
© 2014 Cengage Learning.

When you apply unique, custom styling using the `<video>` element, you can control how your video will appear in a user's mobile device.

Options for Non-HTML5 Browsers

I promised earlier in this chapter that I'd return to the issue of users viewing your site in Internet Explorer versions 6-8.

Do I have to?! After all, this is not an issue for mobile devices, since obviously there are no mobile devices using these decades-old browsers. But there are, as I noted, entrenched user bases who remain locked into IE 6-8 for a variety of reasons.

A minimal option for addressing this audience is to display a message for them explaining that their browser doesn't support HTML5 video. To do that, include a line of code right before the end of the </video> element like the one shown here:

```
<video>
<source src="name.mp4" type="video/mp4">
<source src="name.ogv" type="video/ogg">
Your browser doesn't support the video tag.
</video>
```

If providing accessible video for the IE 6-8 audience is a priority, one option is to encourage them to download a contemporary browser. Here's an example of syntax for that:

```
<video>
<source src="name.mp4" type="video/mp4">
<source src="name.ogv" type="video/ogg">
Your browser doesn't support the video tag.
    Click <a href="http://www.firefox.com">here</a>
    to download the Firefox browser for your operating system.
</video>
```

TESTING AND TROUBLESHOOTING HTML5 VIDEO

HTML5 video isn't *that* confusing. But there are a number of things that can go wrong when you prepare, embed, and upload native video. Let me briefly note a few common problems and explain some pathways to solving them.

If Your Video Doesn't Play in Firefox

If your video is working in most environments, but not in Firefox, chances are the problem lies with your Theora (.ogg or .ogv) file. Try opening the *video* file itself in Firefox.

This process will differ depending on your version of Firefox, but in general you can follow these steps:

1. Choose File > Open File. The Open File dialog box appears.

2. Navigate to your .ogg or .ogv file.

3. Click Open in the Open File dialog.

The video file itself should open in Firefox and start playing, as shown in Figure 8.8. If it doesn't play, here's a quick trouble-shooting checklist:

1. Did your video convert properly to Theora? Or was the conversion corrupted by a flakey Internet connection?

2. Did the video file upload properly? In my experience, OGG files tend to be a bit larger in file size than H.264 files, and sometimes servers or connections that handle an H.264 file fine don't upload the OGG version of a video on the first try.

3. Make sure you're testing in a browser that supports OGG, such as Firefox.

Figure 8.8
Testing a Theora video file in Firefox.
© 2014 Cengage Learning. Source: Xiph.org Foundation.

If Your Video Doesn't Play in an iPhone

If your video is playing okay in other browsing environments (including Safari for desktop/laptop), but won't play properly in an iPhone, the problem could be that you have your sources in the wrong order.

Remember, some iPhone browser versions require that the H.264 be listed *first* in the set of sources. So this syntax will work:

```
<video>
  <source src="file.mp4" type="video/mp4">
  <source src="file.ogv" type="video/ogg">
</video>
```

But this syntax will *not* because the H.264 source is not listed first.

```
<video>
<source src="file.ogv" type="video/ogg">
  <source src="file.mp4" type="video/mp4">
</video>
```

Tip

Troubleshooting H.264 video that doesn't play. If your H.264 video isn't playing, and you've made the fix I noted earlier (putting the H.264 video first in the list of sources), here's a couple things you can do. One, check to make sure it was fully uploaded to a sever. Video files are large, and if there's a hiccup in the server connection, the video file might get corrupted "on the way" to the server. Second, make sure you are testing the H.264 video in a browser that supports that format (like Apple's mobile iOS and Mobile Safari browser).

If Your Video Won't Play Anywhere

If your video file won't play at all, in any browser, chances are your link to the files in the `<source>` element aren't correct. If your video is in the *same folder* as the page with the `<video>` tag, you do not need to specify a path. You can define the source like this:

```
<video>
  <source src="file.mp4" type="video/mp4">
  <source src="file.ogv" type="video/ogg">
</video>
```

But, if your video files are, for example, in a folder named `video`, the path to the video has to be included in the `<source>` element, like this:

```
<video>
  <source src="video/file.mp4" type="video/mp4">
  <source src="video/file.ogv" type="video/ogg">
</video>
```

SUMMARY

Mobile is hot. Video is hot. Mobile video is really hot. But it is also a challenge. Mobile browsers support *native* video, which means you need to prepare and present video in native video formats. Different browsers support different native video formats, so you have to provide more than one video option. And you have to take into account that we still live in a world where not every browser is HTML5-compliant, so you have to provide options for users without HTML5 video.

In this chapter, I showed you how to do all that. Key techniques include:

- Defining video parameters to define size, preloading, autoplay, muting, and display of a control bar (or not).

- Displaying "posters," which is artwork that appears while a video downloads.

- Providing an H.264 and a Theora version of your video, plus some options for users without HTML5-compliant browsers.

- Customizing video display with CSS.

Here are four "take home" points for presenting mobile-friendly video that works anywhere:

- HTML5 video is *native* video, it plays *without* plug-in video player software.

- You must start with an H.264 and a Theora version of your video file.

- The most essential element of the HTML5 for native video is the `<source>` element, this must be defined.

- Customize the display of video with CSS styling for the `<video>` element.

CHAPTER 9

PROVIDING AUDIO FOR MOBILE

Mobile audio, including downloaded audio files and Internet radio stations, makes up a substantial chunk of all mobile web usage. If you don't believe me, ask someone in the music business, where the physical distribution of music has been eclipsed by online music sharing. Or, for a more empirical case, *Mobility Techzone* reports that "Mobile audio, including Internet radio and audio file downloads, now constitutes 12 percent of mobile data volume in North America." ("3 Apps Drive Android Traffic, 4 Apps Drive iOS Traffic," *Mobility Techzone,* by Gary Kim 11/6/2013.)

While Internet radio and commercial music downloads are *mainly* dominated by massive commercial entities (like Pandora, Spotify, or iTunes), smaller projects and institutions—commercial and non-commercial—can and should make effective use of online audio. Among my clients and students are musicians who distribute their own music, spoken word and theatrical performers who distribute audio, clients who provide a "Welcome" audio message, religious institutions that share liturgical music, and authors who provide audio readings of their books. I've even worked with someone who records birdcalls and makes them available for download.

A few examples will help to give you a sense of the potential of video in your mobile projects. The London public transportation system makes quick downloading, easily accessed online instructions available for all their services, as shown in Figure 9.1.

Figure 9.1
Checking audio directions for public transport in London.
Source: TfL™.

Authors Dave Logan, John King, and Halee Fischer-Wright provide potential readers of their book *Tribal Leadership* with an audio of the book's foreword in a nicely accessible mobile format, as shown in Figure 9.2.

Figure 9.2
Listening to an audio of the forward to *Tribal Leadership*.
Source: CultureSync™.

Would you bet money that the United States Supreme Court provides very easily accessible, mobile-friendly audio of oral arguments they hear? If so, you would have won the bet.

The Court provides mobile-ready audio of those arguments at supremecourt.gov, shown in Figure 9.3.

Figure 9.3
Mobile audio for oral arguments at the United States Supreme Court.
Source: SupremeCourt.gov.

There are essentially two steps to the process of presenting mobile audio:

- Preparing mobile-friendly audio in appropriate audio formats.
- Embedding that audio in your mobile site with HTML5.

In this chapter, I'll walk you through both steps. But first, a bit of background on what it means to use *native* audio with HTML5.

USING NATIVE AUDIO WITH HTML5

Essentially, the *native* in native audio means that audio files play in mobile (and other) browsers without requiring the user to download a plug-in app to play the audio. The audio player is, to put it another way, built into the browser.

Until the widespread acceptance of HTML5, there were no effective standards for distribution of audio online. Those of us who lived through that era remember, and not fondly, needing to install separate plug-in players for Windows Media (.wmv) files, Apple's AIFF format (.aiff), perhaps Real Media's audio format (.ra), and the list goes on.

With the adoption of HTML5, there are basically five supported formats:

- AAC
- MP3
- OGG
- WAV PCM
- WebM Vorbis

Support for Native Audio

As we go to press, the current versions of the following browsers *do* support HTML5 native audio:

- Android Browser
- Blackberry Browser
- Chrome
- Chrome for Android
- Firefox
- Firefox for Android
- IE Mobile
- Internet Explorer
- iOS Safari
- Opera
- Opera Mobile
- Safari

Opera Mini does not support HTML5 audio. Opera Mini is a niche browser, but there's no reason not to provide audio for users coming to your site with that browser installed on their mobile devices. When we get to the nuts and bolts of embedding video on a mobile site, I'll suggest options for Opera Mini users.

As is the case with native video (see Chapter 8), there is no *single* native audio format supported in all browsers. You can track the ever-evolving state of support for HTML5 audio and various audio formats at http://caniuse.com/audio. But the bottom line is that for the near and mid-term future, you can safely cover all HTML5-friendly mobile (and other) browsers with just these two formats: OGG and MP3.

Controlling Audio Quality

While you can provide accessible, decent quality audio for any mobile device with either MP3 or OGG format files, those file formats *compress* file size by eliminating some data from the original recorded sound. Compression allows audio to download faster. And, when you produce audio for the web, you have options as to how much compression to apply. More compression creates faster downloads, but lower quality. In the section, "Producing Mobile Audio with Audacity," later in this chapter, I'll focus on how to appropriately compress audio for mobile downloading.

If you require high-quality, uncompressed audio files, you can save your audio to the WAV format. WAV files tend to download substantially more slowly than compressed MP3 or OGG files. They are appropriate for distributing audio at CD quality, such as recorded musical performances. A full exploration of recording and saving WAV files is beyond the scope of this chapter and book, but those of you whose work is focused on producing commercially distributed, high-quality video will want to know that the WAV format is supported in some mobile environments.

Native Audio Means Different Players

Native audio players—the ones built into mobile (and other) browsers—do not all look the same. They provide different controls, and they display controls differently. For example, in Figure 9.4, I've "zoomed in" on the audio player provided by Chrome for mobile.

Figure 9.4
Native audio player in Chrome for mobile.
© 2014 Cengage Learning. Source: Google Inc.

Figure 9.5 shows that same audio file in the native audio player in Chrome for desktop/laptop.

Figure 9.5
Native audio player in Chrome for desktop/laptop.
© 2014 Cengage Learning. Source: Google Inc.

This means, practically speaking, that browsers tend to dictate how audio players display in devices. That's intentional. Much of the impetus behind native audio, to be candid, came from browser distributors who wanted to enforce a consistent user experience throughout their interaction with their mobile device.

How then do developers customize audio player display, and integrate an audio player into their own conceptions of how a mobile site should look and feel? There are three avenues for doing this:

- Defining custom control settings and activity (for example, setting autoplay to start an audio automatically, or hiding controls). This provides a rather minimal set of customization options.

- Creating custom CSS for the `<audio>` element to define colors, spacing, margins, borders, and so on. This allows for quite a bit of unique individualization of audio player display.

- Connecting with JavaScript widgets distributed on the web (or, if you are a JavaScript programmer, creating your own JavaScript). This provides the most customization, but is the hardest to implement and the most likely to create issues for mobile users, including slow downloads. I will introduce you to that option briefly at the end of this chapter.

I'll walk you through each of these options at the end of this chapter, after I show you how to create and embed HTML5 audio.

Preparing Audio Files for Mobile

Audio files are relatively easy to record and prepare for web distribution. By "relatively," I mean they are much easier to create and prepare for distribution than video files. Editing and producing commercial quality-video requires expensive software, computers with powerful processors, and a substantial skill set. Not so for audio. Here, I will walk you through the steps involved in recording and producing mobile-ready audio files using free, open-source software.

Of course this discussion of recording and producing mobile-ready audio will be highly compressed. Recording and producing professional-level audio recordings can be as complex as you want it to be. The techniques I walk you through here are fine for recording and distributing CD-quality performances of you or your client singing and playing your guitar, reading a chapter of your soon-to-be-a-best-seller book, or welcoming clients to your website. If you've been hired to produce an album for a best-selling recording artist, you'll need another level of skills well beyond what I cover here.

Here's the basic equation involved in producing audio for mobile distribution: the higher the quality, the slower the download. If you are distributing music recordings for sale on your website, you will want high-quality audio, and expect users will be patient with download times. Those of you who distribute interviews and lectures do not need the same quality, and your users might well have less tolerance for long download times.

Producing Mobile Audio with Audacity

Audacity is a professional-level audio recording and production application. For the longest time, Audacity has been in my top ten list of free tools for building mobile websites. You can download Audacity for Windows, Mac, or Linux, and learn more about it, at http://audacity.sourceforge.net/download.

Find the link for your operating system and download the application, as shown in Figure 9.6.

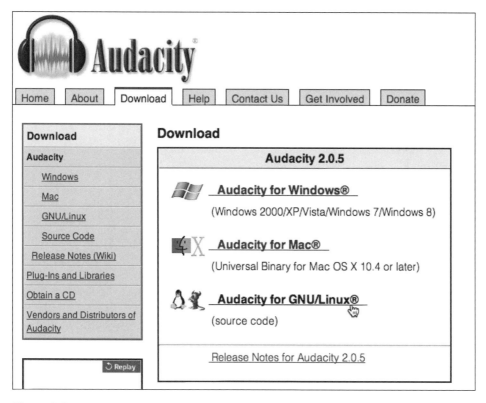

Figure 9.6
Downloading Audacity.
Source: Members of the Audacity development team.

Installing Audacity is pretty intuitive if you've downloaded applications before. If not, the Help tab at the Audacity site provides a manual with detailed installation instructions.

Adding the LAME Plug-In for MP3

There's one more step before you can use Audacity to prepare audio for mobile devices. That step is LAME. I don't mean there's anything "lame" about it, I mean you need to download the LAME plug-in that allows Audacity to export to MP3.

The MP3 format, one of the two essential formats you need to distribute audio over mobile devices, is proprietary. It's owned. It's not open source (like OGG). So Audacity cannot include MP3 export as part of the basic application. Instead, the second step in preparing to use Audacity is to download the separate LAME plug-in that allows Audacity to export to the MP3 format. You do that from http://lame1.buanzo.com.ar/ for Mac users, and http://lame1.buanzo.com.ar/#lamewindl for Windows and other operating systems.

Make sure you download the LAME plug-in for Audacity, not the standalone LAME application for operating systems. I'll illustrate what to look for. When you get to the LAME download site, look for downloads that match your operating system *and specify they are for Audacity.* See Figure 9.7.

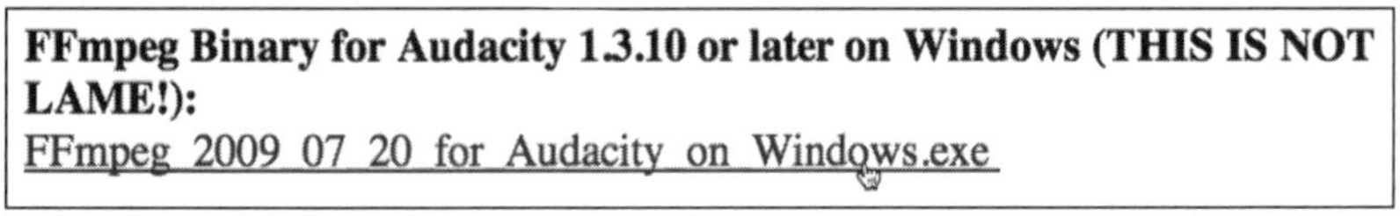

> **FFmpeg Binary for Audacity 1.3.10 or later on Windows (THIS IS NOT LAME!):**
> FFmpeg_2009_07_20_for_Audacity_on_Windows.exe

Figure 9.7
Downloading the LAME plug-in for Audacity.
Source: Buanzo / Arturo Busleiman.

Keep track of where you download the LAME for Audacity files. The first time you export from Audacity to MP3, you'll be asked to navigate to the location where you saved the LAME files.

I realize the Audacity and LAME download sites aren't as elegant as ones you use to download commercial software, but they're pretty intuitive, and they provide a package that produces professional-quality audio, free!

Recording in Audacity

Once you launch Audacity, choose File > New to create a new project. As I've alluded to, Audacity has professional-level control over recording, but you can create high-quality mobile-ready audio without messing with most of those options.

They key settings are as follows:

- *Input device* defines where the input comes from.
- *Input channels* can be mono or stereo.
- *Sample rate* defines audio quality.

Because these settings are key to creating a quality audio experience for your mobile users, I'll walk through them in a bit of detail. Different versions of Audacity have somewhat different interfaces, so your installation may look a little different than the screen caps I use here, but the differences are small enough that I'm confident you'll find the appropriate drop-down menus in your installation.

Choosing an Input Device

Before recording in Audacity, choose an input device from the Input Device drop-down menu in the Audacity toolbar. As I noted, different versions of Audacity have different menus and toolbars, but the Input Device option menu will look pretty close to the one shown in Figure 9.8.

Figure 9.8
Choosing an input device in Audacity.
Source: Members of the Audacity development team.

This setting defines the microphone or other input used to record sound. If you don't have any microphone connected to your laptop or desktop, this will be set to that device's built-in mic automatically. If you do have an external microphone or other input device (if you are feeding a musical instrument directly into your computer, or if you have software that records audio from your computer), you can choose that.

Defining Input Channels

If you have a stereo input device, or if you want to generate two identical stereo tracks from one input channel, you can choose 2 (Stereo) from the Input Channels drop-down in the Audacity toolbar, as shown in Figure 9.9.

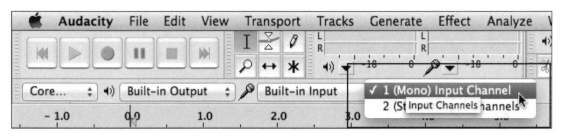

Figure 9.9
Defining stereo input in Audacity.
Source: Members of the Audacity development team.

Keep in mind, stereo recordings are twice as large (and slow) as mono, so if you don't need stereo, choose mono.

Setting a Sample Rate

Setting a sample rate takes some thinking. Low sample rates "sample," or grab, a bit of data from the input audio less frequently. The result is lower-quality audio. High sample rates sample (grab) data from the input more frequently, producing richer, more nuanced sound, but also larger audio files.

Sample rates in Audacity range from 8,000 (which produces audio quality comparable to an AM car radio) to 96,000 (comparable to Blu-ray or DVD quality).

Here's a basic guide to key sample rates:

8,000Hz	Equivalent to the quality of a phone conversation. Users will hear intelligible conversation but not syllables like "s."
22,050Hz	This sample rate provides much better quality audio for conversations, greetings, and fast-loading reading. It is the lowest quality audio setting I would use for music recordings.
44,100Hz	This sample rate produces studio CD quality audio.
96,000Hz	This highest quality sampling rate produces files that take twice as long to download as 44,100 audio files. The quality is not supported in mobile devices, even high-quality ones. In general, 44,100Hz is appropriate for high-quality audio intended for mobile devices.

Use the Project Rate (Hz) drop-down menu on the bottom left of the Audacity screen (shown in Figure 9.10) to set a sample rate *before* recording.

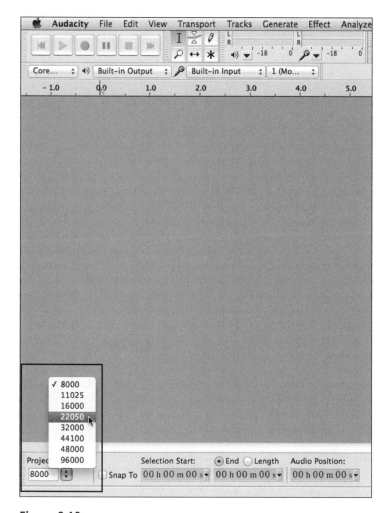

Figure 9.10
Setting a sample rate in Audacity.
Source: Members of the Audacity development team.

Think about the quality/download speed equation (better quality, slower download, lower quality, faster download) when choosing a sample rate. Don't waste a high sample rate on low-quality audio. For example, if you've recorded a phone interview, anything higher than an 8,000Hz sample rate is a waste of data and download time. But if you are selling high-quality recordings of your violin performances, users will expect 96,000Hz CD-quality audio and be willing to wait for it to download into their devices.

Recording and Editing an Audacity Project

Once you've set an input device, channels (mono or stereo), and a sample rate, simply click the Record button in the Audacity toolbar to record. That button is shown in Figure 9.11.

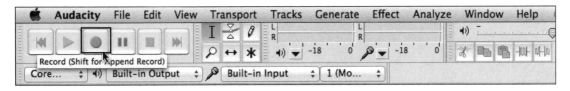

Figure 9.11
Recording in Audacity.
Source: Members of the Audacity development team.

The easily recognizable Pause button pauses recordings, and the equally intuitive Stop button stops a recording. If you've stopped a recording and want to append more to it, hold down the Shift key and click the Record button again.

You can easily select a portion of a recording and delete it by clicking and dragging in a track panel, and then choosing Edit > Remove Audio > Delete, as shown in Figure 9.12.

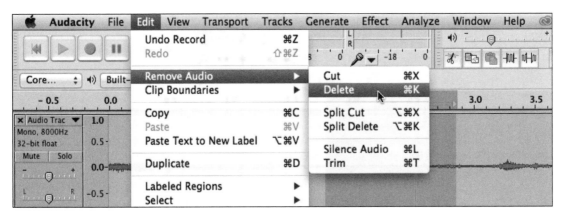

Figure 9.12
Deleting a selected portion of a recording in Audacity.
Source: Members of the Audacity development team.

You'll find many of the tools in Audacity intuitive, like the Play button that lets you listen to your recording. For a full exploration of editing Audacity files, check out the documentation available at http://audacity.sourceforge.net/help/.

Exporting to OGG and MP3

Audacity projects are saved to Audacity's native .aud format, and include many data files for each project. You don't need to save your project to Audacity though, if you are just creating output intended for mobile (and other web) distribution.

To produce mobile-ready audio, you export your recording to OGG and MP3 format. You can do the exporting in either order. Export to MP3 by choosing File > Export and selecting MP3 Files from the Format drop-down menu in the dialog that opens, as shown in Figure 9.13.

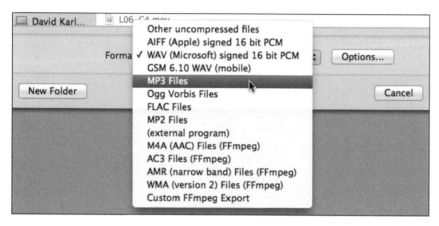

Figure 9.13
Exporting a recording to MP3 in Audacity.
Source: Members of the Audacity development team.

To export to OGG, follow the same steps but choose OGG Vorbis Files.

MP3 Export Options

The Options button in the export dialog in Audacity provides different options for MP3 and OGG. On the basis of the data you collected with your recorded sample rate, you can *compress* the quality of your exported file, and affect the file size, with those options.

For MP3, export options can be customized, but the four options available when you choose Preset provide a sufficient set of options for professional projects. Those presets are:

- *Insane* quality is generally (as suggested by its name) an unnecessary level of quality that adds substantially to file size without recognizable improvement in quality in most devices.

- *Extreme* also generates unnecessarily large files for online distribution.

- *Standard* maintains the overall quality of the recording, and is appropriate for most online distribution.

- *Medium* degrades audio quality but reduces file size.

If you're serious about fine-tuning audio quality and download speed, there is no substitute for trial and error. As you generate and test compressed MP3 audio, you'll find appropriate settings. But if you're not distributing high-quality commercial music recordings, the standard setting should suffice.

Once you've set the options for MP3 export, enter a filename in the Save As field in the Save dialog. Use web-appropriate filenames—no spaces, uppercase characters, or symbols (except for dash or underscore).

When you've set the options and entered a filename, click Save. The Edit Metadata dialog appears. Use this to add information like artist name, genre (if music), and recording date, as shown in Figure 9.14. Then click OK to export the file.

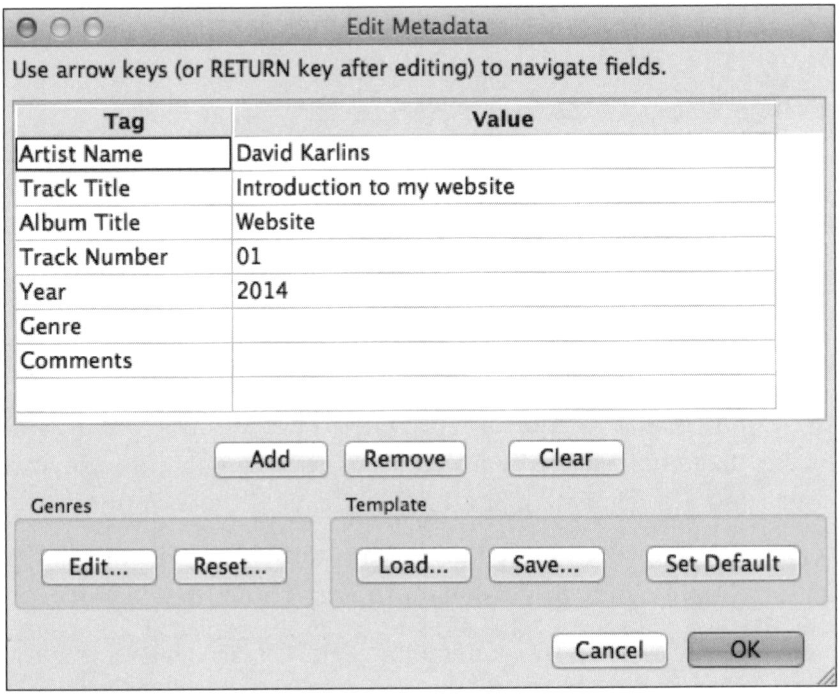

Figure 9.14
Defining MP3 metadata.
Source: Members of the Audacity development team.

Organize your exported MP3 files into a folder so you can easily upload them to your website.

OGG Export Options

The options that appear when you export your recording to OGG format are simple. All export settings are controlled by choosing a value from the Quality slider, shown in Figure 9.15.

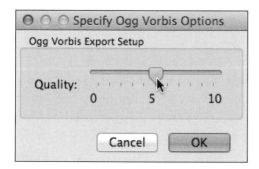

Figure 9.15
Choosing OGG export options from the slider.
Source: Members of the Audacity development team.

The Average (5) setting in the Quality slider for OGG export is equivalent to what is called a bitrate of 160 kilobits/second (kb/s). This is a little bit less quality than the Standard preset for MP3 (which outputs to a slightly higher bitrate). It's an appropriate setting for most files.

What Is Bitrate?

Without getting technical beyond the scope of this chapter, bitrate is roughly comparable to sample rate except that bitrate governs the amount of data *exported* from the recording, while sample rate defines the amount of data collected *during* output.

Professionals tweak bitrate, including using variable bitrates that respond to the kind of sound being transmitted (for example, a silent section of an audio might use a lower bitrate than a section with rapidly changing audio).

Since the "bottom line" for the recording is sampled data, normally it makes sense for amateur or semi-professional sound producers to keep bitrate settings at standard suggested levels.

Proponents of the OGG format claim that the quality of the 5 setting for OGG produces audio quality indistinguishable from the Standard preset for MP3, but produces smaller files. I won't issue a verdict on those claims, but they're credible.

In short, the 5 setting for quality is usually fine.

When you click the Save button in the Export to OGG dialog in Audacity, you'll see the same Metadata dialog that appears when you export to MP3. And, if you've already exported your recording to MP3, the metadata settings you defined appear by default. Click OK to complete the process.

USING HTML5 FOR NATIVE AUDIO

With MP3 and OGG audio files saved to a folder where you can find them, you're ready to embed those files into HTML5 pages that will play "native" in mobile (and other HTML5) browsers.

First, a quick checklist:

- **Are your files exported to MP3 and OGG?** You need files in those formats for mobile HTML5.

- **Did you compress your files appropriately?** The tendency is to create files of too high quality. Remember, your audience is listening, in most cases, with off-the-shelf headphones. Standard quality settings generally work fine for exporting audio for mobile HTML.

- **Are your files saved to the folder with your other website files?** You're going to need to define links to your files in HTML5, and that process is easiest if your MP3 and OGG files are saved to the folder that holds all your other site files.

If your checklist is in order, you're ready to embed HTML5 native video in your mobile site!

Embedding HTML5 Audio

Here is the basic syntax to embed a native HTML5 video in a page:

```
<audio>
  <source src="file.mp3" type="audio/mpeg">
  <source src="file.ogg" type="audio/ogg">
</audio>
```

This example code provides both an MP3 option (the .mp3 file) and an OGG option (the .ogg file). Between the two, this covers the bases for all contemporary browsers.

But nothing is going to happen yet. You need to at least add a player control bar to allow users to listen to the audio. You can do that by simply adding the controls parameter, like this:

```
<audio controls>
  <source src="file.mp3" type="audio/mpeg">
  <source src="file.ogg" type="audio/ogg">
</audio>
```

Here's an example/template you can use. In it, I created a very basic HTML5 mobile page, with jQuery Mobile links, and basic welcome text to introduce a "welcome" message.

```
<!DOCTYPE html>
<html>
<head>
<title>Page Title placeholder text</title>
<meta name="viewport" content="width=device-width, initial-scale=1">
<link rel="stylesheet" href="http://code.jquery.com/mobile/
      1.3.2/jquery.mobile-1.3.2.min.css" />
<script src="http://code.jquery.com/jquery-1.9.1.min.js"></script>
<script src="http://code.jquery.com/mobile/1.3.2/
      jquery.mobile-1.3.2.min.js"></script>
</head>

<body>

<div data-role="page" id="page01">

<div data-role="header" data-theme="a">
<h1>Welcome</h1>
</div>
<div data-role="content">
<h1>Listen!</h1>
<p>To our welcome message</p>
<audio controls>
  <source src="welcome.mp3" type="audio/mpeg">
  <source src="welcome.ogg" type="audio/ogg">
</audio>
</div>
<div data-role="footer">
<h4>(c)2014</h4>
</div>
```

```
</div>
</div>
</body>
</html>
```

This produces a simple, inviting audio player like the one shown in mobile Chrome in Figure 9.16.

Figure 9.16
Playing an audio file in a mobile device.
© 2014 Cengage Learning. Source: Google Inc.

Setting Audio Play Parameters

The `src` parameter is the only required parameter for HTML5 audio. But as I noted, in order to let users play, pause, stop, or change volume, you need to add the `controls` parameter.

You can also define autoplay, which starts an audio playing as soon as a page opens. As with autoplay videos, some users will resent it if a loud audio track begins playing when they open a page. But there is a time and place for carefully considered autoplay audio.

The basic options for audio include autoplay and looping.

Autoplay launches an audio file, even without a user clicking the Play button. And looping repeats an audio. Here is the syntax for a video element that displays autoplay:

```
<audio autoplay>
```

Here's the syntax to loop a video to play repeatedly:

```
<audio loop>
```

You can combine parameters. The following example defines an audio element with `autoplay` and `loop`:

```
<audio autoplay loop>
```

Options for Mobile Browsers without Native Audio Support

The basic syntax I showed you to embed HTML5 audio with controls will work in any mobile browser except—at this writing—Opera Mini.

Well, first of all, you don't want to exclude Opera Mini users from hearing your audio. And secondly, providing a non-HTML5 option will allow users of other environments (like older desktops) without an HTML5 browser installed to hear your audio.

One option is to add an error message encouraging the user whose browser does not support HTML5 audio to download a browser that *does* support HTML5. Here's the sample code for that:

```
<audio controls>
<source src="welcome.mp3" type="audio/mpeg">
<source src="welcome.ogg" type="audio/ogg">
<!--error message -->
Sorry, your browser does not support HTML5 audio.Please install a contemporary browser.
</audio>
```

Another option is to provide a direct link to an MP3 file. That will play in a user's environment, but without a native player. Almost every computer has some kind of application or plug-in that can play an MP3 file, so this is a good solution. But to make it even better, you could provide access to an OGG file as well. Here's the sample code for that:

```
<audio controls>
<source src="welcome.mp3" type="audio/mpeg">
<source src="welcome.ogg" type="audio/ogg">
<!--error message -->
Download <a href="welcome.ogg">welcome.ogg</a> or
                <a href="welcome.mp3">welcome.mp3</a>
</audio>
```

Again, this audio won't play in a nice, mobile-friendly native player. But one way or another, it will almost certainly launch a player of some kind in a user's system, and play either the OGG or MP3 file, depending on which link a user clicks.

STYLING AUDIO ELEMENTS

The easiest way to customize the display of a native audio player is to define a style for the `<audio>` element in CSS.

Although you can't define attributes like height, width, background color, or border with audio tag parameters, you can define them with CSS.

Here's a template that can be added to the `<audio>` element of an HTML5 web page, or a CSS style sheet:

```
audio {
padding: 15px;
border:2px gray solid;
width:75%;
background-color:black;
}
```

The result looks something like Figure 9.17.

Figure 9.17
Customizing the display of a native audio player.
© 2014 Cengage Learning. Source: Google Inc.

While mobile devices (and other environments) will display native audio player controls with their own characteristics, the CSS you apply will appear in all of them. So, for example, the same audio displayed in Figure 9.17 in Chrome for Mobile looks different in Firefox for laptops. But, as shown in Figure 9.18, the CSS still applies, giving the audio player a consistent look and feel across different native audio environments.

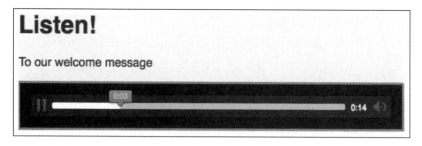

Figure 9.18
Customizing the display of a native audio player.
© 2014 Cengage Learning. Source: Google Inc.

USING JAVASCRIPT-BASED CUSTOM AUDIO PLAYERS

I noted in introducing this chapter that one option for designing custom audio players is to use JavaScript-based audio players.

Do JavaScript-based players cut against the logic of native audio players? Yes, they do. In two ways:

- Native players are supported and "backed" by browser publishers (like Google's Chrome, Apple's Safari, and others), and relatively stable.

- Native players are designed to provide an integrated aesthetic experience for users. In fact, this was a key reason that the late Steve Jobs gave for Apple's refusal to support the Flash Player in iPhones and iPads.

So, for those reasons, I lean toward suggesting you avoid JavaScript-based custom players that impose a different aesthetic, and rely on less stable coding than native browser-based audio players.

That said, there are readers who want to know how to implement JavaScript-based audio players because they provide a higher level of customization than the parameters available in native players.

The most accessible source for JavaScript-based audio players is jPlayer (www.jplayer.org). jPlayer is free and open. It allows developers who can work with JavaScript to build cross-platform audio (and video) players and embed them into web pages.

Benefits and features of jPlayer include:

- jPlayer is cross-browser—It produces players that work in more than one browser.

- jPlayer is a JavaScript library developed as a jQuery plug-in—It meshes well with jQuery Mobile sites because it shares common basic code with the jQuery Mobile source code saved at Central Distribution Network (CDN) sites.

- Finally, jPlayer handles Adobe Flash based audio (and video) files.

Figure 9.19 illustrates a custom player designed with jPlayer.

Figure 9.19
A custom audio player built with jPlayer.
Source: Stark Palace.

You'll find instructions for downloading and using jPlayer at http://jplayer.org.

Summary

Audio is a major part of the mobile browsing experience. HTML5 native audio makes audio files easy to play and inviting in mobile environments.

The caveat is that native audio has to be compressed to both MP3 and OGG to be (more or less) universally supported. Also, native audio players are defined by the browser, meaning the designer's options are limited when it comes to customizing how audio is presented.

In this chapter, I showed you how to address both these challenges. Key techniques include:

- Exporting audio files to MP3 and OGG format.

- Maximizing audio compression for faster downloading.

- Embedding audio files with the HTML5 `<audio>` tag.
- Applying `controls`, `autoplay`, and `loop` parameters where appropriate.
- Customizing audio player display with CSS.

Here are a four "take home" points for presenting mobile-friendly audio that works anywhere:

- HTML5 audio is *native* audio, it plays *without* plug-in audio player software.
- You must start with an MP3 and an OGG version of your audio file.
- The most essential element of the HTML5 for native audio is the `<source>` element; it must be defined. You'll almost always want to include the `controls` parameter so users can play, pause, change volume, or stop the audio.
- You can customize the display of audio with CSS styling for the `<audio>` element.

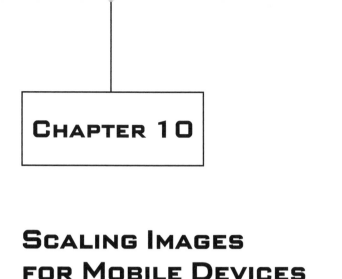

CHAPTER 10

SCALING IMAGES
FOR MOBILE DEVICES

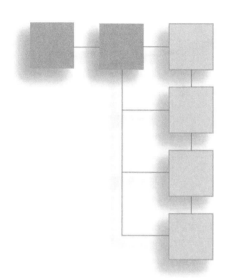

Images are, of course, a large part of the mobile browsing experience. But presenting images is a particularly vexing challenge for mobile designers using HTML5. Why? Because image files, in JPEG, PNG or GIF format, are not easily scalable.

For example, a 320px wide image will download quickly, and be of sufficient quality and resolution to display on an older (lower resolution) smartphone. But that image, displayed full-screen width on an iPad or Android tablet, will look pixilated and grainy. Conversely, an 1,800px wide version of the same image will display with acceptable quality on a high-resolution tablet, but will take unnecessarily long to download and not display properly on a smartphone.

Different mobile devices will try to handle this challenge differently. The results are often unsatisfactory. For example, a 600px wide circle displays fine when viewed in a large tablet or laptop, as shown in Figure 10.1.

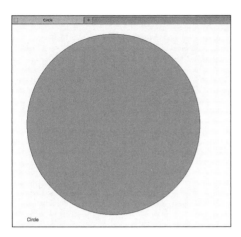

Figure 10.1
Viewing a 600px wide circle on a laptop.
© 2014 Cengage Learning.

Different mobile devices handle image scaling differently, and sometimes, some of them will automatically rescale an image to fit the viewport. But oftentimes not. The same 600px circumference circle simply doesn't fit in the viewport of my iPhone. The result is not at all the same, as shown in Figure 10.2.

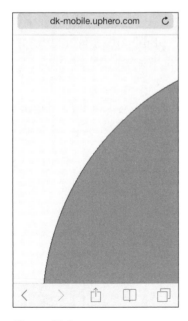

Figure 10.2
Viewing a 600px wide circle on a smartphone.
© 2014 Cengage Learning.

One solution is still in the conceptual stage. The Responsive Images Community Group (http://responsiveimages.org/) is proposing a couple alternative new HTML tags (a `<picture>` element and/or a `srcset` attribute for the `<img>` tag) that would allow designers to specify *different* image files depending on the size of a user's viewport. This is an intriguing initiative, but don't start using it yet! So far, neither option is supported by browsers.

In short, designing with images for mobile still requires finding ways to package a "one-size-fits-all" image into a multi-sized viewport world. And in general, that means including images with large enough size to display properly in a large tablet, which means burdening smartphone users with unnecessary download time. I'll show you how to do that in this chapter, using CSS3 media queries. The result will be an image that rescales to display properly in different viewports (widths), as shown in Figure 10.3.

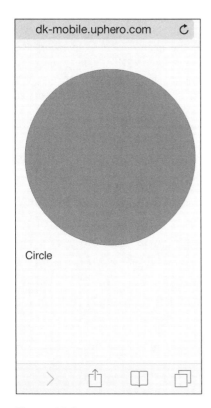

Figure 10.3
Viewing a 600px wide circle on a smartphone, rescaled with a media query.
© 2014 Cengage Learning.

In this chapter, I'll also introduce the value of saving artwork in SVG format. While you can't use SVG images for photos, you can use them for other artwork. And SVG images are vector-based image files. That means they *are* scalable—they can expand (or contract) with no loss of resolution, and no increase in file size.

SCALING IMAGES FOR MOBILE DEVICES

As I noted in the introduction to this chapter, it would be nice if designers could specify *different* image files to display in different viewports. That way users with large tablets would see a high-resolution image, but users with smartphones would not have to twiddle their thumbs waiting for that large image file to download and ultimately display as a small image on their screen.

Apply Progressive or Interlacing Downloading

When you prepare image files for websites in general, and especially when you create images for mobile websites, apply progressive or interlacing downloading when you save the images in your image-editing software. Progressive downloading (applied to JPEG images) or interlacing (applied to PNGs) causes images to "fade in," which means they go from low resolution to higher resolution, as they download into a user's device, as opposed to appearing "line-by-line" starting at the top of the image. This makes the process of waiting for an image to download over a 3G or 4G/LTE connection less unpleasant.

But such is the world we live in. So the most practical way to rescale images for different viewports is to use CSS3's @media query rules to resize images for different viewports.

There are different techniques for creating and applying an @media query to scale images. I'll walk you through a basic and simple but effective approach using an example of an image that is 1024 pixels wide and 768 pixels high. That image can display effectively at full size in high-end tablets with viewports of at least 1024 pixels in width. But on a smaller tablet or smartphone, the image is truncated (cut off) on the sides and/or the bottom, forcing a user to mess around with her fingers and thumbs to try to squeeze the image into the device's viewport.

One effective solution is to create a CSS3 media query that sizes the image depending on the device viewport.

Sizing Images with Media Queries

CSS3 media queries allow designers to provide different CSS styles for different size viewports (screen widths). CSS3 media queries are closely associated with responsive design—creating websites that rescale and change how (and if) content is displayed based on viewport. Responsive design, media queries, and CSS3 are not the focus of this book, but media queries provide the most effective existing technique to displaying images in different sizes in different devices. And so, without going into an extensive exploration of CSS3 or media queries, I'll explain how to use them to rescale images for different mobile devices.

The syntax for defining a media query in CSS3 involves defining a media type (like print or screen), and—most importantly—defining a viewport width. So conceptually, you can define a CSS style for viewports of 480px or less (for smartphones), larger than 480px but narrower than 1024px (for larger smartphones and smaller tablets), and 1024px or greater (for large tablets, as well as for desktops and laptops).

Then, once you've defined a media query, you can define specific styles for any element or combination of elements that will apply *only within that media query*. I'll walk you through a specific example next.

Scaling Images with Media Queries

The CSS code for a media query can be defined in a linked CSS file, or in the `<head>` element of an HTML5 web page. For HTML5 web pages that use jQuery Mobile to provide an interactive, animated experience, it usually makes sense to include the CSS style definition right in the `<head>` element of the HTML page, because jQuery Mobile sites are typically comprised of a single HTML page.

I'll provide an example of defining code in the `<head>` element that provides three sizes for `<img>` elements, depending on viewport. This example has three media queries, one for viewports of 480px or smaller, one for viewports larger than 480px wide but narrower than 1024px, and one for viewports that are 1024px or wider.

Defining a Media Query for Images in a `<figure>` Element

If I was building a full-fledged responsive design site, I might well have specific styling for dozens or hundreds of styles, or sets of styles. Here, however, we're focusing on scaling images, so I'm only going to define one style that will apply to `<img>` elements inside an HTML5 `<figure>` element. The `<figure>` element, by the way, optimizes images for search engines, and it is a good practice to put images inside a `<figure>` element. I'll show you an example of how to do this after I walk through defining the CSS required for the media query.

For this template, I'm using an image with the same height and width (similar to the circle example I used in the introduction to this chapter). You will adapt the dimensions in this template to your own artwork. So, for example, if you are displaying images that are 600px wide and 400px high, you'd maintain a 3:2 ratio between width and height when you downscale the image display for small devices.

Defining a Media Query in the *<head>* Element

I've included the entire content of a sample <head> element to make it easier to use this code as a template:

```
<!DOCTYPE html>
<html>
<head>
<title>Page Title</title>
<meta name="viewport"content="width=device-width, initial-scale=1">
<link rel="stylesheet"
href="http://code.jquery.com/mobile/1.4.0/jquery.mobile-1.4.0.min.css"/>
<script src="http://code.jquery.com/jquery-1.10.2.min.js"></script>
<script src="http://code.jquery.com/mobile/1.4.0/
      jquery.mobile-1.4.0.min.js"></script>
<style type="text/css">

@media screen and (max-width: 480px) {
figure img {
width:256px;
height:256px;
}
}

@media screen and (min-width: 481px) and (max-width: 1023px) {
figure img {
width:512px;
height:512px;
}
}

@media screen and (min-width: 1024px) {
figure img {
width:600px;
height:600px;
}
}

</style>
</head>
```

And here's how the HTML to display this figure (in all devices) would look:

```
<figure>
<img src="filename.png" alt="circle">
<figcaption>caption </figcaption>
</figure>
```

Applying Media Queries to Multiple Image Sizes

With the relatively simple example I've explored so far, you could resize all images inside `<figure>` elements in different devices. I wanted to keep the example simple to focus on the concept and technique. But obviously there will be occasions where you want to rescale images to *different* sizes within a mobile website.

A good solution is to create a set of class styles. Class styles can be appended to any element. So, for example, the following class style (defined with a ".." in front of the style name) resizes an image in a mobile device to 256px high and 256px wide.

```
<style type="text/css">

@media screen and (max-width: 480px) {
.small-image {
width:128px;
height:128px;
}
}

@media screen and (min-width: 481px) and (max-width: 1023px) {
.small-image {
width:256px;
height:256px;
}
}

@media screen and (min-width: 1024px) {
.small-image {
width:512px;
height:512px;
}
}

</style>
```

It would be applied in HTML as shown here:

```
<figure>
<img class="small-image" src="filename.png" alt="circle">
<figcaption>caption</figcaption>
</figure>
```

You can use this class style technique to create a set of images sizes for different sizes (and shapes) of images, in different devices.

Conceptual Approaches to Scaling Mobile Images

Normally I advise students and clients to keep their image sizes relatively standard. In part this is to keep the process of designing mobile sites simplified. But even more importantly, too many image sizes and shapes creates a cacophonous, cluttered look and feel to a site. Mobile sites don't need a lot of image sizes.

Take a look at how the BBC handles image sizing. At their site scale for laptops, desktops, and large tablets, images are large. But the point I'm focusing on here is that they tend to be the same size throughout an article. Take a look at the image in Figure 10.4, which, from the beginning article, is 624px wide.

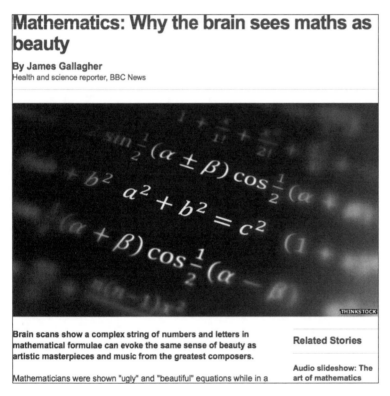

Figure 10.4
A standard-sized image at the BBC website scaled for full-sized screens.
Source: BBC.

As a reader scrolls down the article, other images are the same width, like the one shown in Figure 10.5.

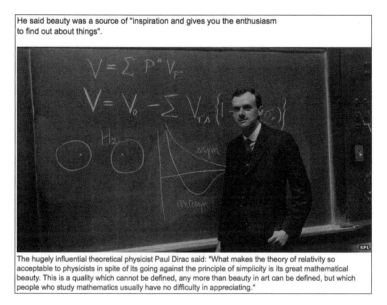

He said beauty was a source of "inspiration and gives you the enthusiasm to find out about things".

The hugely influential theoretical physicist Paul Dirac said: "What makes the theory of relativity so acceptable to physicists in spite of its going against the principle of simplicity is its great mathematical beauty. This is a quality which cannot be defined, any more than beauty in art can be defined, but which people who study mathematics usually have no difficulty in appreciating."

Figure 10.5
A consistently sized image at the BBC website provides an inviting, uncluttered browsing experience.
Source: BBC.

What happens when you go to the BBC's mobile site? Here images have been rescaled to fit nicely into a smartphone viewport, as shown in Figure 10.6.

Figure 10.6
A mobile-sized image at the BBC website.
Source: BBC.

And, you see that images are *consistently* sized, as shown in Figure 10.7.

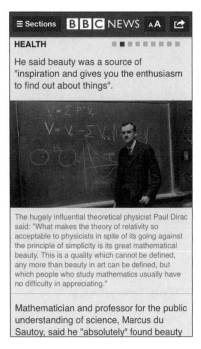

Figure 10.7
Mobile-sized images at the BBC website tend to be the same width.
Source: BBC.

Later in this chapter, I'll provide a case study that produces results similar to the way images are displayed with consistent widths at the BBC site, using SVG format images.

Am I arguing that *every* image in a well-designed, mobile-friendly site has to be the same width? No. But I am encouraging you, both for practical and aesthetic reasons, to organize images for a mobile site with *generally consistent* widths.

Scalable Artwork with SVG

Having briefly surveyed the range of potential and future solutions to scaling images for mobile devices, and having walked through how to apply media queries as a practical solution for scaling mobile images, it's time to look at an emerging technology with limited but real applicability to presenting scalable artwork in mobile pages. I'm talking about SVG format.

SVG format, as I briefly explained in the introduction to this chapter, is a *vector-based* image format. Unlike the JPEG, PNG, and GIF formats, image data is not saved pixel-by-pixel, but essentially as a series of lines and fills. That allows SVG files to be tiny, and for SVG images to scale up or down without loss of quality or resolution.

SVG format is widely supported in mobile (and desktop/laptop) browsers. At this printing, the list of browsers that support SVG includes iOS Safari, Opera Mini, Android Browser, Blackberry Browser, Opera Mobile, Chrome for Android, Firefox for Android, and IE Mobile.

Tip

For updated information on mobile browser support for SVG format, see http://caniuse.com/svg.

Using SVG Images

The SVG image format is not as widely known or used as bitmap (raster or pixel) based formats like JPEG and PNG. But it's not a niche format either. You can find SVG images everywhere.

To quickly access a wide range of SVG artwork to experiment with, try searching for "images svg," as shown in Figure 10.8.

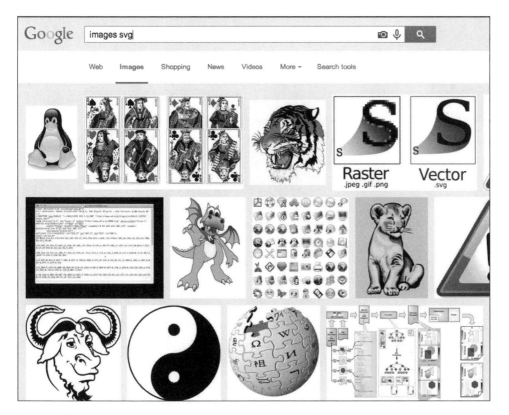

Figure 10.8
Search results for SVG images.
Source: Google Chrome™.

Or, you can create your own SVG artwork. Contemporary drawing programs like Adobe Illustrator, OmniGraffle Pro, and CorelDRAW will export illustrations to SVG format.

Tip

Some raster-based photo-editing applications also have some capacity to export to SVG format, but trying to export raster-based photos to SVG format does not produce acceptable image quality. In short, SVG format is not for photos.

The gray circle I used early in this chapter, for example, could have been exported to SVG format. In Figure 10.9, I've added a gradient fill, and then done just that. I replaced the plain gray circle with an SVG images, and along the way I added a gradient fill.

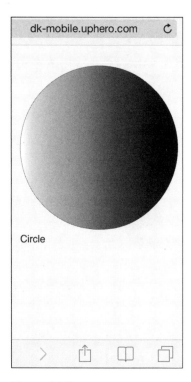

Figure 10.9
Viewing an SVG image with a gradient fill on a smartphone.
© 2014 Cengage Learning.

The SVG replacement image I created resizes fine in any browser viewport. Figure 10.10 shows it in a full-sized browser.

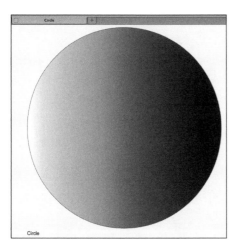

Figure 10.10
Viewing an SVG image with a gradient fill in a full-sized browser.
© 2014 Cengage Learning.

SVG Dos and Don'ts

The short version of SVG dos and don'ts is:

- *Do* use SVG format whenever possible for artwork, logos, line drawings, maps, and illustrations.

- *Do not* use SVG format for photos.

That leaves a lot of space in the "do" category. In general, the use of SVG format is underrated by mobile designers. Why? Because the importance of scalability did not present itself with the same urgency when artwork was scaled just for display in desktops and laptops.

SVG has real advantages. My SVG circle maintains the same smooth gradient no matter how much I zoom in, in any browser, as shown in Figure 10.11.

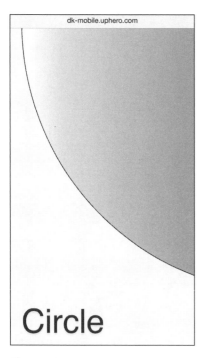

Figure 10.11
Viewing an SVG image with a gradient zoomed in.
© 2014 Cengage Learning.

Pursuing the example of my gradient-filled circle, even though I added substantial content to the image (the gradient fill) when I converted it from PNG to SVG, my SVG image is one-third the size of the original PNG image. That means it downloads into my smartphone three times as fast as the PNG.

SVG Case Study

This sidebar walks through a specific example of implementing an SVG image in a mobile page. A typical application of an SVG image includes a class style that sizes the image, and then uses the `SVG` tag to place the image. The CSS class style can be in a separate CSS file, embedded in the HTML, or in the `<head>` element of the HTML page.

In the following example, I've defined a simple style for sizing an SVG image, and then embedded the image. Here's the syntax for that.

In the `<head>` element of the HTML page:

```
<style type="text/css">
. fullWidth {
width: 100%;
}
</style>
```

And then, in the `<body>` element, here's the syntax to embed the SVG image:

```
<img src="filename.svg" class="classname" />
```

Here's another example. In the `<head>` element of the HTML page:

```
<style type="text/css">
.fullWidth {
width: 100%;
}
</style>
```

And then, in the `<body>` element:

```
<img src="picture.svg" class="fullWidth" />
```

CLOSING OBSERVATIONS ABOUT IMAGES IN MOBILE DEVICES

In this chapter, I introduced you to a number of options for providing mobile-friendly images. Scaling PNG, JPEG, or GIF images solves the problem of properly sizing images in a mobile device, but it does not solve the problem of reducing file size to speed up downloading. Using SVG images does solve the problem of speeding up download time, and SVG images scale up or down (larger or smaller) without distortion. SVG is an under-rated solution for providing artwork in mobile environments—especially for icons, drawings, and other line-based artwork. However, the SVG file format is not a practical solution for photos.

I also noted that there are options for scalable image tags in development. As I alluded to in the beginning of this chapter, the `<picture>` and/or `<srcset>` tags are scalable image tags under consideration by the World Wide Web Consortium (W3C). These tags would provide options for serving different images into different viewports or environments. The downside is that, if implemented, these tags will be very difficult to maintain in older (and current) browsers that do not support these tags. And, it is unclear at this time what impact on download time these tags might have, since they require that different images be downloaded into browsers *after* a browser detects the user's viewport and environment.

There are a number of JavaScript solutions available that detect the browsing environment and display different images. But they too are complicated to implement, and significantly slow down pages—in effect cancelling out any download time improvement they provide by substituting smaller images in mobile devices.

Finally, sites with relatively unlimited back-end server coding resources can build server-side solutions that generally detect connection speeds and viewport, and serve different images depending on the user's device and connection speed. But these solutions also slow down pages.

Those of you interested in following research and work on these options, and possible solutions in development, will find the following online resources worth checking out:

- For discussion of the potential for the HTML5 `<picture>` element, see "HTML5 <PICTURE> ELEMENT" at http://html5hub.com/html5-picture-element.

- For an exploration of using JavaScript to provide alternate image files, see "Automate Your Responsive Images With Mobify.js" at http://mobile .smashingmagazine.com/2013/10/24/automate-your-responsive-images-with-mobify-js/ and "Truly Responsive Images with responsive-images.js" at http://davidwalsh.name/responsive-design.

- For an overview of responsive image options, see "Choosing a Responsive Image Solution" at http://mobile.smashingmagazine.com/2013/07/08/choosing-a-responsive-image-solution/.

SUMMARY

The starting point for this chapter is: Images in mobile sites need to be smaller than images in full-sized sites. To which you are likely responding, "duh." But the big question is how do you achieve this? There is, at this point, no HTML5 element that provides the ability to insert different sized images in different sized browsers.

So, the most practical solution is to provide a single image that will appear in smartphones, small tablets, large tablets, and full-sized browsers in your web pages, and then to scale that image using CSS3 media queries.

This solution provides properly-scaled images for different viewports, but it has a problem. Small device users have to wait for unnecessary data to download, since the image *file* size (not display size) is the same for a smartphone user as it is for a desktop user.

There's no perfect answer to this conundrum. But an effective technique is to use SVG format illustrations when possible. SVG images can be saved with relatively small file sizes (compared to PNG, JPEG, or GIF artwork). And they do not degrade in quality when displayed at large sizes. SVG format works for drawings, but not for photos.

In this chapter, I showed you how to present the same image file in different sizes in different viewports:

- Use one image file in your HTML code.

- Create a CSS3 media query that displays that image at different sizes, depending on the viewport of a user's device.

- As a general rule, both for design efficiency and for aesthetic purposes, standardize on one or a small number of image sizes in mobile pages.

- For non-photo illustrations, use scalable, fast-loading SVG file format artwork.

Here are four "take home" points for effective image display in mobile devices.

- Do *not* apply a one-size-fits-all approach to web images. Forcing mobile users to scrunch, squeeze, and zoom in and out to see an image is a big turn-off.

- Try not to use too many image sizes in your mobile page. That creates a cluttered, noisy, uninviting environment for users.

- Use just one image file for every browsing environment, but rescale it for different devices using CSS3 media queries.

- When planning and preparing a mobile site, as much as possible, have artwork prepared in SVG format—those images download faster and maintain quality in any device.

Part IV

Using HTML5 to Manage Mobile User Interaction

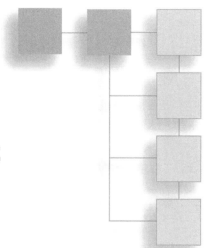

CHAPTER 11

BUILDING MOBILE-FRIENDLY FORMS

Forms turn websites into a two-way street. A retail website can present a product; a form can take an order for that product. A social activist website can make a compelling case for a cause, a form can sign up new volunteers. A band's website can promote their music, a form at the site can build a mailing list so when the band plays the Budokan stadium in Tokyo they fill the house. You get my drift here. Forms are essential.

However, forms require users to enter data like their email address, the color of a product they want to order, the number of items they wish to purchase, or the date they want their product to arrive. Designing forms that make it easy, even inviting, to provide that data is a challenge in full-sized websites. It is a bigger (or should I say smaller?) challenge in mobile devices, where users have to battle awkward keyboards (in most cases), pointer-less interfaces, and of course small screens.

In this chapter, I' show you how to resolve those challenges to provide convenient, attractive, mobile-friendly forms.

In this chapter, you explore:

- HTML5 input types for accessibility and data validation.
- HTML5 output for calculation.
- HTML5 datalists for painless and accurate data input.
- Connecting mobile forms to server-based scripts to manage form data.

LOOKING AT SOME MOBILE-FRIENDLY EXAMPLE FORMS

In introducing this chapter, I argued that collecting data through forms is the single most "interactive" element of a website. Let me expand on that, and be a bit more assertive: if you're not taking full advantage of forms in your website, you're not getting your "money's worth" out of the site—both figuratively and literally.

On the literal level, forms can sell products. You don't need the resources of a Walmart or Target to design and produce forms. Custom Ink sells T-shirts online with your logo, and provides a mobile-friendly form so customers can get an instant price quote, shown in Figure 11.1.

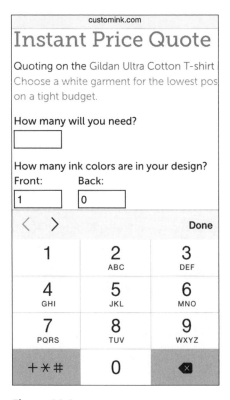

Figure 11.1
A quick, mobile-accessible form provides price quotes from Custom Ink.
Source: Custom Ink™.

Forms can build invaluable e-lists of people who are interested in your site content, and agree, and want, to be kept up-to-date with mailings. Every cause that is serious about attracting support has such a form. For example, Figure 11.2 shows the signup form at autism-society.org.

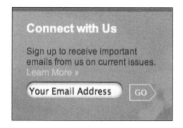

Figure 11.2
An inviting signup form at autism-society.org.
Source: Autism Society™.

Advertisers and sponsors purchase ads on blogs, and at websites based on the number of "registered visitors," which are people who sign up at a website to be members, users, or some other form of joining the site's community. E-list signup forms collect names of people interested in getting involved with your school district, your library, your theater group, or your campaign. It's hard to imagine a site that should not have a signup form.

The same goes for feedback forms. Feedback forms are highly underrated. They provide priceless insights into what users are finding at your site, and how they feel about it. The school cafeteria serving students at the College of Saint Benedict and Saint John's University is cool enough to provide a handy feedback form for students to evaluate their meals from their smartphones—it's shown in Figure 11.3.

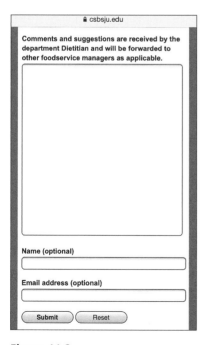

Figure 11.3
Rating the food at College of Saint Benedict and Saint John's University.
Source: College of Saint Benedict and Saint John's University.

Search boxes help visitors find what they need at your site. And I'm convinced search boxes play a particularly important role in mobile sites, where a limited amount of content fits on the site's home page, and users have to rely on search boxes to find content that doesn't fit on the home page. Sites with unlimited development resources, like YouTube, provide easy-to-find and easy-to-use search boxes, as shown in Figure 11.4. So can you.

Figure 11.4
Searching for videos on YouTube.
Source: YouTube™.

And of course e-commerce purchase forms convert visitors to your site into sales of your product or service. Zipcar rents cars to people in big cities, on the go, and makes their registration form mobile-friendly, as shown in Figure 11.5.

Figure 11.5
Registering at Zipcar.
Source: Zipcar™.

WHAT MAKES A FORM MOBILE-FRIENDLY?

In the introduction to this chapter, I illustrated a few mobile-friendly forms. Some of them were created by big entities with vast design resources. Others by mom-and-pop level enterprises. This emphasizes the point that there's no reason why any developer can't build inviting, mobile-friendly forms.

But I'll let you in on something I encountered in putting together the set of examples I used in the introduction to this chapter: Well designed, mobile-accessible forms were hard to find! You'd be surprised (perhaps) at the array of companies who *do* have relatively limitless design resources, who provide really *un*friendly mobile forms. In effect, they are telling users looking to purchase an item, join a movement, or sign up for information on their smartphones and tablets to buzz off and take their business elsewhere.

Which means, I suppose, there is plenty of work for you (and me) to do, building mobile-accessible forms for ourselves and others.

What am I referring to when I talk about mobile-friendly forms? To survey what makes a form mobile-friendly, it helps to start with what makes a form mobile-*un*friendly.

I'm going to dissect a bad form. In order not to hurt anyone's feelings (or subject myself or the publisher to a lawsuit!), I'll use a form I create. Check it out in Figure 11.6.

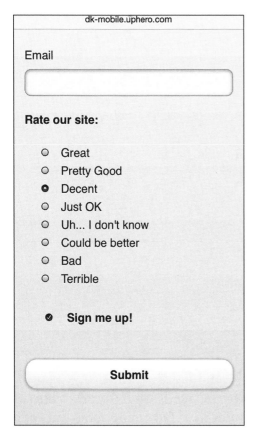

Figure 11.6
A not so mobile-friendly form.
© 2014 Cengage Learning.

Based on what I've discussed so far, you have probably identified some problems with this form. But let's break those down. First of all, when users enter an email address, their mobile devices will not detect that what is being asked for is an email address. So a standard keyboard will display, as shown in Figure 11.7.

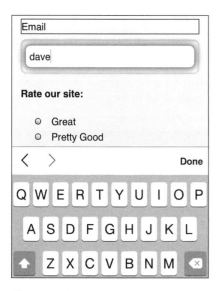

Figure 11.7
Attempting to enter an email address in a mobile form without an email keyboard is tedious and frustrating.
© 2014 Cengage Learning.

Later in this chapter, I'll walk through how to identify an input field as an email address. When you do that, most mobile devices will present users with a special keyboard that includes email-useful characters like the @ symbol shown in Figure 11.8.

Figure 11.8
Entering an email address in a mobile form with an email keyboard enabled is much easier!
© 2014 Cengage Learning.

Also, the set of radio buttons provided in this form is not mobile-friendly. It takes up too much precious mobile real estate, for one thing. Those tiny radio buttons are so hard to tap that a user intending to rate my site "Decent" can easily mis-tap and rate me "Just OK" by accident. A better solution is a mobile-friendly, compact slider that takes up less space, and is easy to drag on a mobile screen, like the one in Figure 11.9.

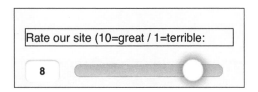

Figure 11.9
Sliders work well in mobile forms.
© 2014 Cengage Learning.

I'm picking just a couple examples, more or less at random, to illustrate how important it is to design specifically *mobile-friendly* forms. There are other problems with the example in Figure 11.6. For instance, the tiny checkbox to get on the email list is—well, tiny—and that makes it hard to tap on a mobile device.

So, the bulk of this chapter is devoted to customizing form input fields to make them mobile-accessible. But first, I want to quickly review the basic HTML5 required to build any form.

CREATING INVITING FORMS WITH HTML5 INPUT TYPES

The basic concept behind HTML forms is that all form input fields have to be inside a `<form>` element. So every form opens with `<form>` and closes with `</form>`. I'll emphasize this because it is the biggest single mistake designers make when building forms:

Tip

All input fields must be inside a *single* `<form>` element.

Every form needs an action. The `action` parameter determines what happens to the form content. In professional-level forms, that action is a link to a script, written in a server-side programming language like PHP, that manages that form data. Depending on the complexity of the script, the data may get entered into a mailing list database, or it might be used as search content and produce search results.

In the last sections of this chapter, I'll explain how to link to server-side form-handling scripts. But for testing purposes, and for low-level forms, you can define an action that simply sends the form content to an email address. Here's the syntax for that:

```
<form id="myForm" action="mailto:email@email.com">
form content here
</form>
```

And a form generally needs a Submit button to activate the `form action` parameter (and submit the content). A form with a Submit button has this basic syntax:

```
<form id="myForm" action="mailto:email@email.com">
form content here
<input type="submit" name="submit" id="submit" value="Submit">
</form>
```

You can substitute your own text for `"Submit"` inside the button element, for example:

```
<input type="submit" name="submit" id="submit" value=
    "Click here to submit this form">
```

And forms often have a Reset button instead. Here is the syntax for that:

```
<input type="reset" name="reset" id="reset" value="Reset">
```

Here, again, you can use any text for `"Reset"` inside the element, for example:

```
<input type="reset" name="reset" id="reset" value=
      "Click here to clear this form">
```

Using Input Types

The basic syntax for adding an input field to a form is:

```
<input type="type" name="name">
```

In the previous syntax, a type (like `text` or `email`) is followed by a name that identifies the field.

Every input (field) in a form needs a unique name. That's how the data that gets collected is sent to its destination, whether that is an email to you, or an entry into a complex order form at a large company.

Input types can, and generally should, have a label and an ID that links the label to the input field. The `<label>` element defines a label that displays in a browser for an `<input>` element. Labels are an important accessibility technique in general because when a user clicks on the text anywhere within the `<label>` element, it focuses (makes active) the associated input field.

The following syntax adds an ID and an associated label to an `input` element:

```
<label for="name">label content:</label>
<input type="type" name="name" id="name"
```

Tip

Some (but not many) input types require a value. I'll explain how those work when I walk you through specific examples, including a value slider.

Let me review and emphasize the relationship between a label and an input field: the `name` value in the `label` for the "name" parameter must *match* the value of the `id="name"` parameter in the `<input>` element. Here's an example to reinforce the point:

```
<label for="lastname">Last name:</label>
<input type="type" name="name" id="lastname">
```

Tip

If you are working in an environment with back-end (server) programming resources, or you are skilled at setting up a database on your server, and feeding data into and pulling data out of that database, be especially careful in naming inputs. Databases do not handle input (field names) well if they contain spaces or special characters. So, for example, use `id="myForm"` instead of `id="my form"`.

To summarize the key elements and parameters in an input:

■ The input *type* defines the *type* of content being collected. This is key to making input fields accessible in mobile devices, and I'll walk through how to assign input types in detail next in this chapter.

■ The input *name* is a unique identifier for the content that is collected. It does not display in the form itself, but is associated with the content that is collected. So, for example, if a field name is `email` and the collected input is `dave@dave.com`, that data will be sent in as `email:dave@dave.com`.

■ The input *label* appears on a user's screen, and is a tappable part of the input, allowing mobile users to quickly select a checkbox or a radio button, or focus on a text input field.

■ The input *ID* is useful in associating a label with an input field, and can also be used for formatting. The attribute of the `<label>` tag should be identical to the ID attribute of the related element to bind them together.

Surveying HTML5 Input Types

HTML5 has substantially beefed up the set of available field types. These field types do a number of things:

■ They activate helpful widgets in some cases (like a color palette for the color input type).

■ They provide a level of validation, so that, for example, if a user tries to enter `Dave` as an email address, an email input type will prompt the user that this doesn't look like a valid email address.

■ They activate specific keyboards in mobile devices (like a keyboard with .com as a button) when a user is asked to enter a URL.

I'll examine some examples next, but first, a caveat. Support for the helpful widgets, validation, and specific keyboards are device and browser dependent. As mobile (and desktop) browsers more and more fully embrace HTML5, that support will grow.

So what does this mean for a designer? It means that the features you enable in mobile devices to make forms more inviting and accessible will not all work everywhere. Where they do work, users will have a more pleasant experience entering form data. Where they don't, they won't. At least not yet. But users in environments that do not support all HTML5 input types will still have functional forms. They just won't have all the bells and whistles that work in environments with full support for HTML5.

Tip

To track the exact (and ever-evolving) state of mobile (and desktop) browser support for different HTML5 form features, check in at http://caniuse.com/#feat=forms.

Here, I'll demonstrate some of the ways different browsers support different HTML5 input types. In the next section, I'll break down the syntax for defining these input types.

The `email` input type usually generates a keyboard in mobile devices that includes useful keys for entering email addresses, as shown in Figure 11.10.

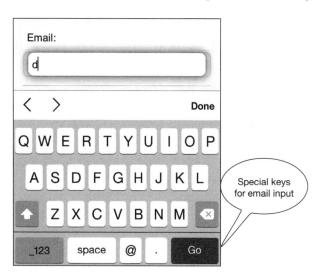

Figure 11.10
Email input types prompt mobile devices to display an email-friendly keyboard.
© 2014 Cengage Learning.

The color input type activates a color palette. Not all browsing environments support these handy features, but those that do allow users to choose colors for input forms in an inviting way, as shown in Figure 11.11.

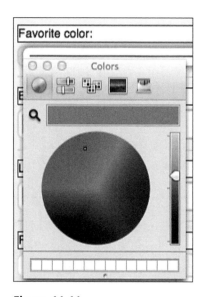

Figure 11.11
In some browsing environments, color input types prompt users with a color palette.
© 2014 Cengage Learning.

The date input type works differently in different devices. In many mobile environments, it provides a date-selection interface like the one in Figure 11.12.

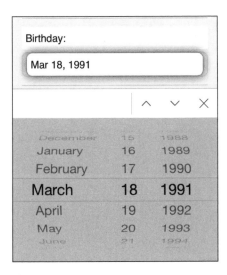

Figure 11.12
Choosing a date in a mobile phone.
© 2014 Cengage Learning.

In other environments, the date input type prompts a browser to display a calendar, like the one in Figure 11.13.

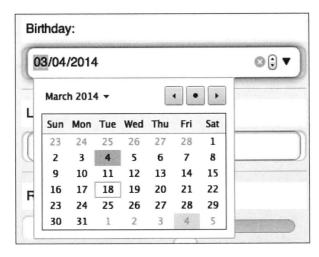

Figure 11.13
Choosing a date in Chrome.
© 2014 Cengage Learning.

Numbers are often a hassle to enter into a form on mobile devices. Some of my mobile device keyboards offer quick access to numbers, but others don't. Using the number input type prompts mobile devices to display a number keyboard instead of the alphabetical keyboard that is the default in most of them. Figure 11.14 shows a numeric keyboard activated automatically, prompted by a number input type.

Figure 11.14
Entering a number in a number input field in Chrome for mobile.
© 2014 Cengage Learning.

And here, let me note again that different devices have different ways of interpreting input types. For example, entering number values can be a hassle on laptops as well—most users aren't as quick to find numbers as letters on their keyboards. So laptop/desktop browsers provide features that make it easier to enter values in number input fields as well. Figure 11.15 shows a spinner that displays for number input fields.

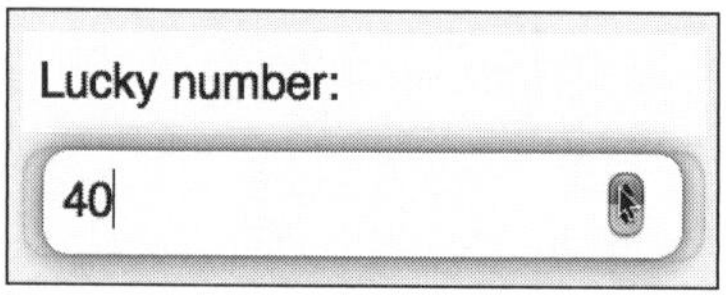

Lucky number:

40

Figure 11.15
Entering a numeric value in a number input field in Chrome for laptops.
© 2014 Cengage Learning.

Phone numbers can also be tricky to enter in a mobile device. Most mobile device browsers support the phone input type with a handy, ready-for-phone special keyboard, like the one shown in Figure 11.16. The phone keyboard even toggles nicely to display characters like * (for extensions).

Figure 11.16
Entering a phone number in a phone input field.
© 2014 Cengage Learning.

I won't display or preview how every input type appears in mobile browsers, but before closing this show-and-tell section and getting into the syntax needed for input types, take a look at how the url (that's lowercase when coded, even though we normally write URL in uppercase letters) input type works.

Here again, the input type prompts mobile devices for a custom keyboard—this time it includes .com as a one-tap button shown in Figure 11.17. Nice, right? Have you ever noticed, when entering your URL into a form, that this feature appears? That's because the designer was tuned in to HTML input types and included a url input.

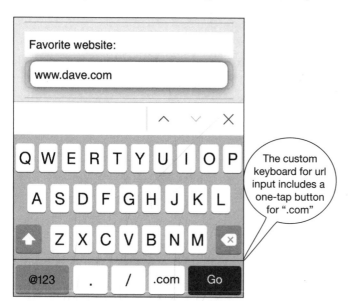

Figure 11.17
Entering a URL into a custom keyboard prompted by a `url` input field.
© 2014 Cengage Learning.

Syntax for HTML5 Input Types

As I noted early in this chapter (but it was a while ago so here it is for quick reference), the basic syntax for an HTML5 input element with a label is:

```
<label for="name">Name:</label>
<input type="type" name="name" id="name"/>
```

Some input types have other parameters as well. Those include `value` (a number value), `min` (a minimum value), and `max` (a maximum value). I'll walk you through how these parameters work when I show you how to define a `range` input type.

At the end of this chapter, after I cover both syntax and styling for input elements, I'll provide a full template that you can use to build HTML5 input forms. But here, I'll quickly provide examples for the most useful input types.

Example Input Forms

Here's a basic `text` field with a label `Name:` to collect a user's name:

```
<label for="name">Name:</label>
<input type="text" name="name" id="name">
```

Here's a basic `email` field with a label `Email:` to collect a user's email address:

```
<label for="email">Email:</label>
<input type="email" name="email" id="email" />
```

Here's a basic `color` field with a label `Favorite color:` to collect a user's selected color:

```
<label for="color">Favorite color:</label>
<input type="color" name="color" id="color" />
```

Here's a basic `date` field with a label `Birthday:` to collect a user's birthday:

```
<label for="birthday">Birthday:</label>
<input type="date" name="birthday" id="birthday" />
```

Here's a basic `number` field with a label `Lucky number:` to collect a number from a user:

```
<label for="number">Lucky number:</label>
<input type="number" name="number" id="number" />
```

Here's a basic `tel` field with a label `Phone:` to collect a user's phone number:

```
<label for="phone">Phone:</label>
<input type="tel" name="phone" id="phone" />
```

Here's a basic `url` field with a label `Favorite website:` to collect a URL:

```
<label for="url">Favorite website:</label>
<input type="url" name="url" id="url" />
```

I promised an example using other input parameters: `value`, `max`, and `min`. Here's that example, applied to a `range` element to collect a number between 0 and 10, with a label asking users to rate a site:

```
<label for="rating">Rate this site (10 is best):</label>
<input type="range" name="rating" id="rating" value="5" min="0" max="10" />
```

By tweaking these examples, you can put together a wide range of forms that mobile users will find inviting to fill out.

Providing Placeholder Text

Placeholder text appears in an input element *until* a user starts to type in that field. Placeholder text can take the place of a label, but I wouldn't recommend that. I've discussed how labels aid in accessibility both in mobile devices, and for touch-impaired users who have difficulty selecting an input field on a form in any environment. But placeholder text can supplement a label, and provide more assistance to users. In Figure 11.18 for example, the placeholder text suggests that users can enter a nickname in the name field.

Figure 11.18
Placeholder text.
© 2014 Cengage Learning.

The syntax for a placeholder is simply `placeholder="content"` within an `<input>` field. The following code adds placeholder text to a name field:

```
<label for="name">Name:</label>
<input type="text" name="name" id="name" placeholder="Enter a nickname" />
```

Placeholder text can be useful with many input types. Figure 11.19 shows a form in a mobile device with prompts and tips for user input, to make the experience more pleasant and intuitive.

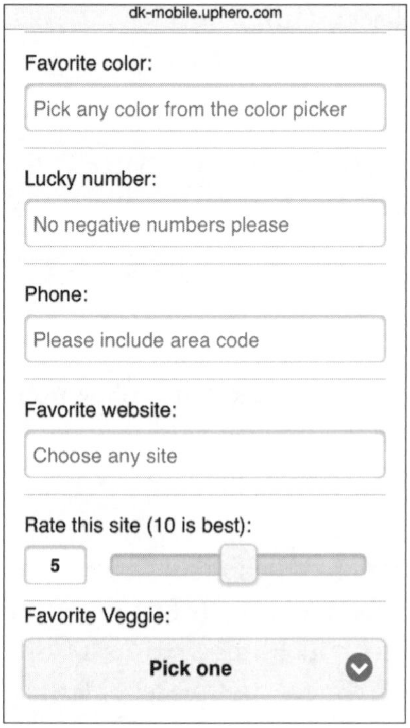

dk-mobile.uphero.com

Favorite color:

Pick any color from the color picker

Lucky number:

No negative numbers please

Phone:

Please include area code

Favorite website:

Choose any site

Rate this site (10 is best):

5

Favorite Veggie:

Pick one

Figure 11.19
Placeholder text applied throughout a mobile form.
© 2014 Cengage Learning.

Validating Input with HTML5

Validation, as applied to designing web forms, means testing data before it is submitted. You might, for example, want to make sure that if you are asking for the age of a user, she doesn't enter 1987. You could do that by defining a maximum value for an input field. You can also make fields required.

There are essentially three ways to validate form data:

- Using server-side scripts that test data. These scripts are supplied by back-end coders, or services (like those listed at the end of this chapter) that provide forms linked to their own databases.

- Client-side scripts, which are scripts that run in a browser. These are written in JavaScript.

- Using HTML5.

The first two options are more reliable because they don't require an HTML5-compliant browser. The last option—HTML5 validation—is much easer, because it is accomplished with just a bit of HTML code.

Where Do You Get Validation Scripts?

Server-side validation scripts are built into different resources distributed with forms. Some of these resources are open-source or proprietary but free. Others cost money. They include mail list managers like MailChimp (mailchimp.com), search engines like FreeFind (freefind.com), or Google forms (you find these in the documentation for Google Docs). There are also resources that generate scripts for your forms. I'll catalog a couple of my favorites at the end of this chapter. Or, you can hire a back-end coder to write these scripts for you in PHP.

JavaScript validation scripts are written by people who know JavaScript (a good resource is *JavaScript: The Web Technologies Series,* by Don Gosselin; ISBN-10: 0538748877).

Tip

The following examples use HTML5 validation. They work in browsers that support HTML5 validation. For updated information on the state of browsers that support or are in the process of adopting support for HTML5 forms, including validation, see http://caniuse.com/forms.

To require a user fill in an input field, add `required` inside the `<input>` element. Here's an example of a required email form. I'll include the label and other input content:

```
<label for="email">Email:</label>
<input type="email" name="email" id="email" placeholder=
    "Email is required" required />
```

If this input field is submitted in a form, in a browser that supports HTML5 validation, an error message appears like the one in Figure 11.20.

Figure 11.20
A validation error message.
© 2014 Cengage Learning.

As I mentioned earlier in this chapter, simply defining an input type provides a level of validation. For example, if you define an input field as an `email` type, and a user tries to submit the form without an @ symbol in that field, he will see an error message like the one in Figure 11.21.

Figure 11.21
An email input validation error message.
© 2014 Cengage Learning.

The `min` and `max` parameters define a minimum or maximum value for the input field. Here's sample syntax for a number input that must be at least zero, but no more than 100:

```
<input type="number" name="number" min="0" max="100">
```

If the user tries to enter a value outside of those parameters, he sees an error message like the one shown in Figure 11.22.

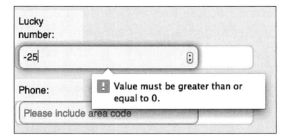

Figure 11.22
A number minimum validation error message.
© 2014 Cengage Learning.

DEFINING A SELECT MENU OR DATALIST

Select menus, also known as select option menus, and sometimes referred to as drop-down menus (three names for one input form!), are handy in any environment. Select menus present a list of options for the user. Select menus save users time and hassle—one tap (or click) and they see a long list from which they can choose an option. And select menus improve the accuracy of input. If users had to type the name of their state or country into every form, there would be too many misspelled states and countries, and the collected data wouldn't be worth much.

Figure 11.23 demonstrates a form at the mobile site for Dollar Rent A Car.

Figure 11.23
Choosing a month from a select menu.
Source: Dollar Rent A Car™.

But select menus have a special role in mobile forms. Because they pack a lot of content into a single row in a form, they're particularly handy for giving users access to a ton of options in a tiny space. For example, if I want to collect users' choices for favorite vegetable (invaluable info for health food sellers who create targeted emailings when there are seasonal locally grown veggies in stock), I can give users dozens of choices without clogging up screen space, as shown in the form in Figure 11.24.

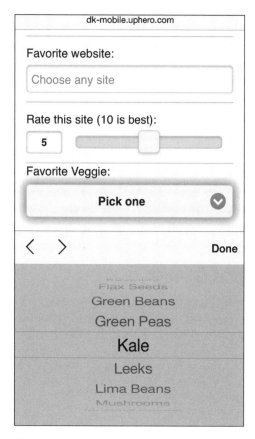

Figure 11.24
Choosing from a select menu in a home-grown form.
© 2014 Cengage Learning.

When a user taps on the menu, she can easily pick from the list of options. Most mobile devices provide a very accessible way to choose options from a spinner that appears at the bottom of the screen, as shown on the bottom half of Figure 11.24.

Defining a Select Menu

The syntax for a select menu involves defining the menu with a `select` tag, and the options with `option` tags. The option `value` parameter is submitted with the form, and the text between the open and close `option` tags displays for users.

Here's an example:

```
<select name="veggie" id="veggie">
<option value="0">Pick one</option>
<option value="1">Asparagus</option>
<option value="2">Avocado</option>
<option value="3">Barley</option>
<option value="4">Beets</option>
<option value="5">Bell Peppers</option>
<option value="6">Black Beans</option>
<option value="7">Bok Choy</option>
<option value="8">Broccoli</option>
<option value="9">Brussels Sprouts</option>
<option value="10">Cabbage</option>
</select>
```

Tip

You'll find copy-and-paste code for this example at http://dk-mobile.uphero.com/#ch11.

Let me explain the value attribute in this example. In a database the numbers would correspond with actual names or item numbers. If this is to be received by email and handled by a person it would be better to have the actual names as values, so again be careful with the naming of the values. Some of the scripts that process this info for email or to a database may not like spaces and special characters, so `Bell Peppers` would be `BellPeppers` or `bellPeppers`.

Also might be a good idea to put in something about the attribute selected, where 1 option is preselected.

Looking for a Jump Menu?

Jump menus look a bit like select menus, but they employ JavaScript to function as navigational elements, without a server-side form action. If you're inclined to dive into JavaScript and create one, you'll find helpful resources at http://jquery-plugins.net/tag/dropdown-menu.

Defining a Datalist

The HTML5 `<datalist>` element works something like a select menu, but it filters the set of options as a user types characters. And, a datalist allows a user to enter an option not listed in the menu.

The `<datalist>` element defines a list of options for an `<input>` element. This works like an auto-complete feature. Users see a list of options that match the character string they type into the input field, as shown in Figure 11.25.

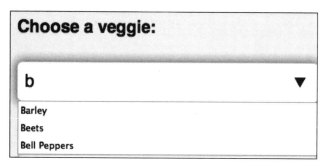

Figure 11.25
Using a datalist.
© 2014 Cengage Learning.

The `<datalist>` tag is used to provide an auto-complete feature on `<input>` elements. Users will see a drop-down list of predefined options as they input data. The `<input>` element's `list` attribute connects the input options with the `<datalist>` element.

Tip

The `<datalist>` tag is not supported in Internet Explorer 9 and earlier versions, or, at this writing, in Safari.

Here's an example:

```
<input list="veggies" name="veggies">
<datalist id="veggies">
<option value="asparagus">Asparagus</option">
<option value="artichoke ">Artichoke</option>
<option value="cabbage">Cabbage</option>
```

```
<option value="corn">Corn</option>
<option value="cucumber">Cucumber</option">
</datalist>
```

CREATING FORM OUTPUT ELEMENTS

I saw a study noting how many basic skills people are losing because we rely on our digital devices to do things like do simple calculations. Humans are losing the ability to do simple math without a calculator? I'm not that upset about that since I never had basic math skills in the first place. But in any event, even those of us who are not mathematically challenged find ourselves jumping to the calculators on our smartphones when we need to figure out a tip, split a tab, or figure out how many calories we've consumed in a day.

But why make smartphone or tablet users toggle over to their calculator apps while filling out a form? If form input requires doing some math, you can provide a simple calculator right in an HTML5 mobile page.

The key is that form *output* is managed through a distinct form. That is, unlike form input fields, each output has its own form. The basic syntax for multiplying two values, a and b, for example, is:

```
<form oninput="x.value=parseInt(a.value)*parseInt(b.value)">
<input type="number" id="a">*
<input type="number" id="b">=
<output name="x" for="a b">
</output>
</form>
```

Note that the <output> element is in its own form. This form action is managed by a tiny bit of JavaScript. So little JavaScript, in fact, that I figured we could slip it into the book. The first line defines the calculation in JavaScript, embedded in the <form> tag. The * in that line of code denotes that the a value and the b value are multiplied.

If you want to add the numbers, you replace the * symbol with a + sign. To subtract, you use a - sign. And to divide, you use a / symbol.

This code also defines a box for the output. Figure 11.26 illustrates an output form.

Figure 11.26
Multiplying with an output form.
© 2014 Cengage Learning.

STYLING MOBILE FORMS

Much of the styling in mobile forms is defined by the set of JavaScript and CSS files that make jQuery Mobile work. And part of the toolset for customizing forms and form fields lies in the jQuery Mobile toolkit. Specifically, the `<div data-role="fieldcontain">` tag defines some useful spacing and other attributes for form elements.

You can also customize the appearance of mobile forms with the `data-theme=` parameter in many form elements.

Finally, you can use basic CSS styles to define color, padding, and other attributes of form elements. I'll walk you through all three of these options next.

Using the Fieldcontain Element

A *fieldcontain* (short for field container) encloses a label and an input or other form element within a sort of box. The syntax is:

```
<div data-role="fieldcontain">
label and input element go here
</div>
```

A `<div data-role="fieldcontain">` element is used to wrap around a label, and a field (usually an input element). Here's an example of using a `fieldcontain div` around an email field:

```
<div data-role="fieldcontain">
<label for="email">Email:</label>
<input type="email" name="email" id="email">
</div>
```

Let's do a "before and after" exercise. Figure 11.27 shows an email field without being wrapped in a `<div data-role="fieldcontain>` element.

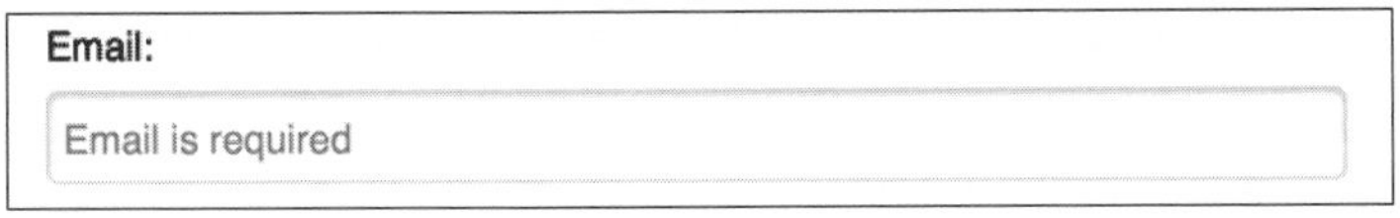

Email:

Email is required

Figure 11.27
An email field and label without a `<div data-role="fieldcontain>` element.
© 2014 Cengage Learning.

When I add a `<div data-role="fieldcontain>` element, the field takes on a width and padding that adapts to the width of the viewport for an inviting, uncluttered look and feel, as shown in Figure 11.28.

Email: Email is required

Figure 11.28
An email field and label with a `<div data-role="fieldcontain>` element.
© 2014 Cengage Learning.

Tip

The actual configuration of how the `<div data-role="fieldcontain>` element configures form fields has changed with different versions of jQuery Mobile, but in general, it aligns labels and input fields in the same row when a device viewport is at or wider than a set width, but puts them in separate rows when the device viewport is very narrow.

Applying Theme Swatches

In Chapter 5 of this book, I walked through how to design custom color swatches and other styling elements using jQuery Mobile ThemeRoller. I won't rehash that whole exploration here. But I will draw on what I covered there and focus on how this applies to theming input fields in forms.

As I explained in Chapter 5, when you define color swatches for data-themes (like a, b, c and so on), you can activate the Inspector to see which swatch panel holds the formatting options for the element you want to format. Here's how that applies to defining a color swatch for an input element.

In ThemeRoller, be sure the Inspector is activated, as shown in Figure 11.29.

Figure 11.29
Activating the Inspector in ThemeRoller.
Source: jQuery Mobile™.

Then, with the Inspector activated, click on a form element for the swatch you are defining. For example, in Figure 11.30, I'm defining background color and text color for the Text Input field in Swatch A.

Figure 11.30
Styling an input field in ThemeRoller.
Source: jQuery Mobile™.

In a similar way, you can define styling for options (in select menus), radio buttons, and checkboxes.

Defining Styles

For full-scale reformatting of how forms look in your site, head to jQuery Mobile Theme-Roller. But you can tweak some individual form elements by simply defining a style for them in the <head> element of your jQuery Mobile page.

For example, I can define a black background, white text, and a bit of padding for my labels with this CSS:

```
<style>
label {
background-color:black;
color:white; padding:
2px; }
</style>
```

The effect is shown in Figure 11.31.

Figure 11.31
A styled mobile label element.

© 2014 Cengage Learning.

Tip

Why not do all your mobile form styling with CSS? Why rely on jQuery Mobile ThemeRoller? The answer is twofold. One, the CSS for jQuery Mobile sites is so complex it is an Augean task—a superhuman challenge—to sort through it and edit it. The second is that tinkering with the CSS in jQuery Mobile-based HTML5 sites produces unpredictable results, exactly because the CSS for jQuery Mobile is so complex and so integrally connected to the JavaScript that makes jQuery Mobile pages so much fun. For instance, when I added the two pixels of padding in the previous code, it forced a line break between labels and fields. Not a particularly bad thing in this case—one might argue it makes the form more inviting in a smartphone. At the very least, be prepared to endure some trial-and-error if you experiment with applying your own CSS to jQuery Mobile forms.

MANAGING FORM DATA WITH PHP SCRIPTS

I hate to close a chapter on building forms for mobile devices without addressing what happens to form input. In general, this is where the HTML book ends, and the PHP or other book on back-end scripting takes up. But in today's world, designers need to know how to prototype forms, test them, and connect them to existing scripts.

Normally a `form action` parameter defines a link to a PHP script, and defines whether the server hosting that script requires `post` or `get` as an upload method. Here's the basic syntax:

```
<form action="http://script.php" method="post or get">
```

So where do those scripts come from? You or your programming team might create these scripts, upload them to your server, and connect them to databases that manage the data. Or, more typically for smaller-scale enterprises, you get a link to a script supplied by the developer of the back-end script.

A third option is to use an online resource that generates back-end scripts and prototype forms that you then customize with your own styling.

How does all this fit into *mobile* form implementation? In a word, nicely. The back-end scripts that manage input data are hosted on a server, and run well in any environment.

Generating Scripts with Online Resources

As I noted, there are many online resources that generate PHP scripts to manage form data. Generally these scripts simply collect form data, and send it to you through email.

You can, by the way, just add a `form action` that emails content submitted in a form using the visitor's email client. This is a simple way to test forms, but not usually satisfactory because it reveals your email address to the user, and the user's email address to you.

But here's the `form action` code for that option:

```
<form action="mailto:email address" method="post" enctype="text/plain">
```

For more complex form-handling scripts, I recommend two free online resources:

- The HTML/PHP Form Generator at http://www.phpform.info/htmlform.php.
- The Feedback Form Wizard at TheSiteWizard, http://www.thesitewizard.com/wizards/feedbackform.shtml.

Both these resources walk you through generating all the PHP you need to manage input form data for forms you design. The form generator at TheSiteWizard is shown in Figure 11.32. It is easier to use than the HTML/PHP Form Generator, but less flexible. It generates a simple feedback form that you can customize styling for.

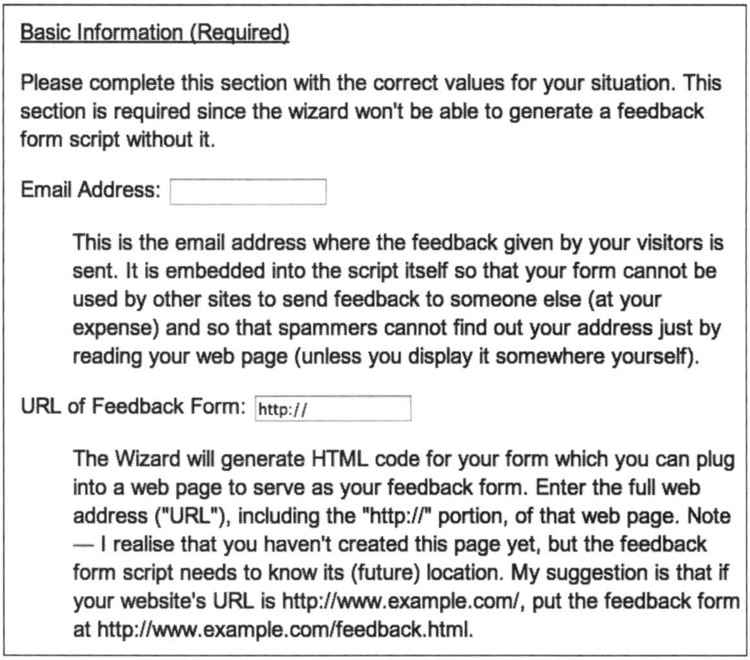

Basic Information (Required)

Please complete this section with the correct values for your situation. This section is required since the wizard won't be able to generate a feedback form script without it.

Email Address: [_____]

> This is the email address where the feedback given by your visitors is sent. It is embedded into the script itself so that your form cannot be used by other sites to send feedback to someone else (at your expense) and so that spammers cannot find out your address just by reading your web page (unless you display it somewhere yourself).

URL of Feedback Form: [http://_____]

> The Wizard will generate HTML code for your form which you can plug into a web page to serve as your feedback form. Enter the full web address ("URL"), including the "http://" portion, of that web page. Note — I realise that you haven't created this page yet, but the feedback form script needs to know its (future) location. My suggestion is that if your website's URL is http://www.example.com/, put the feedback form at http://www.example.com/feedback.html.

Figure 11.32
Generating PHP for a form with TheSiteWizard.
Source: TheSiteWizard™.

The HTML/PHP Form Generator is more powerful than TheSiteWizard, and a bit more involved. It allows you to collect form data in a web page, while the PHP script generated by TheSiteWizard only sends form data to you at an email address.

And, as shown in Figure 11.33, the HTML/PHP Form Generator has a preview window so you can see the form fields you generate script for on the screen as you define them.

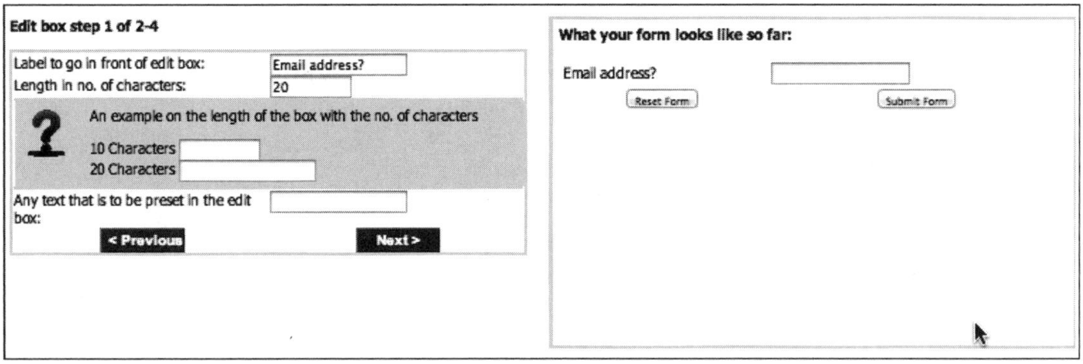

Figure 11.33
Generating PHP and previewing a form with the HTML/PHP Form Generator.
Source: Paul Roberts, ROBO Design Solutions™.

Acquiring PHP Scripts from Online Resources

While you can manage input data from dozens or hundreds of users with scripts generated using the PHP generator resources I just described, that's not sufficient to manage thousands of instances of user input. And most of us are aiming to have thousands of people fill in our signup forms, our feedback forms, or order forms.

There are a wide range of online resources that provide server-side scripts to manage search boxes, signup forms, feedback forms, and other forms.

Here are a few I recommend:

- MailChimp is a powerful e-list manager that generates forms and scripts to collect email addresses and send out e-newsletters. The site provides forms and links to scripts to manage them. You define a form using WYSIWYG tools at mailchimp.com, and you get HTML code for your form that includes a defined `form action` parameter. At this writing, MailChimp is free for your first 500 names.

- Search boxes are available from Google (www.google.com/cse) and FreeFind (www.freefind.com). What site can't use one?

- Forms to store data in databases can be generated from Google Docs. While working with a spreadsheet in Google Docs, click the Insert menu and select Form.

All these resources, and more that you will find online, provide very helpful and detailed documentation for how to connect your form to the necessary script with an action link.

A Mobile-Friendly HTML5 Form Template

The following code creates a form with the key form elements explored in this chapter, as well as a separate output form for calculation.

Tip

You'll find this code at http://dk-mobile.uphero.com/#ch11.

```
<h3>Tell us about yourself</h3>
<div data-role="main" class="ui-content">
<form name="form1" method="post" action="">
<div data-role="fieldcontain">
<label for="name">Name:</label>
<input type="text" name="name" id="name" placeholder="Enter a nickname">
</div>
<div data-role="fieldcontain">
<label for="email">Email:</label>
<input type="email" name="email" id="email" placeholder="Email is required" required/>
</div>
<div data-role="fieldcontain">
<label for="color">Favorite color:</label>
<input type="color" name="color" id="color"
    placeholder="Pick any color from the color picker"/>
</div>
<div data-role="fieldcontain">
<label for="number">Lucky number:</label>
<input type="number" name="number" id="number"
    placeholder="No negative numbers please" min="0">
</div>
<div data-role="fieldcontain">
<label for="phone">Phone:</label>
<input type="tel" name="phone" id="phone"
    placeholder="Please include area code"/>
</div>
<div data-role="fieldcontain">
<label for="url">Favorite website:</label>
<input type="url" name="url" id="url"
    placeholder="Choose any site"/>
</div>
<div data-role="fieldcontain">
<label for="rating">Rate this site (10 is best):</label>
<input type="range" name="rating" id="rating" value="5" min="0" max="10"/>
</div>
<label for="veggie">Favorite Veggie:</label>
```

```html
<select name="veggie" id="veggie">
<option value="0">Pick one</option>
<option value="1">Asparagus</option>
<option value="2">Avocado</option>
<option value="3">Barley</option>
<option value="4">Beets</option>
<option value="5">Bell Peppers</option>
<option value="6">Black Beans</option>
<option value="7">Bok Choy</option>
<option value="8">Broccoli</option>
<option value="9">Brussels Sprouts</option>
<option value="10">Cabbage</option>
<option value="11">Carrots</option>
<option value="12">Cauliflower</option>
<option value="13">Celery</option>
<option value="14">Collard Greens</option>
<option value="15">Corn</option>
<option value="16">Cucumber</option>
<option value="18">Eggplant</option>
<option value="19">Flax Seeds</option>
<option value="20">Green Beans</option>
<option value="21">Green Peas</option>
<option value="23">Kale</option>
<option value="24">Leeks</option>
<option value="25">Lima Beans</option>
<option value="26">Mushrooms</option>
<option value="27">Mustard Greens</option>
<option value="28">Navy Beans</option>
<option value="29">Olives</option>
<option value="30">Romaine Lettuce</option>
<option value="31">Spinach</option>
<option value="32">Summer Squash</option>
<option value="33">Sweet Potato</option>
<option value="34">Swiss Chard</option>
<option value="35">Turnip Greens</option>
<option value="36">Winter Squash</option>
</select>
<h4>Choose a veggie:</h4>
<input list="veggies">
<datalist id="veggies">
<option value="Asparagus">
<option value="Avocado">
```

```
<option value="Barley">
<option value="Beets">
<option value="Bell Peppers">
</datalist>
<div data-role="fieldcontain">
<label for="birthday">Birthday:</label>
<input type="date" name="birthday" id="birthday"
     placeholder="Not required"/>
</div>
<button>Submit</button>
<button type="reset">Reset</button>
</form>
Calculate here
<form oninput="x.value=parseInt(a.value)*parseInt(b.value)">
<input type="number" id="a">*
<input type="number" id="b">=
<output name="x" for="a b">
</output>
</form>
```

Summary

In this chapter, I walked through how to use many different HTML5 form tools—input types, output, and datalists. I showed how HTML5 form elements can be used to make input more inviting and fun in mobile devices, as well as how you can make the experience of collecting form data from mobile users effective and accurate.

Consistent use of HTML5 input types, and taking full advantage of other HTML5 form tools has a cumulative effect. It makes your forms stand out, attracts users, and generates more output and more accurate content.

In this chapter, I covered:

- HTML5 form basics.
- Using HTML5 input types for styling, for native widgets to make input easier, and for validation.
- How to use new HTML5 features to calculate in a form.
- How to connect a form to a script.

Here are four "take home" points for effective forms in mobile devices.

- Entering data in mobile devices, without mice, with small screens, and with limited space in the viewport requires seriously distinct forms.

- HTML5 form elements, combined with jQuery Mobile, make form entry much more inviting in mobile devices.

- Enclosing mobile forms in a `<div data="fieldcontain">` element improves display in different devices.

- Mobile forms connect just fine with server-side scripts that handle data using scripting languages like PHP. You can generate those scripts yourself, or use online resources that provide scripts for e-lists, search boxes, and other forms.

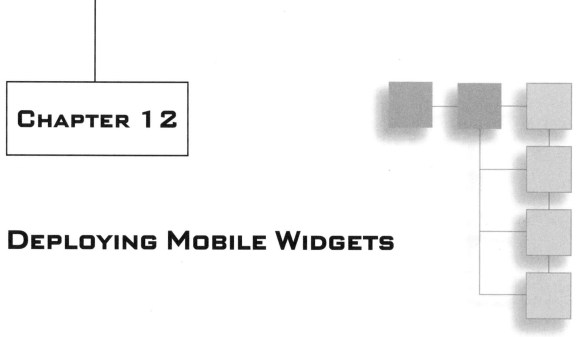

CHAPTER 12

DEPLOYING MOBILE WIDGETS

Widgets allow designers to add animation and interactivity to mobile sites without much, or even any, coding skills in JavaScript. And templates can greatly aid productivity in building sites.

In this chapter, I show you how to integrate and customize widgets from jQuery Mobile's library. I focus in some detail on the popup widget, because it's useful in its own right, and a good model to develop your chops at integrating jQuery Mobile widgets into your HTML5-based mobile sites.

I also show you how to take advantage of one of the online resources that jump-starts mobile page development.

In this process, you will:

- Survey jQuery Mobile's set of widgets.
- Create, customize, define parameters for, and stylize popups.
- Define and style mobile link buttons.
- Use available templates to expedite mobile site development with HTML5.

UNDERSTANDING THE ROLE OF WIDGETS

The term "widget" goes way, way back—it was used when teachers or textbooks needed to discuss an element of the production process and needed a generic term that could mean any product.

In web design, it can mean a lot of things. But in general, and as used here, a widget is a packaged set of commands that creates an object that can be used in a website and is customizable.

Widgets can be created using a range of programming languages. In the scope of mobile website development explored in this book, widgets are generally some mix of HTML5, CSS3, and JavaScript.

Examples of mobile web design widgets include:

- Animated buttons
- Popup content
- Popup dialogs
- Tabbed panels

Widgets are the essential tool in building blogs with blog-composing tools like WordPress, where sites are essentially built by dragging widgets ranging from slideshows to text boxes onto a page.

When I advocate taking full advantage of jQuery Mobile's library of widgets, am I steering you in the direction of WordPress-style, cookie-cutter mobile sites? Am I leading you down the path to generic websites, where users will say to themselves, "Didn't I just see that same page design at the last site I visited?" No. But you can build unique, completely custom page designs without reinventing the wheel or avoiding efficiency-enhancing tools.

Widgets, JavaScript, and Mobile

The animation and interactivity that makes widgets pop up, fade away, spin, and more comes from JavaScript. But how JavaScript powers a widget can vary. In some cases, the developers of widgets require designers using their widget to be familiar with, and edit, JavaScript. Other times, that is not necessary. I'll be focusing on how you and I, HTML5 mobile designers not using JavaScript, can use widgets that don't require JavaScript editing.

Grand Central Station for widgets that mesh well and easily with jQuery Mobile-based mobile sites is the jQuery Mobile widgets page: http://api.jquerymobile.com/category/widgets.

The set of jQuery Mobile widgets includes shortcuts for creating mobile page elements I've covered in other parts of this book. For example, the Page widget generates a `<div data=role="page">` element. That's handy, but doesn't add anything substantial to the skill set you already have from Chapter 2 of this book.

At the other extreme, the Loader widget is only used in conjunction with slow-loading JavaScript programs, and isn't useable in its own right as a mobile page element. But most jQuery Mobile widgets that require little or no JavaScript programming on the part of a designer are useable this way, and are very handy.

Using Widgets from jQuery Mobile

The list of jQuery Mobile widgets at http://api.jquerymobile.com/category/widgets can be a bit overwhelming. As I alluded to earlier, some of those widgets are easy to set up but don't do anything particularly dramatic—like the one that generates a `<div data-role="page">` element. Others don't do anything unless they're integrated into a JavaScript program, and are available as Application Programming Interface elements (APIs).

What Is an API?

An Application Programming Interface (API) means something different in different contexts. But essentially, an API is a set of instructions and/or standards that allow programmers to "connect" their programs with web interfaces. APIs are made public by publishers of software applications, like browsers.

You have all seen or used APIs, maybe even without knowing it. Here are a few examples: Google maps, Twitter, and Facebook. They all have systems (programs) that you can tap into with an API (which gives you limited access to elements of the program) and retrieve data. For example, you can use Google Maps to find a nearby restaurant; you can share a thought with Twitter; and you can "like" someone on Facebook. As a web developer/designer it is relatively easy to add complex features to your sites with APIs.

How do you do that? The process is different for each API. You basically read the documentation for the API so you know what is possible and how to implement it. Implementing an API can be as simple as adding a link, or as complex as writing substantial code.

You can think of the system behind the API as building blocks and of implementing an API as a way to put the blocks together and display them.

Caution

When you implement APIs in your website you have to keep track of the source (proprietary or open source) that delivers the service. API providers sometimes disappear or change or remove APIs.

Table 12.1 lists six jQuery Mobile widgets that I think most readers will find quite useful.

Table 12.1 Useful jQuery Mobile Widgets

Widget	Function
Button widget	Creates a button. 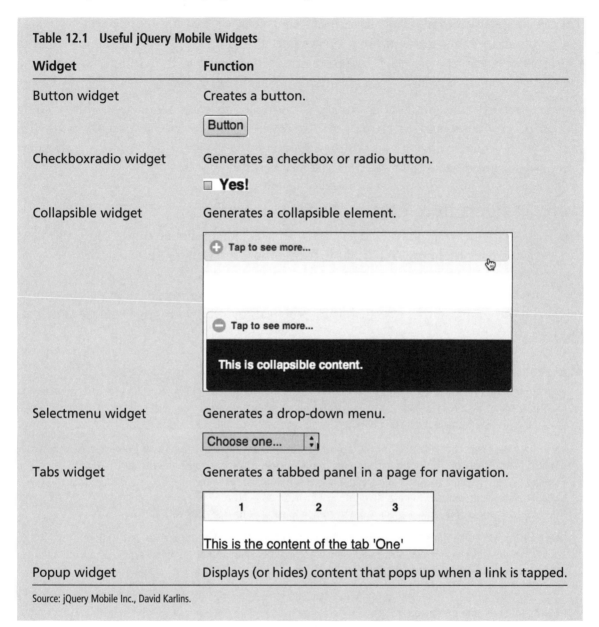
Checkboxradio widget	Generates a checkbox or radio button.
Collapsible widget	Generates a collapsible element.
Selectmenu widget	Generates a drop-down menu.
Tabs widget	Generates a tabbed panel in a page for navigation.
Popup widget	Displays (or hides) content that pops up when a link is tapped.

Source: jQuery Mobile Inc., David Karlins.

I'm going to focus on the popup widget in this chapter, both because it is a helpful element, and because it provides a good way to explore how to use other widgets. And on that basis, I'll show you how to use the widgets listed in the table as well.

To give you a feel for how jQuery Mobile widgets fit into mobile design, Figure 12.1 shows a mobile page with widget-generated checkbox, button, and collapsible element.

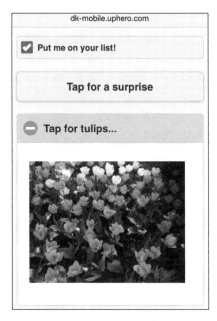

Figure 12.1
Using jQuery Mobile widgets to create interactive mobile elements.
© 2014 Cengage Learning. Source: jQuery Mobile Inc.

Select menus provide access to sets of options, without cluttering up precious mobile page space. Figure 12.2 shows a mobile page with a select menu generated with the Selectmenu widget.

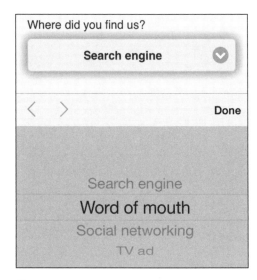

Figure 12.2
Providing easy access to options with a widget-generated Select menu.
© 2014 Cengage Learning. Source: jQuery Mobile Inc.

Another technique for packing extra content into a mobile page is to provide tabbed elements. You'll see tabs in many commercial mobile sites. Expedia.com, for example, provides icon-identified tabs for flights, hotels, vacation packages, cars, cruises, and things to do—all packed neatly into the top row of a smartphone viewport, as shown in Figure 12.3.

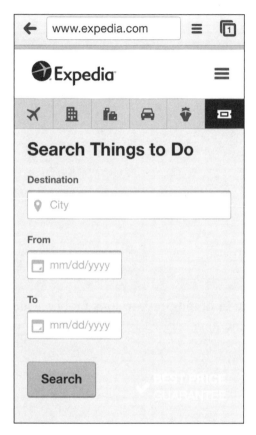

Figure 12.3
A set of tabs packs links into an inviting tabbed navigation bar.
Source: Expedia™.

With jQuery widgets, you and I can generate sets of tabs as well. Figure 12.4 shows a mobile page with a set of basic tabs, produced quickly and easily with a jQuery Mobile widget.

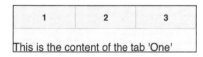

Figure 12.4
A widget-generated set of tabs for a mobile page.
© 2014 Cengage Learning. Source: jQuery Mobile Inc.

CREATING A POPUP WIDGET

Popup widgets provide a good entry into the world of jQuery Mobile widgets. They're easy to define. They don't require any additional JavaScript coding from a designer. The only JavaScript needed to implement them is provided by the standard links to the Content Delivery Network (CDN) files for jQuery Mobile.

And, they're useful!

A basic popup widget can be an inviting way to include extra, optional content in a page. For example, popups can provide clickable definitions. The link in Figure 12.5 clues users in to the fact that tapping on the link will provide them with a definition of the term "link."

Figure 12.5
Prompting users to tap a link for a popup definition.
© 2014 Cengage Learning. Source: jQuery Mobile Inc.

When the link is tapped, the definition appears in a basic popup, as shown in Figure 12.6.

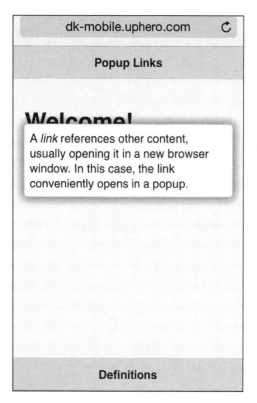

Figure 12.6
Viewing a popup definition.
© 2014 Cengage Learning. Source: jQuery Mobile Inc.

When a user taps outside the popup (or presses Esc on a laptop or mobile or external keyboard), the popup disappears.

Coding a Basic Popup

The basic syntax for defining a popup widget is

```
<a href="#popup1" data-rel="popup">Display Popup</a>
<div data-role="popup" id="popup1">
<p>Popup content.</p>
</div>
```

In this code, the first line defines a link, with a target (#popup1), a defined relationship (data-rel="popup"), and text that displays for the link.

The second tag opens the `<div data-role="popup">` element, with the parameter `id="popup1"`.

The content *within* the `<div-data-role="popup">` element displays *only* when the link is tapped (or clicked).

By itself on a page, this code displays a link like the one in Figure 12.7.

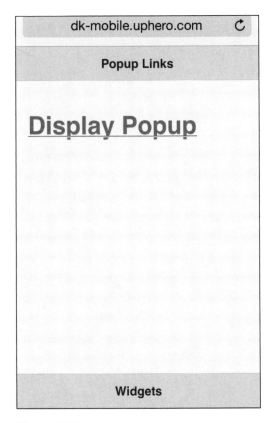

Figure 12.7
A very basic popup link.
© 2014 Cengage Learning. Source: jQuery Mobile Inc.

When tapped, the popup displays the text shown in Figure 12.8.

Figure 12.8
Popup linked text.
© 2014 Cengage Learning. Source: jQuery Mobile Inc.

Adding Other Popups

Each individual popup has a link and popup content. The link and the popup content are connected by a common ID—the link opens the defined ID, and the defined ID has popup content that does not display unless the link is tapped.

This means that when you create multiple popups on a page you need to define distinct IDs for each popup content. For example, the following code defines a second popup that could accompany the one in the previous code sample in the same HTML page:

```
<a href="#popup2" data-rel="popup">Display Popup 2</a>
<div data-role="popup" id="popup2">
<p>Second Popup content.</p>
</div>
```

A second popup using this code appears like the one in Figure 12.9.

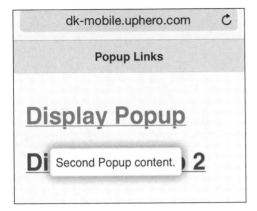

Figure 12.9
Adding a second popup to a page.
© 2014 Cengage Learning. Source: jQuery Mobile Inc.

Tip

I'll provide code for a developed popup example at the end of this chapter. And you can find copy-and-paste ready code at dk-mobile.uphero.com.

Theming Popups

In Chapter 5 of this book, I explained how to generate custom themes and custom color swatches. You might want to pop back there for review. Once you have *defined* a custom theme, you can apply custom theme swatches to a popup. For example:

```
<a href="#popup1" data-rel="popup" data-theme="a">Display Popup</a>
<div data-role="popup" id="popup1" data-theme="a">
<p>Popup content.</p>
</div>
```

In this example, you simply substitute any color swatch you defined with ThemeRoller for a.

You can test this technique even if you don't have a custom theme from jQuery Mobile ThemeRoller handy. The default color swatch for a popup is a, so try switching to b.

Tip

The default theme for jQuery Mobile includes two different color swatches, a and b.

Here's a code sample you can use to experiment with embedding an image in a popup, and using swatch b to add a theme to the popup.

```
<h1><a href="#popup3" data-rel="popup">
Display the jQuery Mobile graphic</a>
</h1>
<div data-role="popup" id="popup3" data-theme="b">
<h1> The jQuery Mobile graphic....
</h1>
<p>
<img src="http://api.jquerymobile.com/
            jquery-wp-content/themes/jquery/images/
            logo-jquery-mobile.png" width="300" height="auto">
</p>
</div>
```

Let me emphasize something: the `data-theme` property is added to the `div data-role="popup"` element, not to the link element.

The previous code includes a bit of embellishment—the display and popup content are both in `<h1>` elements. Figure 12.10 shows how this code appears in a mobile browser.

Figure 12.10
A popup styled with a data-theme.
© 2014 Cengage Learning. Image source © jQuery Mobile.

Tip

This technique—applying a data-theme to a widget-generated element—is applicable to almost any widget, not just to popups.

Transitioning Popups

Popups (and other widgets) can have multiple transitions. They can pop—of course—the transition where they appear or disappear. But popups can also fade, flip, turn, flow, and more.

To animate a popup with a transition, add the transition parameter to the *link* portion of the popup. Here's an example, applying a flip transition:

```
<h1><a href="#popup4" data-transition="flip" data-rel="popup">
Display the jQuery Mobile graphic</a>
</h1>
<div data-role="popup" id="popup4" data-theme="b">
<h1> The jQuery Mobile graphic....
</h1>
<p>
<img src="http://api.jquerymobile.com/
          jquery-wp-content/themes/jquery/images/
          logo-jquery-mobile.png" width="300" height="auto">
</p>
</div>
```

The possible transition parameters are:

- Pop
- Fade
- Flip
- Turn
- Flow
- Slide
- Slide fade
- Slide up
- Slide down

Positioning Popups

By default, popups open centered vertically and horizontally over the link that launched the popup. But you can change that.

I find that it is often more inviting if the link appears visible, or partly visible, even with the popup active. You center the location of a popup using the `data-position-to` attribute. When you do so, you change the element over which the popup centers when it appears.

Options include:

- `data-position-to="window"` centers the popup within the open browser window.

- `data-position-to="header"` centers the popup over the header.

- `data-position-to="footer"` centers the popup over the footer.

Figure 12.11 shows a popup centered in a browser window.

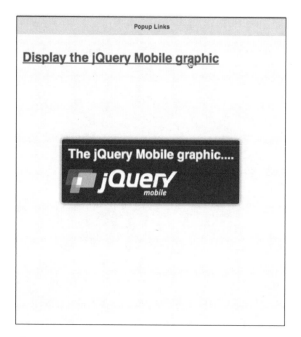

Figure 12.11
A popup centered in a browser window.
© 2014 Cengage Learning. Image source © jQuery Mobile.

Tip

Popup placement is somewhat "intelligent." In some situations, a popup wouldn't look right if directly centered over the element to which it is associated with a `data-position-to` parameter. So the widget adjusts for that. The width of any popup will be limited to the width of the window minus a tolerance of 15px on either side. Also, tolerance from the edges of the window (15px from each of the sides and 30px from the top and the bottom) will be added when the popup fits inside the window. Popups with a height larger than the viewport will overflow the top and bottom edges of the browser window, requiring vertical scrolling. There are other constraints on the degree to which a popup is centered over an element to which it is associated. Don't try to over fine-tune popup placement; the widget generally knows best. For the best sense of how popup placement will be applied, examine your results in a mobile device.

Formatting a Popup as a Button

In the examples so far, I've worked with a popup triggered by simple text. These popups provide tooltip-type effects. But button-launched popups add another dimension of interactivity, as shown in Figure 12.12.

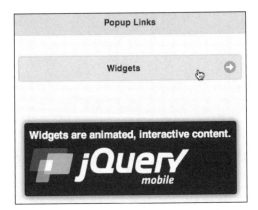

Figure 12.12
A button popup.
© 2014 Cengage Learning. Image source jQuery Mobile.

The parameter to define a popup as a button is:

```
data-role="button"
```

Here's an example you can experiment with:

```
<h1>
<a href="#popup5" data-transition="flip" data-rel="popup"
data-position-to="window" data-role="button"
data-icon="arrow-r" data-iconpos="right"> Widgets</a>
</h1>
<div data-role="popup" id="popup5" data-theme="b">
<h3> Widgets are animated, interactive content.
</h3>
<p>
<img src="http://api.jquerymobile.com/jquery-wp-content/
                themes/jquery/images/logo-jquery-mobile.png"
                width="300" height="auto">
</p>
</div>
```

Tip

Code for a developed model of the popup examples in this chapter is available at http://dk-mobile.uphero.com/#ch12.

Adding and Positioning Icons and Arrows

You'll find it helpful to add and position arrows in a number of widgets. Here, I'm focusing on adding icons to popup buttons. But listviews, for example, are often enhanced with right-positioned arrow parameters, as shown in Figure 12.13.

Figure 12.13
A listview with right-positioned right arrows.
© 2014 Cengage Learning. Source: jQuery Mobile Inc.

To configure a button icon, use the `data-icon=` parameter and one of the values in the following table.

Possible data icons are:

Icon	Parameter
Left arrow	`data-icon="arrow-l"`
Right arrow	`data-icon="arrow-r"`
Up arrow	`data-icon="arrow-u"`
Down arrow	`data-icon="arrow-d"`
Delete	`data-icon="delete"`
Plus	`data-icon="plus"`
Minus	`data-icon="minus"`
Check	`data-icon="check"`
Gear	`data-icon="gear"`
Refresh	`data-icon="refresh"`
Forward	`data-icon="forward"`
Back	`data-icon="back"`
Grid	`data-icon="grid"`
Star	`data-icon="star"`
Alert	`data-icon="alert"`
Info	`data-icon="info"`

By default, all icons in buttons are placed to the left of the button text. But you can change that. Other data positioning options include:

Right	`data-iconpos="right"`
Top	`data-iconpos="top"`
Bottom	`data-iconpos="bottom"`

Here's an example of a right-arrow, positioned on the right of a button:

```
data-icon="arrow-r" data-iconpos="right"
```

And here's how that button looks in a popup; see Figure 12.14.

Figure 12.14
A popup button with a right-positioned right arrow.
© 2014 Cengage Learning. Source: jQuery Mobile Inc.

A Popup Template

If you'd like a template to use for applying popup widgets, the following code will serve as a start. It incorporates the popup transitions, positioning, icons and icon positioning, data-theming, and other parameters explored in this chapter.

Tip

You can find this code at http://dk-mobile.uphero.com/#ch12.

```
<!doctype html>
<html>
<head>
<meta charset="UTF-8">
<title>Mobile Widgets</title>
<meta name="viewport" content="width=device-width, initial-scale=1">
<link rel="stylesheet" href="http://code.jquery.com/mobile/
                    1.4.1/jquery.mobile-1.4.1.min.css" />
<script src="http://code.jquery.com/jquery-1.10.2.min.js"></script>
<script src="http://code.jquery.com/mobile/1.4.1/
                    jquery.mobile-1.4.1.min.js"></script>
</head>
<body>
<div data-role="page" id="page01">
<div data-role="header"><h1>Popup Links</h1></div>
<div data-role="content">
<h1><a href="#popup1" data-transition="flip" data-rel="popup"
      data-position-to="window" data-role="button"
      data-icon="arrow-r" data-iconpos="right">
Widgets</a>
</h1>
<div data-role="popup" id="popup1" data-theme="b">
<h3> Widgets are animated, interactive content. </h3>
<p>
<img src="http://api.jquerymobile.com/
          jquery-wp-content/themes/jquery/images
          /logo-jquery-mobile.png" width="300" height="auto">
</p>
</div>
</div>
</div>
</body>
</html>
```

Navigation Buttons

In exploring the popup widget in depth, I mentioned defining buttons. But you might be wondering how to define a button that acts simply as a regular link, not as a popup. I'll walk through that. It won't take long since the previous exploration of popups gave you a basic conception of how buttons, icons, and icon positioning works.

The basic syntax for a button link is:

```
<a href="#" data-role="button">Link text</a>
```

Here's an example that integrates the data-icon and data-iconpos parameters:

```
<a href="#page01" data-role="button"
        data-icon="arrow-u" data-iconpos="right">
Home
</a>
```

Placed inside a footer, that home button looks like the one in Figure 12.15.

Figure 12.15
A link button with a right-positioned up arrow.
© 2014 Cengage Learning. Source: jQuery Mobile Inc.

GENERATING A TABBED NAVIGATION BAR

The jQuery Mobile tabbed navigation bar is a highly useful and easy-to-implement widget for building navigation bars in headers, footers, or within page content. Early in this chapter (back in Figure 12.3) I showed you how high-resource development teams like the ones that built the Expedia website use tabbed navigation bars with icons in the header.

You can use tabbed navigation bars in headers, like in the Expedia.com example. But you don't have to; you can place a tabbed navigation bar anywhere.

A few rules for the jQuery Mobile Navbar widget:

- Tabbed navbars can have between one and five tabs.
- Navbar tabs are always equal in width:
  With a two-tab navbar, each tab is half the width of the available space.
  With a three-tab navbars, each tab is one-third the width of the available space.
  With a four-tab navbars, each tab is one-quarter the width of the available space.
  With a five-tab navbars, each tab is one-fifth the width of the available space.
- If a navbar has more than five tabs, a new row of tabs is generated.

Navbars often rely on icons to indicate navigation targets. That makes sense, given the limited real estate in mobile pages. The Verizon mobile site, for example, shown in Figure 12.16, provides a tabbed navigation bar with icons indicating their product line, a search box, the shopping cart, and an extended menu.

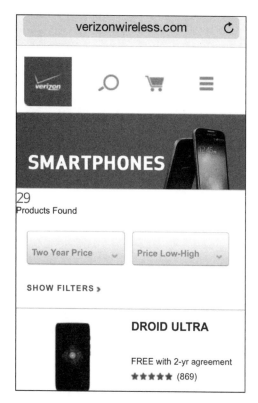

Figure 12.16
Verizon's mobile site uses a four-tab navigation bar.
Source: Verizon™.

I'll show you how to use icons in widget-generated navigation bars in this section of this chapter, as well as how to create navigation bars that include text.

Defining a Navbar

Navbar widgets are created with HTML5 coding that defines an unordered list of links wrapped in a `<div data-role="navbar">` element.

As I noted, spacing is pre-set as part of the jQuery Mobile CSS. Each tab within a navbar is equal in width.

The basic syntax for a navbar is:

```
<div data-role="navbar">
<ul>
<li>
<a href="#">text</a>
</li>
<li>
<a href="#">text</a>
</li>
<li>
<a href="#">text</a>
</li>
<li>
<a href="#">text</a>
</li>
<li>
<a href="#">text</a>
</li>
</ul>
</div>
```

The links in the code (indicated with "#") are replaced with real links, and placeholder text with real link text. The previous code creates the navbar in Figure 12.17.

Figure 12.17
A navbar with placeholder text.
© 2014 Cengage Learning. Source: jQuery Mobile Inc.

Using jQuery Mobile 1.4's Extended Data Icon Set

jQuery Mobile provides navbar icons that can be used by applying a data-icon attribute. This substantial set of icons is larger than the ones available for buttons that I introduced you to earlier in this chapter (see "Formatting a Popup as a Button").

The icons are SVG format images, which download quickly and rescale without distortion in any sized viewport. jQuery Mobile's Content Delivery Network CSS files include links to PNG versions of the icon images for environments without support for SVG images.

Here's a list of available icon names:

- action
- alert
- arrow-d
- arrow-d-l
- arrow-d-r
- arrow-l
- arrow-r
- arrow-u
- arrow-u-l
- arrow-u-r
- audio
- back
- bars
- bullets
- calendar
- camera
- carat-d

- carat-l
- carat-r
- carat-u
- check
- clock
- cloud
- comment
- delete
- edit
- eye
- forbidden
- forward
- gear
- grid
- heart
- home
- info

- location
- lock
- mail
- minus
- navigation
- phone
- plus
- power
- recycle
- refresh
- search
- shop
- star
- tag
- user
- video

Impressive, right? Get your money's worth out of these free and fast-downloading icons.

You can see the current set of available navbar icons here: http://api.jquerymobile.com/icons.

For quick reference, Figure 12.18 shows this set.

Figure 12.18
The icon set for jQuery Mobile's Navbar widget.
Source: jQuery Mobile Inc.

The syntax for adding an icon is as follows:

```
<a href="# data-icon="icon name">text</a>
```

In the syntax, `icon name` is replaced with a real icon name from the list at http://api. jquerymobile.com/icons.

Here's an example with placeholder text for five icons.

```
<div data-role="navbar">
<ul>
<li>
<a href="# data-icon="icon name">text</a>
</li>
<li>
<a href="# data-icon="icon name">text</a>
```

```
</li>
<li>
<a href="#" data-icon="icon name">text</a>
</li>
<li>
<a href="#" data-icon="icon name">text</a>
</li>
</li>
<a href="#" data-icon="icon name">text</a>
</li>
</ul>
</div>
```

Again, if you're using this code as a template, the links in the code (indicated with "#") should be replaced with real links, the placeholder *text* with real link text, and the *icon name* with real icon names. This code creates the navbar shown in Figure 12.19.

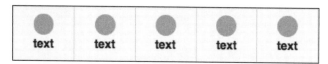

Figure 12.19
A five-tab navbar with placeholder text and icons.
© 2014 Cengage Learning. Source: jQuery Mobile Inc.

Tip

You'll find code for a completed, developed sample of a page with navbars in the header and footer at http://dk-mobile.uphero.com/#ch12.

Embedding a Navbar in a Header or Footer

Navbars do not have to be embedded in headers or footers. But that's often where users will look for navigation options. So navbars are, often, best placed in a header, a footer, or both.

By the way, if you want to add a navbar to the top of the page, you can still have a page title and buttons, like the layout in Figure 12.20.

Figure 12.20
A navbar in a header with a header title.
© 2014 Cengage Learning. Source: jQuery Mobile Inc.

The code for the navbar in Figure 12.20 serves nicely as a template for a page with a five-column navbar that has icon links. Here's that code:

```
<!DOCTYPE html>
<html>
<head>
<title>Navbar no style</title>
<meta name="viewport" content="width=device-width, initial-scale=1">
<link rel="stylesheet" href="http://code.jquery.com/mobile/1.4.2/
                         jquery.mobile-1.4.2.min.css" />
<script src="http://code.jquery.com/jquery-1.10.2.min.js"></script>
<script src="http://code.jquery.com/mobile/1.4.2/
            jquery.mobile-1.4.2.min.js"></script>
</head>
<body>
<div data-role="page">
<div data-role="header">
<h1>Header content</h1>
<div data-role="navbar">
<ul>
<li><a href="#" data-icon="home">Home</a></li>
<li><a href="#" data-icon="video">Video</a></li>
<li><a href="#" data-icon="info">Info</a></li>
<li><a href="#" data-icon="comment">Talk</a></li>
<li><a href="#" data-icon="mail">Email</a></li>
</ul>
</div>
</div>
```

```
<div data-role="content">
Page content
</div>
</body>
</html>
```

Of course you will choose different icons and define your own links when you adapt this code.

Tip

Remember, the code for a completed, developed sample of a page with navbars in the header and footer is at http://dk-mobile.uphero.com/#ch12.

What about embedding a navbar in a footer? The basic concept is the same as for a header. In the following example (the template), I've assigned a `data-position="fixed"` property to the footer so it "sticks" to the bottom of a page as users scroll through page content. And, again, you'll customize this example with your own content when you use it in your own mobile site.

Positioning Icons

Icons can be positioned at the top, bottom, left, or right of any text within a navbar tab. By default, icons are added above the text. Icon positioning is defined for an entire navbar, not for each specific icon. That makes sense, right? If the icons were positioned differently within a navbar, the effect would be cluttered and chaotic.

The syntax for positioning an icon within a navbar is: `data-iconpos="position"`, where the position is one of these four self-explanatory values:

- left
- right
- bottom
- top

Here's an example:

```
<div data-role="navbar" data-icon-pos="bottom" >
```

A Full Navbar Template

For quick reference, here's the code for an entire page with navbars in the header, content, and footer:

```html
<!DOCTYPE html>
<html>
<head>
<title>Navbar no style</title>
<meta name="viewport" content="width=device-width, initial-scale=1">
<link rel="stylesheet" href="http://code.jquery.com/mobile/1.4.2/
                        jquery.mobile-1.4.2.min.css" />
<script src="http://code.jquery.com/jquery-1.10.2.min.js"></script>
<script src="http://code.jquery.com/mobile/1.4.2/
            jquery.mobile-1.4.2.min.js"></script>
</head>
<body>
<div data-role="page">
<div data-role="header">
<h1>Header content</h1>
<div data-role="navbar">
<ul>
<li><a href="#" data-icon="home">Home</a></li>
<li><a href="#" data-icon="video">Video</a></li>
<li><a href="#" data-icon="info">Info</a></li>
<li><a href="#" data-icon="comment">Talk</a></li>
<li><a href="#" data-icon="mail">Email</a></li>
</ul>
</div><!-- /navbar -->
</div><!-- /header -->
<div data-role="content">
<h1>Go to...</h1>
<div data-role="navbar" data-icon-pos="bottom" >
<ul>
<li><a href="#">Home</a></li>
<li><a href="#">Video</a></li>
<li><a href="#">Info</a></li>
<li><a href="#">Talk</a></li>
<li><a href="#">Email</a></li>
<li><a href="#">Email</a></li>
</ul>
</div><!-- /navbar -->
```

```
<p>Page content</p>
<p> </p>
<div data-role="navbar">
</div>
</div>
<div data-role="footer" data-position="fixed">
<h1>Footer</h1>
<div data-role="navbar" data-iconpos="bottom">
<ul>
<li><a href="#" data-icon="home"></a></li>
<li><a href="#" data-icon="video"></a></li>
<li><a href="#" data-icon="info"></a></li>
<li><a href="#" data-icon="comment"></a></li>
<li><a href="#" data-icon="mail"></a></li>
</ul>
</div>
</div>
</div>
</div>
</body>
</html>
```

Tip

You can see an example of a page with navbars in the header, content, and footer of a page at http://dk-mobile.uphero.com/tabbed-navbar.html.

Theming Navbars

Navbars inherit the data-theme assigned to their containers. So, for example, the following code applies `data-theme="b"` to a navbar within a header:

```
<div data-role="header" data-theme="b">
<h1>Header themed B</h1>
<div data-role="navbar">
<ul>
<li><a href="#" data-icon="home">Home</a></li>
<li><a href="#" data-icon="video">Video</a></li>
<li><a href="#" data-icon="info">Info</a></li>
```

```
<li><a href="#" data-icon="comment">Talk</a></li>
<li><a href="#" data-icon="mail">Email</a></li>
</ul>
</div>
</div>
```

Tip

Check out Chapters 4 and 5 of this book for a full exploration of assigning data-theme properties to elements, and creating and applying your own custom themes and color swatches.

With default themes, the previous code creates the header and navbars in Figure 12.21.

Figure 12.21
A themed navbar in a header.

© 2014 Cengage Learning. Source: jQuery Mobile Inc.

Custom Glyphs

Before closing the discussion of navbars, I want to make you aware of the availability of custom icon sets. As I noted earlier, rather enthusiastically, jQuery Mobile comes with a nice set of free icons for navbars—dozens of them in fact. And low-budget designers can get a lot of mileage from these.

But there are times when you may want to purchase customized sets of icons. One of the best sources is glyphish.com. The site refers to icons as *glyphs,* which is a term used to define sets of symbols in typography. They sell over 1,000 customized icons, in sets created specifically for Apple's iOS operating system, Android, and other environments. Figure 12.22 shows some of the icon sets available. The glyphish.com site also provides hundreds of free icons you can use if you follow the licensing rules at the site.

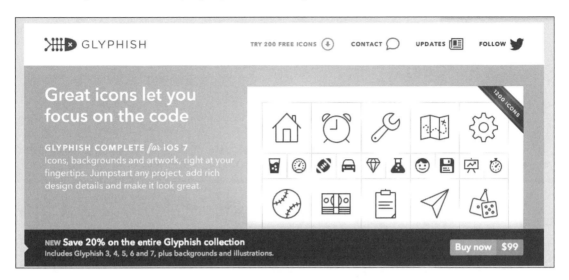

Figure 12.22
Custom fonts from glyphish.com.

Source: glyphish.com™, jQuery Mobile Inc.

Summary

In previous chapters of this book, I've emphasized that HTML5—backed by the JavaScript (and CSS) package that comes with jQuery Mobile—provides tools for vibrant, inviting, accessible mobile websites. I'm not backing off on that assertion! Just to quickly review the case, HTML5 plus jQuery Mobile allows you to include:

- Animated, interactive navigation listviews (see Chapter 3)
- Custom themes and color swatches (see Chapters 4 and 5)
- Collapsible content (see Chapter 6)
- Native audio and video (see Chapters 8 and 9)
- Accessible images (see Chapter 10)
- Mobile-friendly input forms that provide calendar prompts for dates, color palettes for color input, and other handy features for users (see Chapter 11)

In this chapter, I introduced you to another dimension of integrated animation and interactivity—jQuery Mobile widgets.

I showed you how to use three widgets:

- Popups provide content that "pops up" on a page.

- Navigation buttons make it easy for mobile users to follow links.

- Navbars generate automatically formatted navigation elements that work in headers, footers, or content areas of mobile `<div data-role="page">` elements.

In the course of examining these three widgets, I showed you how to customize parameters like transitions (for popups, like flip or slide); styling; and deploying jQuery Mobile's nice set of free icons.

Through exploring these three widgets (popups, buttons, and navbars), you were exposed to how widgets work in general.

Here are four "take home" points for effective deployment of jQuery Mobile widgets:

- Widgets in general add layers of animation and interactivity to mobile sites.

- jQuery Mobile widgets integrate smoothly and efficiently into jQuery Mobile sites since they utilize the same centrally distributed JavaScript and CSS that makes jQuery Mobile tick.

- Some jQuery Mobile widgets are designed for JavaScript programmers to adapt and integrate into scripting, but many do not require any knowledge of JavaScript to implement—the parameters and content are defined completely with HTML5.

- The community of jQuery Mobile programmers continues to develop new, useful widgets, expanding the scope of what you can do with mobile sites.

Chapter 13

Building a Complete Mobile Presence

This book is focused on building mobile websites with HTML5. And I've emphasized the value of connecting that HTML5 with the library of tools at jQuery Mobile to add script-free animation and interactivity. But where does that leave a developer who needs a presence for large viewport users with laptops and desktops?

There are a number of possible approaches to that issue. One is to simply allow desktop/laptop users to view content and pages built for mobile. Another approach is called *responsive web design* (RWD). Another option is to provide completely distinct content for desktop/laptop users and mobile users. I'll explain these and other approaches in this chapter, and walk you through some solutions.

And, I'll show you how to implement features like caching (storing) page content in devices, implanting a live chat, and using geolocation, to provide an app-like experience with a mobile site.

In this process, you will learn:

- How to understand different strategies for providing distinct laptop/desktop and mobile content.

- How to detect mobile devices and divert users from desktop/laptop pages to mobile content.

- How to optimize search engine results when creating duplicate content for laptop/desktop users and mobile users.

- How to include features like caching, geolocation, and live chat in your mobile site.

Differentiating Between Mobile and Full-Sized Pages

Let's examine four options for managing the relationship between mobile and laptop/desktop sites. Those options are essentially:

- Simply allowing laptop/desktop users to view mobile content.

- Using responsive web design to provide content that adapts to different viewports.

- Building native apps for mobile users and HTML pages for laptop/desktop users.

- Building a separate desktop/laptop site, and then detecting mobile users and diverting them to mobile-friendly pages.

This chapter emphasizes the last option for a number of reasons that I'll explain shortly. But before getting to that, I want to explore the other options for addressing the needs of non-mobile users.

Providing the Same Content for Mobile and Laptop/Desktop Users

This might seem like a radical proposition: Why not simply allow laptop/desktop users to view the content you build for mobile users? I'm going to make an argument that this is not a bad idea in many cases.

It is still the case that many websites that lack the resources of the "big boys," enterprises with huge design and development resources, do not provide an acceptable mobile presence. Given the radical shift taking place as we "speak," with users migrating to mobile devices for their web activity, that is simply out of synch with the real needs of users.

Look at it this way: Sites designed for laptop/desktop environments, with multiple columns, reliance on mouse hovering, color schemes that don't work outdoors, or that are so full of "rich media" that they take endless minutes to download over 3G, 4G, and LTE connections are terribly off-putting for mobile users. But sites designed *without* those elements, with mobile-friendly animation and interactivity, can provide a perfectly acceptable experience for laptop/desktop users.

For example, Monster Energy Company, the company that makes the Monster Energy drinks, has the resources to promote itself through sponsorship of sporting events like motocross, BMX bike competitions, mountain biking, snowboarding, skateboarding, and car racing. So, they can afford to have separate content for their mobile and desktop/laptop sites. Figure 13.1 shows Monster Energy's full-sized site.

Figure 13.1
Monster Energy's laptop/desktop site.
Source: Monster Energy Company™.

But what if laptop/desktop users ended up at Monster Energy's mobile site? Figure 13.2 shows that site, viewed in a full-sized viewport on a laptop.

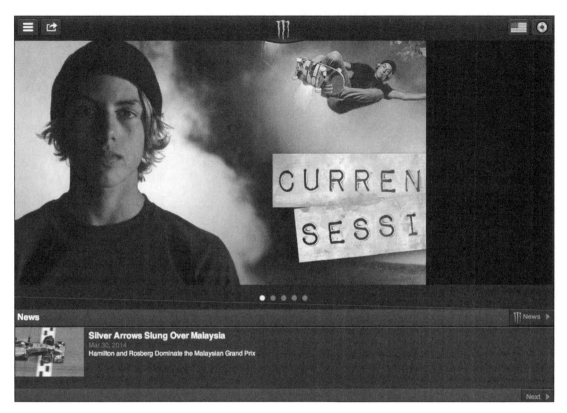

Figure 13.2
Monster Energy's mobile site viewed in a full-sized laptop viewport.
Source: Monster Energy Company™.

Not too shabby, right? If—and this is not the case—but if Monster Energy only had the juice to build a single site, their mobile site would probably be a better than average experience for laptop/desktop users.

Tip

You can check out Monster Energy's mobile site from a laptop or desktop by going to http://mobile.monsterenergy.com/.

As you browse the web with your mobile device, check out and study sites that would work well in laptop/desktop browsers. Henry's, the Canadian digital camera retailer, has a mobile site that is inviting on a laptop, with tabbed navigation, images that fill the page, and bright colors that look great inside in controlled lighting and outside in bright sun. Figure 13.3 shows the Henry's site in a laptop viewport.

Figure 13.3
Henry's mobile site is inviting when viewed in a full-sized laptop viewport.

Source: Cranbrook Glen Enterprises Ltd.

In sum, there are situations where a nicely designed mobile-friendly site provides a perfectly acceptable experience for users in any environment.

What Is Progressive Enhancement?

While we're on the subject of making mobile sites work well in laptop/desktop environments, the concept of *progressive enhancement* deserves a mention.

As more powerful browsers emerged on the web-browsing stage, with support for HTML5 and other cutting edge features, designers began to talk about "graceful degradation." The concept was that they would design with tools that exploited the latest features in HTML and CSS, but build in options so that the site still functioned in older browsers. For example, older browsers don't support some gradient backgrounds that rely on CSS3, so a graceful degradation approach would substitute a solid color background for a gradient as necessary.

And as mobile browsing became a big factor, the approach of graceful degradation was at times used to provide content that "degraded" gracefully from laptop/desktop devices to mobile browsers. For example, designers might create sites that used hover-based drop-down navigation menus in laptop/desktop environments, but substituted mobile-accessible menus for mobile users.

The approach of progressive enhancement flips the script, and starts with design for devices and environments that don't support high-speed Internet connections or other elements. At this stage of the game, progressive enhancement can be applied in the form of a mobile-first approach to web page design, with additional features added for laptop/desktop users.

Using Responsive Web Design

Responsive web design (RWD) is an approach that generally relies on providing the same basic content, but with different styling in different viewports. *The Boston Globe's* website is often cited as a positive model of well-implemented RWD. Visitors to the site (bostonglobe.com) in a full laptop/desktop viewport see a three-column page design like the one in Figure 13.4.

Figure 13.4
The Boston Globe site viewed in a laptop-sized viewport.
Source: *The Boston Globe*™.

In a tablet-sized viewport, the *Globe's* site changes layout, providing two columns instead of three, as shown in Figure 13.5.

Figure 13.5
The Boston Globe site viewed in a tablet-sized viewport.
Source: *The Boston Globe*™.

In a smartphone-sized viewport, the *Globe's* site changes layout, stacking all three columns into a single column of content, as shown in Figure 13.6.

Figure 13.6
The *Boston Globe* site viewed in a smartphone-sized viewport.
Source: *The Boston Globe*™.

Many experts have written extensively on how to build RWD sites, and a full exploration of the approaches and techniques involved is beyond the scope of this book. But here I identify a few key points to put RWD in perspective:

■ Responsive web design generally relies on using media queries in CSS style sheets to provide distinct page designs for different viewports.

■ RWD usually involves using the *same* basic HTML in different viewports, but with *different* styles applied depending on viewport.

- RWD provides distinct styling based on a user's *viewport*—the width of the browser window.

- RWD does *not* provide different styling (or content) based on a user's *device*. Instead, different styling is based on the viewport.

How does this approach relate to the approach in this book of building *mobile* sites? The answer is complex. RWD *differs* from building mobile-first sites in important ways. RWD does not provide fundamentally distinct content for mobile users, instead it adapts content for mobile users. RWD does not, in the main, provide mobile-specific animation and interactivity that is available from jQuery Mobile.

At the same time, it is possible to take the techniques you've learned in this book and combine them with RWD to build sites that start with jQuery Mobile and HTML5, and then adapt to different viewports. To put that another way, you can take a jQuery Mobile-based website and apply RWD techniques to it.

Native and Mobile Apps

What's the difference between a mobile website built with jQuery Mobile, using techniques and providing features covered in this book, and a mobile web application (or app for short)?

The basic answer is nothing. They are the same thing. A "mobile app" generally means a website that looks and feels like an app in a mobile device—one with animated navigation, mobile-friendly effects, and a slew of helpful features such as, for example, the handy form tools you explored in Chapter 11 of this book.

A *native* mobile app is one that runs in a mobile device without a browser. That's the main difference between *native* mobile apps and mobile *web* apps. Native apps are operating system-specific. So, for example, to reach the widest range of mobile users, a native app has to have different versions for Android, Apple's iOS, Microsoft's Mobile operating system, and Blackberry's operating system. Plus, a handful of other mobile OSs. Of course many apps are only built for Android and iOS, but even in those instances, the apps have to be built completely differently, from the ground up, using high-end programming languages.

How different are mobile web apps and native web apps? To quote an article on the subject at Wikipedia.com, "The distinction between mobile web applications and native applications is anticipated to become increasingly blurred..."

Yelp, for example, provides a mobile-friendly experience for users who download their native app and search for a good taco in Palm Springs, as shown in Figure 13.7.

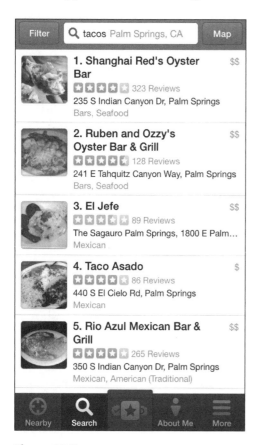

Figure 13.7
The Yelp native app.
Source: Yelp™.

Users who visit the Yelp site (www.yelp.com) in mobile devices have a similar and positive experience searching for tacos in Palm Springs, as shown in Figure 13.8.

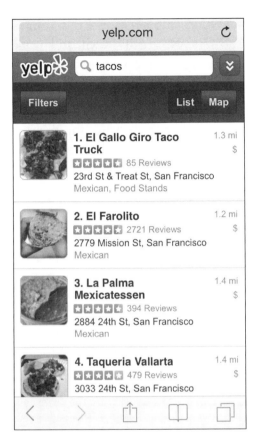

Figure 13.8
The Yelp mobile site.
Source: Yelp™.

If the user experience for a web app, built with HTML5 and jQuery Mobile on the one hand, and a native app requiring much more programming resources is similar, why do enterprises with virtually unlimited resources build apps? Mainly for commercial reasons, not for additional functionality. You cannot, for example, sell a mobile web app from iTunes or Google Play, but you can sell a native app. But designers with limited resources can provide a highly inviting app experience without building native apps.

Providing Distinct Sites for Laptop/Desktop and Mobile Users

If you have the resources to do so, you can provide a higher quality experience for all users by providing distinct websites for laptop/desktop users and mobile users.

Am I contradicting my earlier advice, where I argued that in many cases building a mobile-first site can satisfy the needs of laptop/desktop users? Not really. I will still argue that in this day and age, if your choice is between building a laptop/desktop site that doesn't work well in mobile devices, and building a mobile-friendly site that works okay in a laptop/desktop environment, the second option is preferable.

But, again—if you have the resources—you can provide an optimal experience for all users if you build two distinct sites. In the following section of this chapter, I walk through how to integrate and mesh a distinct laptop/desktop site with a mobile site.

DETECTING AND DIVERTING MOBILE USERS

Scenario: You have a website you built with laptop/desktop users in mind. More recently, you've built a separate mobile site that provides a fantastic experience for users with mobile devices.

Challenge: How do you detect mobile users and divert them to the mobile-friendly site, while leaving laptop/desktop users at the site you built for them?

And, how do you handle the challenge of providing two, essentially parallel, sites? How do you optimize search engine results when you are providing similar content in two different sites?

I'll walk you through solving those issues now.

Detecting Mobile Devices

If you want to detect users' devices and provide an appropriate site depending on the results, you need to integrate some JavaScript. JavaScript can detect a user's operating system and redirect a user to a specific URL based on the operating system. And, since different devices use different operating systems, detecting an operating system allows JavaScript to divert users to a site matched to their devices.

One implication of this is that you can actually provide specific mobile sites for different mobile devices. A one-size-fits-all is not required. Want to provide different content for iPad users than the pages you supply to Android users? You can do that.

Here's the process:

1. Detect users' devices when they come to your website.

2. Leave users with a laptop/desktop computer at the version of your site designed for them.

3. Send users with mobile devices to a mobile-friendly page built with HTML5 and jQuery Mobile.

To do this, open the HTML file of the home page of your web page built for laptop/desktop users. In the `<head>` element of that page, enter this short JavaScript code:

```
<script type="text/javascript">
//<![CDATA[
var mobile = (/iphone|ipad|ipod|android|blackberry|mini|windows\sce|
             palm/i.test(navigator.userAgent.toLowerCase()));
if (mobile) {
document.location = "mobile-ver.html";
}
// ]]>
</script>
```

This script detects users' devices and diverts them to a page—in this example, that page is `mobile.html`.

Tip

Another source for a JavaScript that detects devices can be found at http://detectmobilebrowsers.com/.

As I noted earlier, you can actually tweak this script (even without knowing JavaScript) by editing the list of devices in the line:

```
var mobile = (/iphone|ipad|ipod|android|blackberry|mini|windows\sce|palm/i.test
(navigator.userAgent.toLowerCase()));
```

For example, if you wanted iPad users, with their wide screens, to stay at your laptop/desktop site, you would remove `ipad` from the set of mobile devices, like this:

```
var mobile = (/iphone|ipod|android|blackberry|mini|windows\sce|palm/i.test
(navigator.userAgent.toLowerCase()));
```

Some sites provide mobile users with an option to view the "full" site (the laptop/desktop version). Amazon.com does this, as shown in Figure 13.9.

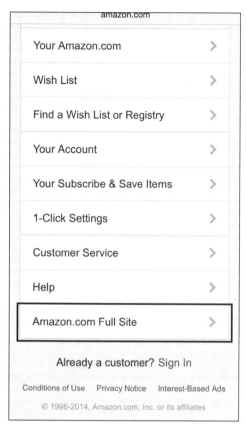

Figure 13.9
A link to Amazon's full site in a mobile device.
Source: Amazon.com™.

Caution

If you elect to provide an option for mobile users to view the full site, one solution is to link to a duplicate version of the laptop/desktop page that does *not* include the script that redirects them to the mobile page.

Managing Separate Mobile URLs

Providing parallel content for mobile and laptop/desktop users in separate web pages presents challenges in maintaining good search engine results. The Google search engine supports three approaches to smartphone-optimized sites:

- Responsive web design sites that provide all devices with the same URLs. As I explained earlier in this chapter, RWD provides content in different viewports using the same URL. That makes search engine optimization easy, because with RWD, all users see content in the same URL.

- Sites that dynamically serve all devices using the same URLs. This involves a high level of back-end programming and is an approach beyond the scope of this book and beyond the skillset of most designers.

- Finally, the option I've focused on in this chapter—sites with *separate* mobile and desktop URLs. I'll explain how to manage these pages to optimize search engine results.

Before I walk you through the solution, let's examine the problem quickly. If you build a site with different URLs for desktop/laptop content and mobile content, you might save one page as `index.html` and the other (mobile) page as `mobile.html`. But the pages have the same essential content. And when users search Google for your site, you don't want a whole batch of alternate pages to pop up, confusing them.

Here's how Google advises you to address this:

- Between two (or more) pages with similar content, aimed at different devices, specify a "canonical" (preferred) page.

- On the laptop/desktop page, add a `link rel="`*canonical*`"` tag pointing to the corresponding preferred URL.

- In the coding for your mobile page, add a special `link rel="`*alternate*`"` tag pointing to the corresponding alternate.

This helps Google discover the location of your site's mobile pages.

Here's an example, where the laptop/desktop page is `www.full.html` and the home page for mobile users is `www.mobile.html`. The canonical (preferred) page—the one to which search engine results point—is the laptop/desktop page.

In the mobile page, add the following code in the `<head>` element:

```
<link rel="alternate" href="http://www.mobile.com" >
```

And in the laptop/desktop page:

```
<link rel="canonical" href="http://www.full.com" >
```

Tip

The reason for making the laptop/desktop page canonical here is that we have just explored how to place a script in the `<head>` element of that page that will divert users with mobile devices to a mobile site. So by making the laptop/desktop page the preferred (canonical) page, both the laptop/desktop and the mobile audiences will end up at their appropriate pages.

This two-way (bidirectional) annotation helps the Google search engine's technology correctly identify content and correctly handle the relationship between laptop/desktop pages and mobile pages.

Tip

If you don't combine the search results of your laptop/desktop and mobile pages, one negative result will likely be that your search engine rankings will be lower, because visits will be divided between mobile and laptop/desktop pages.

If they are treated separately, both desktop and mobile URLs are shown in desktop search results, and their positions may be lower than they would otherwise be.

Enhancing Mobile Web Apps

In surveying the differences between native mobile apps and web mobile apps—earlier in this chapter—I noted that one advantage native mobile applications have over web mobile apps is that native apps can function, at least partially, without an Internet connection.

The native mobile app for the *New York Daily News,* for example, makes content available even when its readers are away from an Internet connection. They emphasize this feature to readers, as shown in Figure 13.10.

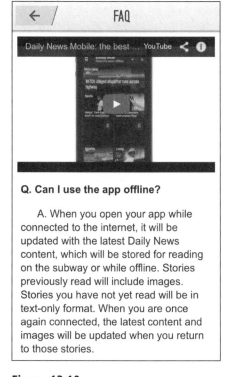

Figure 13.10
The *NY Daily News* mobile app works when readers are offline.
Source: *New York Daily News*™.

Caching has been one of the big advantages of native apps over mobile apps, but that's changing. With HTML5, you can *cache* (store) content in a browser and make that content available even when your mobile users lose their Internet connection. And, by the way, you can define a cache without JavaScript—just using HTML5. I'll show you how to configure your mobile site to make that happen in the next section of this chapter.

Another feature usually associated with native apps is the ability to detect a user's location, called *geolocation*. Geolocation is often associated with an element that can frame content provided by a remote server. HTML5 provides solutions for both these challenges.

Geolocation can be implemented as an HTML5 API—an application programming interface. API means different things in different contexts. In general (in relation to computer programming), API defines how software components can be programmed to interact with each other. APIs reduce the amount of coding required to implement features, and in this case, HTML5's geolocation API makes it easy for JavaScript coders to implement interactive maps, directions, and other location-based interactivity in mobile sites.

The new ⟨canvas⟩ element in HTML5 essentially provides a programmable space in a mobile (or any) web page.

The HTML5 geolocation API can be combined with a ⟨canvas⟩ element to produce a "You Are Here" interactive element in a mobile page. While this requires JavaScript coding, there are plenty of pre-built JavaScript libraries that HTML5 coders can adapt, customize, and integrate into their mobile sites. I'll show you how to do that as well.

Caching Content

I've noted that caching is now available with HTML5. You don't need to be a high-level programmer writing native apps to use it. But how important is caching?

Caching makes a big difference in places like New York City where mobile users spend considerable time underground and out of Internet range. Mobile users driving through large stretches of West Virginia who lack Internet access face the same problem. So do travelers stuck on a plane trip without WiFi. They all see a screen like the one in Figure 13.11 And that's no fun!

Figure 13.11
An error message when a user cannot access a mobile web app.
© 2014 Cengage Learning.

Fact is, no matter where your users are found, there will be times when they don't have access to the Internet on their mobile devices. But you don't need to lose connection with them.

The solution is application caching, which:

- Allows users to view at least part of your mobile site without an Internet connection.

- Speeds access to your site content for users who do have Internet connections.

Different browsers have different size limits for cached data, so you don't want to over-do it on cached files. So think about what content is so essential that you want to make it available to users without Internet connections. A general rule of thumb is to restrict cached content to 5MB of data.

Once you've decided which pages to cache, there are two steps to caching content on your site:

1. Creating a cache manifest file that defines which files remain in a user's device.

2. Enabling that cache manifest file.

Defining a Cache Manifest File

Cache manifest files are just text files that you can create with your HTML coding application and then save with a filename extension of `.appcache`.

Tip

It is not a technical requirement that cache files are saved with the `.appcache` extension, but it is standard practice and helps designers identify the cache file.

Cache manifest files have up to three sections:

- CACHE MANIFEST—Files listed under this header are cached after being downloaded for the first time by a user.

- NETWORK—Files listed under this header require a connection to the server, and are *not* cached.

- FALLBACK—Files listed under this header display if the page a user attempts to open is inaccessible because there is no Internet connection.

Here's an example of code for an entire cache file:

```
CACHE MANIFEST:
style.css
image.png
mobile.html
NETWORK:
New-content.html
FALLBACK:
offline.html
```

In this example cache file, three files (`style.css`, `image.png`, and `mobile.html`) are cached. Once users have downloaded them, they remain in their browsers, even when they are on an airplane without WiFi, driving through a remote area of West Virginia, in a New York City subway, or visiting a planet in the solar system without WiFi.

One file (`New-content.html`) is designated to never be cached. This might be a page that contains frequently updated content.

And the content of the file `offline.html` will appear whenever a user tries to open a page but cannot access it because of a lack of an Internet connection.

Caution

Manifest files require ongoing updating because after a file is cached, users will continue to see the cached version, even if the content of the page is updated. To ensure that users see updated content, after you update a page, you should update the manifest file.

Enabling a Cache Manifest

To enable application cache, include the `manifest` attribute in the document's `<html>` tag:

The following example invokes a cache manifest file named `cache.appcache`:

```
<!DOCTYPE HTML>
<html manifest="cache.appcache">
<head>
Head content
</head>
<body>
Body content
</body>
</html>
```

Note that the `manifest` parameter is part of the open `<html>` tag. It is part of the very first information a browser "sees" when a user opens your web page. So, the `manifest` parameter has to be added to the `<html>` tag—*before* the `<head>` and `<body>` elements in an HTML5 page.

Defining Geolocation

As I've explained, geolocation identifies a user's location. That location is often teamed with an application to provide location-specific content. For example:

- A camera app might add location information to a photo taken in a cell phone.
- A retail sales app might provide local sales info to a user.
- A compass app might display a user's current location.
- A news application might provide locally based news content.
- A map app might position a user's location on a map and provide directions to another location.
- A radio station or music app might provide local-specific music programming.
- A weather app might provide local weather.

You get the concept. But here's the sticky part: identifying a user's geolocation poses serious privacy issues. There are many reasons why a user might not want her location identified. So, devices that support geolocation provide options to turn that feature off and on.

Geolocation Privacy Issues

When a user attempts to use an app that relies on geolocation but doesn't have geolocation enabled on his device, he sees an error message and a prompt to change its settings, like the one in Figure 13.12.

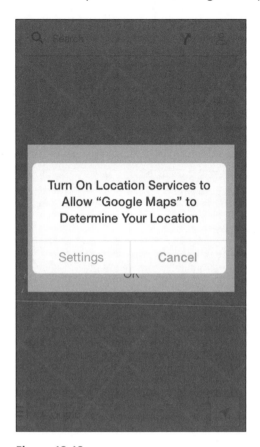

Figure 13.12
An error message when a user cannot access an app that requires geolocation.
© 2014 Cengage Learning.

Users who try to use an app that requires geolocation will be prompted to turn on geolocation and then given the option to open the appropriate section of the Settings screen on their device, as shown in Figure 13.13.

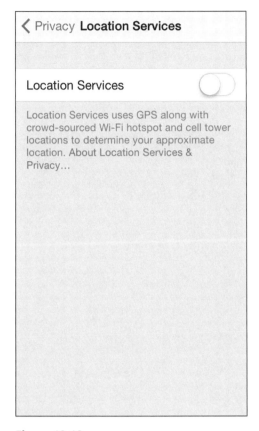

Figure 13.13
Enabling geolocation.
© 2014 Cengage Learning.

Mobile devices generally allow users to pick and choose which apps are allowed to access their location.

Tip

Geolocation is more accurate for devices with GPS, like mobile phones.

Defining a Simple Geolocation Script

There are many online sources that provide templates that can be adapted and customized to provide a basic geolocation element that tells a user where she is located with latitude and longitude parameters. I'll list a few sources for these scripts shortly, but here's one I put together that is simpler than anything I've found online, and that you can use to experiment with. It creates a basic jQuery Mobile HTML5 page with a simple geolocation script.

The code is:

```
<!DOCTYPE html>
<html>
<head>
<meta name="viewport" content="width=device-width, initial-scale=1">
<link rel="stylesheet" href="http://code.jquery.com/mobile/
                        1.4.2/jquery.mobile-1.4.2.min.css">
<script src="http://code.jquery.com/jquery-1.10.2.min.js"></script>
<script src="http://code.jquery.com/mobile/1.4.2/
            jquery.mobile-1.4.2.min.js"></script>
<title>Where Am I?</title>
</head>
<body>
<div data-role="page" id="home">
<div data-role="content">
<h3 id="location">Click the button to get your longitude and latitude:</h3>
<button onclick="getLocation()">Locate me!</button>
<script>
var x=document.getElementById("location");
function getLocation()
  {
  if (navigator.geolocation)
    {
    navigator.geolocation.getCurrentPosition(showPosition);
    }
  else{x.innerHTML="Please change your device
                    settings to enable geolocation.";}
  }
function showPosition(position)
  {
  x.innerHTML="Your latitude is: " + position.coords.latitude +
  "<br>Your longitude is: " + position.coords.longitude;
  }
</script>
</div>
</div>
</body>
</html>
```

In a mobile browser, it looks like Figure 13.14.

Figure 13.14
A simple page to display geolocation.
© 2014 Cengage Learning.

And when the button is clicked, it processes a user's location as shown in Figure 13.15.

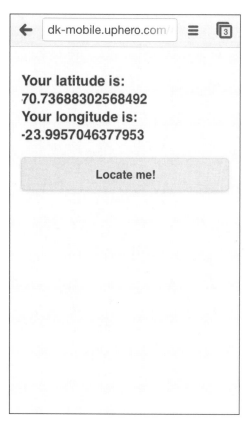

Figure 13.15
Testing geolocation.
© 2014 Cengage Learning.

Obviously the practical uses of this simple implementation of HTML5 geolocation are quite limited. Most mobile users won't find the longitude and latitude of their location that useful. Geolocation is more valuable when combined with apps or JavaScript implementation that identifies a user's location on a map, finds the closest open gas station, or suggests well-reviewed coffee shops nearby.

But I did want to give you an example of a geolocation implementation that you can do with minimal JavaScript, on your own. And I included code that builds a jQuery Mobile-based HTML5 page, so you can apply all the formatting techniques explored in previous chapters in this book. For example, just adding a `data-theme` parameter to the

`<div data-role="page">` element in the code for the geolocation example changes the appearance of the page, as shown in Figure 13.16. That edited line of code is:

```
<div data-role="page" id="home" data-theme="b">
```

Figure 13.16
Applying a jQuery Mobile theme to a geolocation page.
© 2014 Cengage Learning.

With this basic understanding of how geolocation works, you can grab code for more developed geolocation applications. And, depending on your comfort level tweaking JavaScript, you can tinker with and customize settings.

For example, you can grab code from Google's Developers site to create a geolocation map like the one in Figure 13.17.

Figure 13.17
Locating a user with Google's geolocation tool.
© 2014 Cengage Learning.

You'll find the code for this map at https://developers.google.com/maps/documentation/javascript/examples/map-geolocation.

Tip

One of my favorite sources for geolocation content is geoPlugin; see http://www.geoplugin.com. This site has copy-and-paste code for localized weather forecasts, embedded maps, other practical mobile website features. And it serves a community of developers, so the set of geolocation examples is growing.

Using Canvas

The HTML5 `<canvas>` element is another component of HTML5 that, combined with JavaScript, has the potential to create interactive mobile page content.

The concept is the `<canvas>` element can be used to draw graphics in JavaScript. The level of JavaScript required to do anything useful with a `<canvas>` element is pretty intense, and at this point, I haven't found practical uses for it that can be implemented easily by copying and pasting code, or generating the necessary JavaScript. The resource with the most potential is sketch.js, and I'll show you how to use that.

So, while the <canvas> element isn't quite ready for prime time, unless you're a high-powered JavaScripter, it has some interesting potential. For that reason I'll introduce you to it here.

The basic syntax for a <canvas> element is simple:

```
<canvas></canvas>
```

The default size of the canvas is 300px wide and 150px high. Custom sizes, as well as other parameters, can be defined with CSS. For example, you can resize a <canvas> element to 280px wide by 400px high and give it a gray background with the following CSS in the <head> element of a page:

```
<style>
canvas {
width:280px;
height:400px;
background-color:gray;
}
</style>
```

That CSS produces a canvas element like the one shown in Figure 13.18.

Figure 13.18
Customizing a <canvas> element.
© 2014 Cengage Learning.

The most accessible and fun online resource I've found for generating canvas elements with JavaScript is the `sketch.js` script, found at http://soulwire.github.io/sketch.js/.

This script powers a set of animated, interactive elements, some of them shown in Figure 13.19.

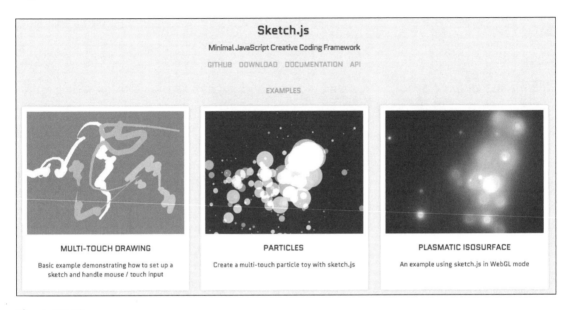

Figure 13.19
JavaScript `<canvas>` applications from `sketch.js`.
Source: Soulwire.co.uk™.

I'll walk you through setting up and implementing one of these applications here. The first step is to download the `sketch.js-master.zip` file from the download link at http://soulwire.github.io/sketch.js/. That link is shown in Figure 13.20.

Figure 13.20
Downloading files from `sketch.js`.
Source: Soulwire.co.uk™.

Copy the `sketch.js-master.zip` file into the folder that holds your website content and extract the contents of the ZIP file there. Unzipping the files creates a folder in your site named `sketch.js-master`. Inside that folder is a subfolder titled `examples`, and inside that folder are HTML5 files you can experiment with. For example, the `drawing.html` file is an interactive page where users can draw shapes, as shown in Figure 13.21.

Figure 13.21
The `drawing.html` canvas page created with `sketch.js`.
Source: Soulwire.co.uk™.

The `particles.html` page generates a wild array of floating particles that react to a user's touch, as shown in Figure 13.22.

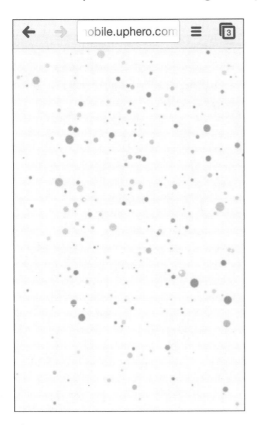

Figure 13.22
The `particles.html` canvas page created with `sketch.js`.
Source: Soulwire.co.uk ™.

Like you, I'll be keeping my eye open for new tools and resources that integrate the `<canvas>` element with accessible JavaScript. But for now, the fun resources at `sketch.js` are a good way to get a feel for the potential of the `<canvas>` element.

Summary

In this chapter, I explained the relationship between mobile web pages and mobile apps. There are actually two kinds of mobile apps—native and web. Native apps run without browsers in mobile devices. They are device-specific. That means an app developed for Android doesn't run in an Apple mobile device and vice versa. Native apps require exponentially more programming skills to build and maintain than mobile apps.

There is one property of native apps that cannot be duplicated in web apps. Native apps can be sold—through Google Play, iTunes, and other online venues—while mobile apps are distributed free. But other than that, there are few features of native apps that cannot be duplicated in web apps.

In this chapter, I showed you how to combine laptop/desktop content with mobile pages. And, I showed you how to implement some of the most valuable features of native apps in web apps:

- You can add a simple JavaScript to a web page to divert mobile users to special mobile-friendly content.

- You can cache content in web apps, so that it is available when users are not connected to the Internet.

- You can include geolocation content, which identifies a user's location, in web apps.

- The HTML5 `<canvas>` element, combined with JavaScript, has the potential to be developed into a highly interactive way for users to interact with mobile sites.

Here are three "take home" points for integrating laptop/desktop pages with mobile-friendly pages:

- Use JavaScript (code provided in this chapter) to identify users coming to your site with mobile devices and to divert them to mobile-specific content.

- Identify laptop/desktop pages with a `canonical` parameter to make it clear to search engines this content is the "first stop" for users and should be listed in link results.

- Identify mobile pages with an `alternate` parameter to make it clear to search engines this content should not be listed in search results.

And here are three "take home" points for integrating interactive app content in your mobile site:

- Use caching to allow users to access some content while out of Internet range.

- Employ geolocation resources, like the template from Google Maps, to provide location-specific content for users.

- Provide fun animated interactivity with content built using HTML5's new `<canvas>` element.

CHAPTER 14

USING TEMPLATES

Templates provide "starter" content that can be customized. And templates are not just for beginners. They allow designers at any level to get a quick start on projects. And good templates provide reliable, tested code.

In this chapter, I walk you through using a jQuery Mobile template to build pages, forms, navbars, buttons, and other useful elements in a mobile website. And I provide tips on how to draw on the previous chapters in this book to make the most of these options.

In this process, you explore:

■ Generating a new HTML5/jQuery Mobile site from a template page.

■ Grabbing navbars and buttons from templates.

■ Using pre-defined CSS themes and color swatches.

■ Building complex forms.

USING JQUERY MOBILE TEMPLATES

Templates can radically speed up the process of building mobile websites. But if you don't understand what is "under the hood," templates either lock you into a pre-fabricated design or can become an unmanageable mess when you try to customize them.

With what you've learned in the previous chapters of this book, you're ready to explore using templates.

In a hurry to build a mobile website? I'm not recommending starting here, at the end of the book, but that (starting at the end) is the kind of thing I might well do if I had to produce a mobile site overnight. If you are starting with this chapter, I'll try to accommodate you by both showing you how to customize the template I introduce you to, and by referring you back to previous chapters for more detail on the key features of a mobile site.

SURVEYING JQUERY MOBILE BOOTSTRAP

There are a number of templates available for building mobile-friendly websites with HTML5, based on jQuery Mobile. The one I'm going to focus on here is jQuery Mobile Bootstrap. I like it for a number of reasons, and I think you will like it for these reasons as well:

- The basic features provided by the jQuery Mobile Bootstrap template synch well with the features for mobile websites covered so far in this book.

- That basic feature set is a nice starting point for mobile sites.

- If you are familiar with the Twitter Bootstrap front-end framework, you'll see that at least in a very initial way, jQuery Mobile Bootstrap attempts to emulate some of the style features of that widely-applied resource for building responsive web pages.

Using jQuery Mobile Bootstrap

Building responsive web pages, including with Twitter Bootstrap, is the topic of another book and beyond the scope of this one. But in brief, Bootstrap is a free collection of tools for generating websites and web applications. It includes HTML and CSS-based templates for fonts, forms, buttons, and navigation elements, as well as optional JavaScript extensions.

You download jQuery Mobile Bootstrap from GitHub. I'll walk you through that process shortly, but the GitHub site is http://github.com/commadelimited/jQuery-Mobile-Bootstrap-Theme.

I should emphasize that the publisher of jQuery Mobile Bootstrap makes no claims that this resource duplicates the feature set of the much more substantial Twitter Bootstrap library. The jQuery Mobile Bootstrap template does adopt the color scheme themes in Twitter Bootstrap, and seems inspired by the concept of providing easy-to-use productivity tools for quickly generating pages. But jQuery Mobile Bootstrap is a dedicated resource for building *mobile* pages.

Examining jQuery Mobile Bootstrap Pages

If you go to https://github.com/commadelimited/jQuery-Mobile-Bootstrap-Theme, you can explore what jQuery Mobile Bootstrap does before downloading the files. There's a helpful overview of what is in the package provided by jQuery Mobile Bootstrap.

Tip

I'm directing you to GitHub to first examine, then download jQuery Mobile Bootstrap. But what is GitHub? It is a hosting service for software development projects that can be downloaded. Some resources at GitHub are free and open source. Others are not. The name comes from the fact that these resources all use the Git version-control system—a revision control and source code management (SCM) program originally designed and developed by Linus Torvalds for Linux and now widely applied. Each GitHub folder includes a complete history and full version tracking capabilities.

At the GitHub page for jQuery Mobile Bootstrap, you can click on links to any of the template pages that come with the template to see how they work. You'll find a list of those files on the GitHub page, shown in Figure 14.1.

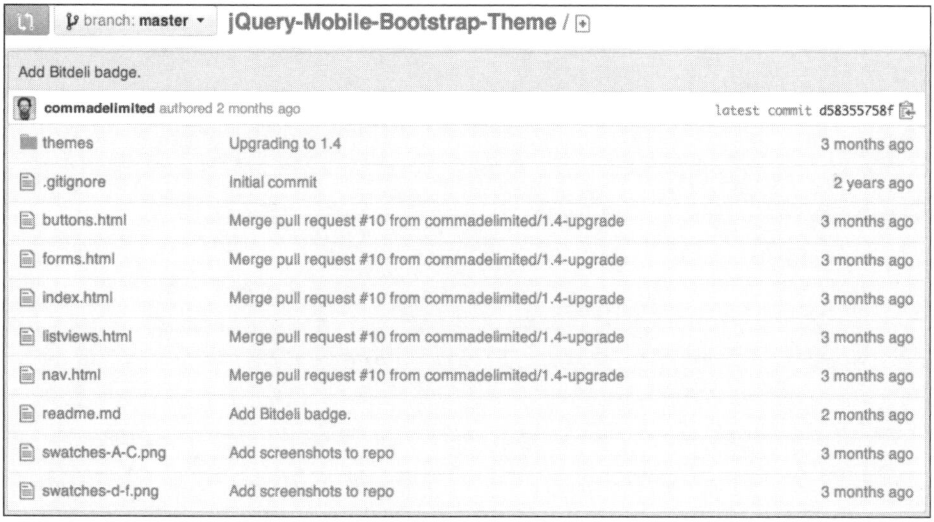

Figure 14.1
Links to files provided with jQuery Mobile Bootstrap.
Source: jQuery Mobile Bootstrap™.

Focus first on the HTML pages that are part of the jQuery Mobile Bootstrap template. They are:

- `buttons.html`

- `forms.html`

- `index.html`

- `listviews.html`

- `nav.html`

You can click on these to see the code for each of these pages. For example, the home page code is:

```
<!doctype html>
<html>
<head>
<meta charset="utf-8">
<meta name="viewport" content="width=device-width,initial-scale=1">
<title>jQuery Mobile Bootstrap Theme</title>
<link rel="stylesheet" href="themes/Bootstrap.css">
<link rel="stylesheet" href="http://code.jquery.com/mobile/1.4.0/
                      jquery.mobile.structure-1.4.0.min.css" />
<link rel="stylesheet" href="themes/jquery.mobile.icons.min.css" />
<script src="http://code.jquery.com/jquery-1.8.2.min.js"></script>
<script src="http://code.jquery.com/mobile/1.4.0/
             jquery.mobile-1.4.0.min.js"></script>
</head>
<body>
<div data-role="page" data-theme="a">
<div data-role="header" data-position="inline">
<h1>jQuery Mobile Bootstrap Theme</h1>
<div data-role="navbar">
<ul>
<li><a href="index.html" data-icon="home" class="ui-btn-active">Home</a></li>
<li><a href="buttons.html" data-icon="star">Buttons</a></li>
<li><a href="listviews.html" data-icon="grid">Lists</a></li>
<li><a href="nav.html" data-icon="search">Nav</a></li>
<li><a href="forms.html" data-icon="gear">Forms</a></li>
</ul>
</div>
</div>
<div data-role="content" data-theme="a">
<a href="https://github.com/commadelimited/
        jQuery-Mobile-Bootstrap-Theme"
        data-role="button" data-icon="star">Get the code</a>
<h2>Overview</h2>
<p>
The jQuery Mobile Bootstrap theme is meant to duplicate the appearance
   of <a href="http://twbs.github.io/bootstrap/">Bootstrap</a>
   within the context of a jQuery Mobile application. Currently
   only the colors are mimicked, but eventually some of the
   components might also work their way into the theme.
```

```
</p>
</div>
</div>
</body>
</html>
```

Figure 14.2 shows the `index.html` page in a mobile browser.

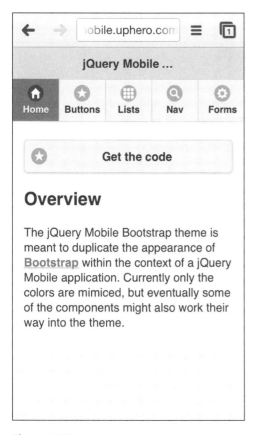

Figure 14.2
The home page template from jQuery Mobile Bootstrap.
Source: jQuery Mobile Bootstrap™.

You'll recognize a number of features here that I've covered in this book. The Forms template—shown in Figure 14.3—includes features covered in Chapter 11.

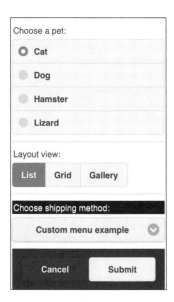

Figure 14.3
The Forms page template from jQuery Mobile Bootstrap.
Source: jQuery Mobile Bootstrap™.

And where there are features in the jQuery Mobile Bootstrap templates that I haven't addressed explicitly in this book, you'll find helpful documentation in the pages themselves. For example, the top of the Forms template includes documentation shown in Figure 14.4.

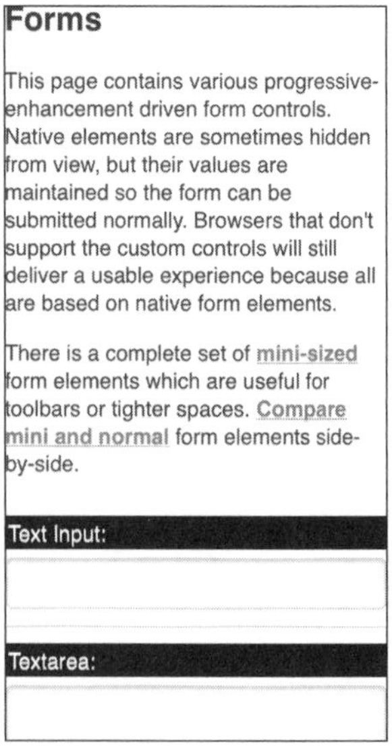

Figure 14.4
Documentation for the Forms page template from jQuery Mobile Bootstrap.
Source: jQuery Mobile Bootstrap™.

Tip

Having emphasized the essential synchronicity between the templates in jQuery Mobile Bootstrap and the approach of this book, the other point I need to make is that every developer, teacher, and writer has a different approach to mobile site design. Consequently, you'll find approaches in the templates from jQuery Mobile Bootstrap that diverge from approaches I recommend in the book. For example, the Template Input form uses checkboxes and radio buttons. In Chapter 11 of this book, I advocate other types of input fields for collecting data from mobile users. But you can handle being exposed to alternative approaches! Part of the reason this topic is covered in the final chapter of the book is so that you have enough exposure to mobile page design with HTML to be able to integrate alternate approaches. And, as I noted, the jQuery Mobile Bootstrap template pages include helpful documentation to help digest and apply techniques that are a bit different than approaches used in this book.

In Chapter 12 of this book, I show you how to create and edit navigation buttons. With that as background, you can implement the jQuery Mobile Bootstrap template for buttons. The code provided for the `buttons.html` page template is going to look pretty familiar:

```
<!doctype html>
<html>
<head>
<meta charset="utf-8">
<meta name="viewport" content="width=device-width,initial-scale=1">
<title>jQuery Mobile Bootstrap Theme</title>
<link rel="stylesheet" href="themes/Bootstrap.css">
<link rel="stylesheet" href="http://code.jquery.com/mobile/1.4.0/
                        jquery.mobile.structure-1.4.0.min.css" />
<link rel="stylesheet" href="themes/jquery.mobile.icons.min.css" />
<script src="http://code.jquery.com/jquery-1.8.2.min.js"></script>
<script src="http://code.jquery.com/mobile/1.4.0/
           jquery.mobile-1.4.0.min.js"></script>
</head>
<body>
<div data-role="page" data-theme="a">
<div data-role="header" data-position="inline">
<h1>jQuery Mobile Bootstrap Theme</h1>
<div data-role="navbar">
<ul>
<li><a href="index.html" data-icon="home">Home</a></li>
<li><a href="buttons.html" data-icon="star"
                       class="ui-btn-active">Buttons</a></li>
<li><a href="listviews.html" data-icon="grid">Lists</a></li>
<li><a href="nav.html" data-icon="search">Nav</a></li>
<li><a href="forms.html" data-icon="gear">Forms</a></li>
```

```
</ul>
</div>
</div>
<div data-role="content" data-theme="a">

<a href="https://github.com/commadelimited/jQuery-Mobile-Bootstrap-Theme"
        data-role="button" data-icon="star">Get the code</a>

<h2>Buttons</h2>

<a href="index.html" data-role="button" data-theme="a"
                      data-icon="star">Swatch A</a>
<a href="index.html" data-role="button" data-theme="b"
                      data-icon="search">Swatch B</a>
<a href="index.html" data-role="button" data-theme="c"
                      data-icon="check">Swatch C</a>
<a href="index.html" data-role="button" data-theme="d"
                      data-icon="info">Swatch D</a>
<a href="index.html" data-role="button" data-theme="e"
                      data-icon="arrow-d">Swatch E</a>
<a href="index.html" data-role="button" data-theme="f"
                      data-icon="delete">Swatch F</a>
</div>
</div>
</body>
</html>
```

That code generates a page with a set of buttons in a navbar at the top of the page—in the
`<header>` element—as shown in Figure 14.5.

Figure 14.5
Template navigation buttons from the jQuery Mobile Bootstrap Buttons template.
Source: jQuery Mobile Bootstrap™.

Tip

The Buttons template from jQuery Mobile Bootstrap includes custom theme links. I'll explain how those work shortly.

The `nav.html` template from jQuery Mobile Bootstrap provides easy-to-copy code for a variety of navigation bars, using the Navbar widget explored in depth in Chapter 12. Figure 14.6 shows some of those bars.

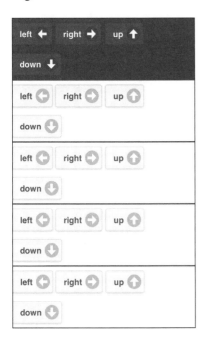

Figure 14.6
Template navigation bars from the jQuery Mobile Bootstrap Buttons template.
Source: jQuery Mobile Bootstrap™.

Finally, the jQuery Mobile Bootstrap template provides handy code for generating a set of listviews. The code is:

```
<!doctype html>
<html>
<head>
<meta charset="utf-8">
<meta name="viewport" content="width=device-width,initial-scale=1">
<title>jQuery Mobile Bootstrap Theme</title>
<link rel="stylesheet" href="themes/Bootstrap.css">
<link rel="stylesheet" href="http://code.jquery.com/mobile/1.4.0/
                     jquery.mobile.structure-1.4.0.min.css" />
<link rel="stylesheet" href="themes/jquery.mobile.icons.min.css" />
<script src="http://code.jquery.com/jquery-1.8.2.min.js"></script>
<script src="http://code.jquery.com/mobile/1.4.0/
            jquery.mobile-1.4.0.min.js"></script>
</head>
```

```html
<body>
<div data-role="page" data-theme="a">
<div data-role="header" data-position="inline">
<h1>jQuery Mobile Bootstrap Theme</h1>
<div data-role="navbar">
<ul>
<li><a href="index.html" data-icon="home">Home</a></li>
<li><a href="buttons.html" data-icon="star">Buttons</a></li>
<li><a href="listviews.html" data-icon="grid"
        class="ui-btn-active">Lists</a></li>
<li><a href="nav.html" data-icon="search">Nav</a></li>
<li><a href="forms.html" data-icon="gear">Forms</a></li>
</ul>
</div>
</div>
<div data-role="content" data-theme="a">

<a href="https://github.com/commadelimited/
          jQuery-Mobile-Bootstrap-Theme" data-role="button"
          data-icon="star">Get the code</a>
<h2>Listviews</h2>
<ul data-role="listview" data-inset="true" data-divider-theme="a">
<li data-role="list-divider">Swatch A</li>
<li data-icon="gear"><a href="">A list item</a></li>
</ul>
<ul data-role="listview" data-inset="true" data-divider-theme="b">
<li data-role="list-divider">Swatch B</li>
<li data-icon="info"><a href="">A list item</a></li>
</ul>
<ul data-role="listview" data-inset="true" data-divider-theme="c">
<li data-role="list-divider">Swatch C</li>
<li data-icon="check"><a href="">A list item</a></li>
</ul>
<ul data-role="listview" data-inset="true" data-divider-theme="d">
<li data-role="list-divider">Swatch D</li>
<li data-icon="grid"><a href="">A list item</a></li>
</ul>
<ul data-role="listview" data-inset="true" data-divider-theme="e">
<li data-role="list-divider">Swatch E</li>
<li data-icon="alert"><a href="">A list item</a></li>
</ul>
```

```
<ul data-role="listview" data-inset="true" data-divider-theme="f">
<li data-role="list-divider">Swatch F</li>
<li data-icon="refresh"><a href="">A list item</a></li>
</ul>
</div>
</div>
</body>
</html>
```

And the generated template looks like the one in Figure 14.7.

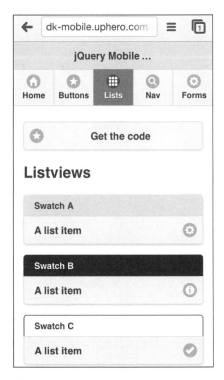

Figure 14.7
The jQuery Mobile Bootstrap Listview template.
Source: jQuery Mobile Bootstrap™.

If you looked at the code for the Listview template carefully (and the code for other pages), you noticed a link to a style sheet file—Bootstrap.css. jQuery Mobile Bootstrap provides this custom CSS file that applies a theme and color swatches to pages. I'll explain how that fits into the picture next, but Figure 14.8 shows that theme, and those color swatches applied to the template listview. Of course, the printed book can't convey the colors, but you can get a basic sense of the themes here.

Tip

You can see an application of the jQuery Mobile Bootstrap CSS theme at http://dk-mobile.uphero.com/listview .html.

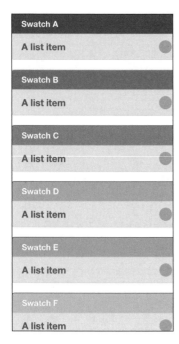

Figure 14.8
The jQuery Mobile Bootstrap listview with a custom theme.

Source: jQuery Mobile Bootstrap™.

Previewing jQuery Mobile Bootstrap Themes

In Chapter 4 of this book, you learned to apply jQuery Mobile data-themes to elements to provide styling and color. In Chapter 5, I showed you how to create custom themes and apply them. To briefly review, every jQuery Mobile page built with HTML5 links to the CSS style sheet provided as part of the default files for jQuery Mobile. But you can create custom CSS files—or themes. Those themes include global style elements, like fonts and button styling. They also include a *set* of color swatches, which you can apply using the data-theme="*x*" parameter (with "x" being a letter from A-Z that invokes a defined color scheme).

The jQuery Mobile Bootstrap comes with a custom CSS file that provides a basic theme and color swatches. Especially now that the powers-that-be in charge of jQuery Mobile decided to strip all coloring from the default jQuery Mobile data-themes (leaving us with two versions of grayscale), quick access to the colorful swatches from jQuery Mobile Bootstrap are handy.

I'll walk through how to download and install those color swatches along with the rest of the resources at jQuery Mobile Bootstrap next.

USING jQUERY MOBILE BOOTSTRAP

The files required to implement jQuery Mobile Bootstrap are easy to access and use. Start at http://dk-mobile.uphero.com/listview.html. Then, there are essentially three ways you can use them:

- You can follow the link to any particular file (see Figure 14.1), open it in a browser, and copy and paste the code into your code editor. This is useful when you only want to grab a single file from the resources at jQuery Mobile Bootstrap.

- You can click the Raw button (shown in Figure 14.9) to open the code for any page in a browser. This displays *just* the code, and you can save that page in the folder in which you have organized all your mobile web page content.

- You can download the entire set of files for jQuery Mobile Bootstrap. That's the approach I'm going to recommend, unless you are confident, comfortable, and competent to manage all the files independently.

Figure 14.9
Accessing raw HTML5 code for the jQuery Mobile Bootstrap Buttons page.
Source: jQuery Mobile Bootstrap™.

Downloading All the Zipped Files

The easiest and most reliable way to implement jQuery Mobile Bootstrap templates is to download the full set of files from the GitHub page. When you do that, you get the HTML page templates, the CSS files for the custom theme, and image files required for icons in the custom themes.

I personally think the Download Zip button for GitHub resources is hard to find in general, and that applies for the jQuery Mobile Bootstrap template as well. So Figure 14.10 should help you locate it. Use that Download Zip button to download all the files required for the jQuery Mobile Bootstrap content. You should unzip the files into the folder you use to store all your mobile page content.

Figure 14.10
Downloading the zipped files for jQuery Mobile Bootstrap.
Source: jQuery Mobile Bootstrap™.

Once you've downloaded and unzipped the files into the folder that contains your mobile site content, you can open and edit any of the template pages.

Customizing a Home Page

When you open the `index.html` file provided by jQuery Mobile Bootstrap in your code editor, you'll note the `<head>` element includes the essential content to make jQuery Mobile pages work. This alone is worth installing jQuery Mobile Bootstrap. It allows you to quickly generate jQuery Mobile pages. That `<head>` content is:

```
<head>
<meta charset="utf-8">
<meta name="viewport" content="width=device-width,initial-scale=1">
<title>jQuery Mobile Bootstrap Theme</title>
<link rel="stylesheet" href="themes/Bootstrap.css">
<link rel="stylesheet" href="http://code.jquery.com/mobile/1.4.0/jquery.mobile.
                          structure-1.4.0.min.css" />
<link rel="stylesheet" href="themes/jquery.mobile.icons.min.css">
<script src="http://code.jquery.com/jquery-1.8.2.min.js">
</script>
<script src="http://code.jquery.com/mobile/1.4.0/jquery.mobile-1.4.0.min.js">
</script>
</head>
```

There are two lines of code to particularly note here. One is the code that links to the custom CSS file provided by jQuery Mobile Bootstrap:

```
<link rel="stylesheet" href="themes/Bootstrap.css">
```

If you used the techniques in Chapter 5 of this book to create your own custom theme using ThemeRoller for jQuery Mobile, then you will want to replace the link to `themes/Bootstrap.css` with a link to your custom theme CSS.

And you will definitely want to replace the `<title>` placeholder text:

```
<title>jQuery Mobile Bootstrap Theme</title>
```

with your own title. For example:

```
<title>Home</title>
```

This defines the text that displays in the title bar of a mobile (or desktop) browser when those browsers display title bar content.

Caution

If you try to open one of the files provided by jQuery Mobile Bootstrap in your browser as a local file (on your own computer, before you upload to a server) and click any of the links in the main navigation, you may get an "Error loading page" message. The reason for this is that some browsers block content that tries to load potential harmful content (in this case the jQuery JavaScript file) that is not in the same domain (when the file is local and JavaScript file is www). This is a problem only when you're attempting to link between different pages. It is not an issue for most of the examples in this book, because all the content is in a single HTML file.

Choosing a Theme

The template `index.html` page provided by jQuery Mobile Bootstrap (and the other templates as well) have `data-themes` assigned to the pages, or to elements within those pages.

Look for `data-theme` parameters within elements like this one that defines the `data-theme` for the `<div data-role="page">` element (and that controls colors for the whole page):

```
<div data-role="page" data-theme="a">
```

Customize the theme by changing the `data-theme` value. For example, to:

```
<div data-role="page" data-theme="b">
```

Tip

Remember, you can find displays of the default jQuery Mobile Bootstrap themes at https://github.com/commadelimited/jQuery-Mobile-Bootstrap-Theme.

Customizing a Navbar

The `navbar.html` template that comes with jQuery Mobile Bootstrap includes sets of pre-built navbars. You'll want to jump to Chapter 12 for full instructions on how to customize (or create) navbars, but here's the quick review.

Navbars are widgets that draw on jQuery Mobile's JavaScript and CSS to generate tabbed navigation bars with between one and five tabs. Each tab takes up the same width on the page, and the tabs are styled to react to taps. You define custom links for each tab, and you can assign and configure icons with them as well.

The template navbar that comes with the `index.html` page template from jQuery Mobile Bootstrap is a great place to start. Here's the code you're looking for in the `index.html` page:

```
<div data-role="navbar">
<ul>
<li>
<a href="index.html" data-icon="home" class="ui-btn-active">Home</a>
</li>
```

```
<li>
<a href="buttons.html" data-icon="star">Buttons</a>
</li>
<li>
<a href="listviews.html" data-icon="grid">Lists</a>
</li>
<li>
<a href="nav.html" data-icon="search">Nav</a>
</li>
<li>
<a href="forms.html" data-icon="gear">Forms</a>
</li>
</ul>
</div>
```

To customize the navbar:

- Substitute your own link for the `a href=` value.

- Substitute any `data-icon` from the set at http://api.jquerymobile.com/icons/.

- Substitute your own link text for the text before the close link (`</a>`) tag.

You can reduce the number of tabs in the navbar by simply eliminating one of the `<li>` (list) elements. But remember, if you try to *add* a tab beyond five, you'll force an additional row of tabs, as shown in Figure 14.11.

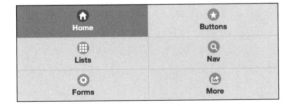

Figure 14.11
Forcing additional rows of icons in a navbar.
© 2014 Cengage Learning. Source: jQuery Mobile Bootstrap™.

Building a Listview

The `listviews.html` template provided by jQuery Mobile Bootstrap provides starter code for a page that includes everything you need for a basic home page—a navbar (which I just discussed as part of the `index.html` template), as well as a listview.

Listviews are examined in depth in Chapter 3 of this book, and I'll refer you there for details on how to configure them. But basically they involve configuring a set of links in a list with a `<div data-role="listview">` element.

The listview in `listviews.html` begins with this tag:

```
<ul data-role="listview" data-inset="true" data-divider-theme="a">
```

As I noted in reference to customizing `<div data-role="page">` elements, you customize the colors for any element by changing the `data-theme`. In this case, the template includes a `data-divider-theme=` parameter that configures the divided list elements used in the template. So you edit the colors of the listview by changing that `data-divider-theme=` value from a to b, c, d, or e (or other themes).

Individual listview items look like this:

```
<li data-icon="gear"><a href="">A list item</a></li>
```

You can customize the data-icon with an icon from the list at http://api.jquerymobile.com/icons. You define a link by entering a URL inside the " " in the `<a href=" ">` code. And you change the link text by replacing A list item with real text.

You can also customize the list divider by editing the placeholder text inside the `<li data-role="list-divider"> </li>` tags with your own text, like this:

```
<li data-role="list-divider">Go to our home page</li>
```

Here's an example of a customized list element:

```
<li data-role="list-divider">Go to our home page</li>
<li data-icon="home"><a href="index.html">Home</a></li>
```

It produces a link like the one shown in Figure 14.12.

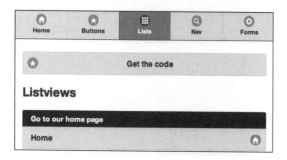

Figure 14.12
A customized listview item.
© 2014 Cengage Learning. Source: jQuery Mobile Bootstrap™.

Building Buttons

In Chapter 12, I explained how important buttons are as navigation tools in mobile pages. They're easy to tap—compared to often frustratingly small and awkward text links. And they're inviting; they draw a user's attention on a small screen.

You can use the `buttons.html` page from the jQuery Mobile Bootstrap template to quickly generate buttons. And, you can copy and paste the button code from that page into other pages to place buttons.

You'll find the template button HTML code in the file `buttons.html`. The first of the set of buttons is created with this code:

```
<a href="index.html" data-role="button" data-theme="a" data-icon="star">
Swatch A
</a>
```

You substitute your own link for `index.html`, your own theme for `data-theme="a"` (replace the `"a"` with another letter), and define a different `data-icon` by replacing `"star"` in the previous code.

Replace `"Swatch A"` with your own link text.

For example, to create a button linking to your home page with the home data-icon, you can use this code:

```
<a href="index.html" data-role="button" data-theme="a" data-icon="home">
Home
</a>
```

That button will look like the one in Figure 14.13. And, as I explained, you don't need to just create these buttons in the `buttons.html` template page; you can copy this button code to any page.

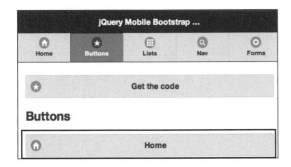

Figure 14.13
A generated Home link button.
© 2014 Cengage Learning. Source: jQuery Mobile Bootstrap™.

Building a Form

Chapter 11 in this book walks through building mobile-friendly forms. And hopefully you get a sense from that chapter that building mobile-friendly forms is a combination of art and science. There are often a variety of ways to collect information from a user. I mention this because the template form that comes with jQuery Mobile Bootstrap uses some form fields (like radio buttons and checkboxes) that I discouraged using in Chapter 11.

As I noted in the introduction to this chapter, you can handle that discrepancy. One of the valuable things about working with templates is that they expose you to alternate design approaches. In particular, I take advantage of the fact that the Forms template from jQuery Mobile Bootstrap includes checkboxes and radio button sets to introduce those options for forms, and expose you to alternatives not covered in Chapter 11.

With that as a disclaimer, so to speak, let me identify some of the key elements in the Forms template provided by jQuery Mobile Bootstrap.

Tip

Remember, input elements *work only* when they are inside a `<form>` element.

Customizing a Form Action

First, let me review the basic element of a form—the `<form>` element. Every form opens with an open `<form>` tag and closes with a `</form>` tag. And every form that does something (usually) includes a form action.

The template code for a form in the jQuery Mobile Bootstrap template doesn't come with an action. Defining actions takes a bit of explaining, so I'll refer you back to the section "Creating Inviting Forms with HTML5 Input Types" in Chapter 11 for an explanation of how to define a form action.

The template open `<form>` element that comes with the form in the `forms.html` page is:

```
<form action="mailto: email@email.com  " method="post">
```

In this code, you replace `email@email.com` with an actual email address.

Tip

For more explanation of how form data is managed, see "Managing Form Data with PHP Scripts" in Chapter 11.

Customizing a Text Input

The most commonly used way to collect data in a form is a `text` input field. The jQuery Mobile Bootstrap `forms.html` has copy-and-paste code for that. That code is:

```
<div data-role="fieldcontain>
<label for="name">Text Input:</label>
<input type="text" name="name" id="name" value=""/>
</div>
```

Here's how you customize this code:

- Substitute your own label text for `Text Input:`.

- Substitute your own field name for the `name` parameter value.

- Substitute your own ID name for the `id` parameter value.

- No content is needed for the `value` parameter.

The template text input field code is enclosed in a `<div data-role="fieldcontain">` element. That `<div data-role="fieldcontain">` element imposes a width on the field based on the width of a user's viewport. This provides helpful styling for form elements, and keeps them from bumping into the edges of a viewport.

And the template includes a `<label>` element. The name parameter value in the `<label>` element must match the name parameter value in the `<input>` element. This creates a label that users can click on to focus on the input field, a handy feature for smartphone users who have to select fields in a form without having the precision pointing that one has with a mouse.

Here's an example of an input form customized to collect a user's name:

```
<div data-role="fieldcontain">
<label for="name">Your name?</label>
<input type="text" name="name" id="name" value=""/>
</div>
```

Figure 14.14 illustrates how that field looks in a form.

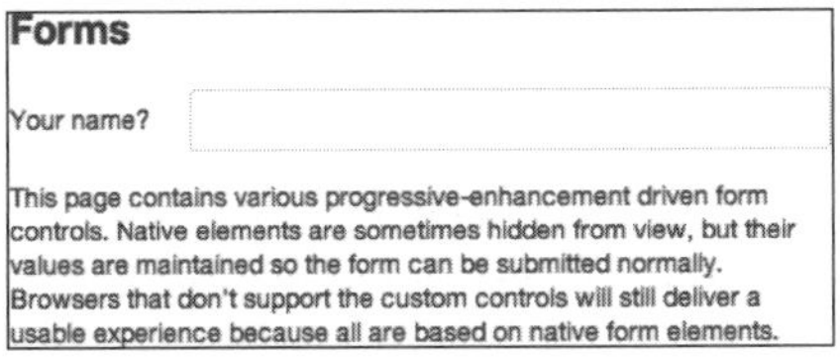

Figure 14.14
A generated text input field.

© 2014 Cengage Learning. Source: jQuery Mobile Bootstrap™.

Customizing a Text Area

Text area inputs allow multiple lines of text. The jQuery Mobile Bootstrap template code for a text area is:

```
<div data-role="fieldcontain">
<label for="textarea">Textarea:</label>
<textarea cols="40" rows="8" name="textarea" id="textarea">
</textarea>
</div>
```

The template `textarea` input field code is also enclosed in a `<div data-role="fieldcontain">` element to control margins. You can customize the width of the text area by changing the `cols` value, and you can customize the height by changing the `rows` value.

The `cols` and `rows` values are not critical for designing input fields for mobile devices. The following example defines a `comments` field with multiple rows.

```
<div data-role="fieldcontain">
<label for=" comments ">Comments:</label>
<textarea name="comments" id="comments">
</textarea>
</div>
```

Figure 14.15 illustrates the `comments` field created with that code.

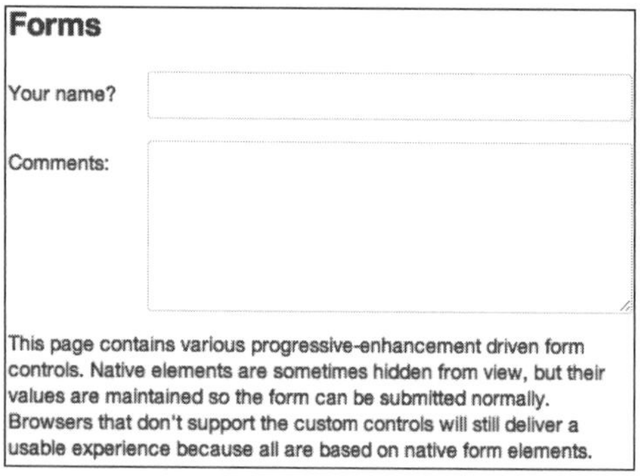

Figure 14.15
A customized `comments` field.
© 2014 Cengage Learning. Source: jQuery Mobile Bootstrap™.

Customizing a Flip Switch

Flip switches, like the one in Figure 14.16, are a really handy, inviting, and fun way for users to enter input into a form.

Figure 14.16
A flip switch.
© 2014 Cengage Learning. Source: jQuery Mobile Bootstrap™.

The template code for a flip switch, with placeholder content italicized, is:

```
<div data-role="fieldcontain">
<label for="slider2">Flip switch:</label>
<select name="slider2" id="slider2" data-role="slider">
<option value="off">Off</option>
<option value="on">On</option>
</select>
</div>
```

Here's an example of a flip switch, with customized code to create a Yes or No flip switch to find out if users will return to your site (like the one in Figure 14.16):

```
<div data-role="fieldcontain">
<label for="slider2">Will you return to this site?</label>
<select name="slider2" id="slider2" data-role="slider">
<option value="no">Yes</option>
<option value="no">No</option>
</select>
</div>
```

Creating a Slider

Sliders are, yes, a hipster term for small burgers, but in the context of mobile web design, there are also an easy way to collect numeric values from users. Rather than making someone type in a value between 1 and 100 to rate your site, for example, you can provide them with a slider that they can drag with their finger.

The template code provided by jQuery Mobile Bootstrap's `forms.html` page for a slider is:

```
<div data-role="fieldcontain">
<label for="slider">Slider:</label>
<input type="range" name="slider" id="slider" value="50"
          min="0" max="100" data-highlight="true"/>
</div>
```

To change that to ask users to rate your site on a scale of 1-100, you only need to edit the `<label>` value:

```
<div data-role="fieldcontain">
<label for="slider">Please rate our site on a scale of 1-100</label>
<input type="range" name="slider" id="slider" value="50"
          min="0" max="100" data-highlight="true"/>
</div>
```

The template form, modified with a customized text, text area, flip switch, and slider created in this section, looks like the one in Figure 14.17.

Figure 14.17
A customized mobile form with a text input, text area, flip switch, and slider.

Tip

The `data-highlight="true"` parameter in the `<input>` element displays the slider with a colored background. The color is defined by the assigned data-theme.

Defining a Checkbox

Personally, I enjoy tapping a flip switch more than clicking a checkbox in a mobile form. But to each his own, and there are clearly times when a checkbox seems right. Users might tend to look for the ubiquitous "Add me to your mailing list" option, for example, as a checkbox, as shown in Figure 14.18.

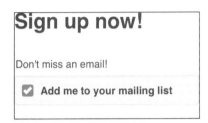

Figure 14.18
A mobile-friendly checkbox.
© 2014 Cengage Learning. Source: jQuery Mobile Bootstrap™.

That template code from jQuery Mobile Bootstrap for a set of checkboxes is:

```
<fieldset data-role="controlgroup">
<legend>Choose as many snacks as you'd like:</legend>
<input type="checkbox" name="checkbox-1a" id="checkbox-1a" class="custom" />
 <label for="checkbox-1a">Cheetos</label>
<input type="checkbox" name="checkbox-2a" id="checkbox-2a" class="custom" />
 <label for="checkbox-2a">Doritos</label>
<input type="checkbox" name="checkbox-3a" id="checkbox-3a" class="custom" />
 <label for="checkbox-3a">Fritos</label>
<input type="checkbox" name="checkbox-4a" id="checkbox-4a" class="custom" />
<label for="checkbox-4a">Sun Chips</label>
</fieldset>
```

I didn't indicate editable code in italics because most of this code isn't necessary. You can simplify this quite a bit for a single checkbox (and there's no real reason to batch checkboxes in a group since users can choose any combination of options from any group of checkboxes). Here's code for the mailing list opt-in illustrated in Figure 14.18:

```
<div data-role="fieldcontain">
<fieldset data-role="controlgroup">
<legend>Don't miss an email!</legend>
<input type="checkbox" name="checkbox-1a" id="checkbox-1a"
                  class="custom" />
<label for="checkbox-1a"> Add me to your mailing list </label>
</fieldset>
</div>'
```

Tip

The <label> value in the previous code example must match the name parameter in the <input> element. By including the label, you make it easy for a user to select the checkbox simply by tapping the label.

Building a Radio Button Control Group

Radio buttons are sets of options from which a user can select only one choice. For example, if you're collecting a user's credit card type, you don't want them to be able to enter both VISA and Master Card for a purchase. Or, if you are asking users to rate a product on a scale of 1–4, you don't want to give them the option of choosing both 2 and 4.

Radio buttons are defined in groups with a single input name, but distinct IDs. The process is a bit tedious, which emphasizes the value of building these sets of buttons from a template! That template code in the forms.html page, with placeholder content italicized, is:

```
<div data-role="fieldcontain">
<fieldset data-role="controlgroup">
<legend>Choose a pet:</legend>
<input type="radio" name="radio-choice-1" id="radio-choice-1"
                  value="choice-1" checked="checked" />
<label for="radio-choice-1">Cat</label>
<input type="radio" name="radio-choice-1" id="radio-choice-2"
                  value="choice-2" />
<label for="radio-choice-2">Dog</label>
<input type="radio" name="radio-choice-1" id="radio-choice-3"
                  value="choice-3" />
<label for="radio-choice-3">Hamster</label>
<input type="radio" name="radio-choice-1" id="radio-choice-4"
                  value="choice-4" />
```

```
<label for="radio-choice-4">Lizard</label>
</fieldset>
</div>
```

The following code customizes this code to collect a user's credit card type.

```
<div data-role="fieldcontain">
<fieldset data-role="controlgroup">
<legend>Choose a credit card type:</legend>
<input type="radio" name="radio-choice-1" id="radio-choice-1"
                  value="choice-1" checked="checked" />
<label for="radio-choice-1">VISA</label>
<input type="radio" name="radio-choice-1" id="radio-choice-2"
                  value="choice-2" />
<label for="radio-choice-2">Master Card</label>
<input type="radio" name="radio-choice-1" id="radio-choice-3"
                  value="choice-3" />
<label for="radio-choice-3">Discover</label>
<input type="radio" name="radio-choice-1" id="radio-choice-4"
                  value="choice-4" />
<label for="radio-choice-4">American Express</label>
</fieldset>
</div>
```

The customized set of radio buttons is illustrated in Figure 14.19.

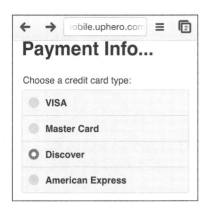

Figure 14.19
A customized set of radio buttons in a mobile browser.

EXPLORING MORE TEMPLATES

Through a rather extensive exploration of the options in the jQuery Mobile Bootstrap template pages, I showed you how you can both save time in generating mobile pages, and take advantage of template code to create elements like radio buttons or sliders without stressing over looking up HTML5 syntax.

There are other options as well for mobile page templates.

The Beginner's Tutorial Coding Web Apps with jQuery Mobile is basically a tutorial. You'll find it at http://spyrestudios.com/beginners-tutorial-coding-web-apps-with-jquery-mobile.

This tutorial is not as complex and full-featured as the jQuery Mobile Bootstrap templates, but that might be just right for a basic page like the one in Figure 14.20.

Figure 14.20
A basic page template from the Beginner's Tutorial Coding Web Apps with jQuery.
Source: Beginner's Tutorial Coding Web Apps with jQuery.

The Free Mobile Template, Mobi—provided by mobi at http://www.mrova.com/free-mobile-template-mobi—provides a set of pre-built pages with features similar to those in jQuery Mobile Bootstrap that I surveyed in this chapter. Figure 14.21 shows a page from the set of available templates.

Figure 14.21
A basic page template from the Free Mobile Template, Mobi.
Source: mobi™ by mRova.

It's not free and it's not a template, but the jQuery Mobile Website Builder site (http://www.jqmbuilder.com) builds jQuery Mobile sites for you for as little as $10. You just enter content into boxes, like those shown in Figure 14.22, and the jQuery Mobile Website Builder generates the HTML5 for you.

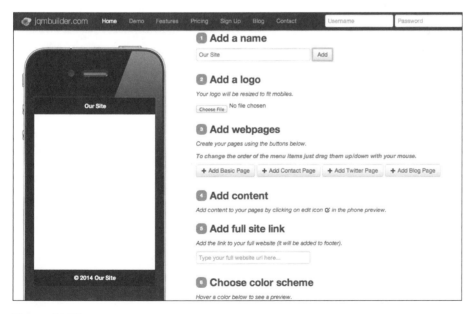

Figure 14.22
No code mobile site building with the jQuery Mobile Website Builder.
Source: jQuery Mobile Website Builder™.

Finally, w3schools.com provides a basic tutorial for coding simple jQuery Mobile sites. The link is http://www.w3schools.com/jquerymobile/. You can experiment with coding using w3schools' "Try It" window, shown in Figure 14.23.

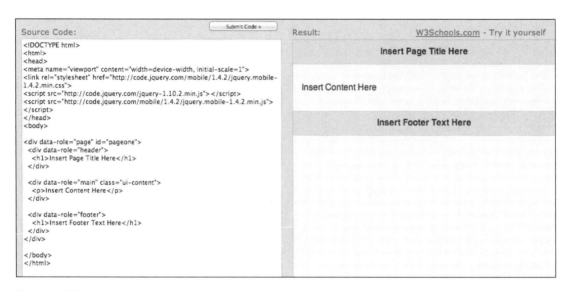

Figure 14.23
Experimenting with jQuery Mobile coding at w3schools.com.
Source: w3schools.com.

SUMMARY

You can save time and get help with coding and syntax by building elements of your mobile site with templates. There is a growing community of jQuery Mobile site designers, and the set of available resources is growing as well.

The jQuery Mobile Bootstrap template provides quick access to a number of mobile page elements I've covered in this book. You'll find them handy in building mobile websites.

In this chapter, I showed you how to use the jQuery Mobile Bootstrap templates to:

- Quickly generate a basic mobile page.
- Access a pre-built set of themes with a variety of color swatches.
- Generate navbar widgets with tabbed navigation links.
- Generate complex forms with a mix of input types.

Here are four "take home" points for getting your "money's worth" out of the jQuery Mobile Bootstrap templates:

- Use the Download Zip option at GitHub to organize all the required files into a single folder.

- Take advantage of the `index.html` template page to start your site.

- Copy and paste elements from the `buttons.html` and `navbar.html` pages into any page.

- When you generate forms, you're well advised to open, edit, and save the `forms.html` template since it includes both complex input types and a defined form to work with.

In this final chapter, I focused on using a valuable template for building an HTML5 mobile page with jQuery Mobile. If you've finished it, you have officially crossed the bridge from learning a technique to increasing productivity. In the process, you've entered the community of women and men building mobile websites with jQuery Mobile. Welcome! I'll see you online, at the book's site (http://dk-mobile.uphero.com/), and beyond.

INDEX